Broadcasting in the United Kingdom

A guide to information sources

Broadcasting in the United Kingdom

A guide to information sources

Barrie MacDonald

Mansell Publishing Limited
London and New York

First published 1988 by
Mansell Publishing Limited, *A Cassell Imprint*
Artillery House, Artillery Row, London SW1P 1RT, England
125 East 23rd Street, Suite 300, New York 10010, U.S.A.

British Library Cataloguing in Publication Data

MacDonald, Barrie
   Broadcasting in the United Kingdom: a guide to information sources.
   1. Great Britain. Broadcasting services. Information sources
   I. Title
   384.54'07

   ISBN 0-7201-1962-6

Library of Congress Cataloging-in-Publication Data

MacDonald, Barrie I.
   Broadcasting in the United Kingdom: a guide to information sources /
   Barrie MacDonald.
      p. cm.
   Includes index.
   ISBN 0-7201-1962-6
   1. Broadcasting—Great Britain—Bibliography. 2. Broadcasting—
   Great Britain—Information services—Great Britain. I. Title.
   Z7224.G7M33   1988
   [HE8689.9.G7]
   384.54'0941—dc 19   88-23392
                                                          CIP

This book has been printed and bound in Great Britain: typeset in Times
Roman by Colset (Private) Ltd., Singapore and printed and bound by
the University Press, Cambridge.

Contents

Introduction

The structure, services and programme output of broadcasting in the United Kingdom have long been admired throughout the world. The British example of broadcasting as a public service, and the solutions to the question of the relationship between broadcasters and the state (of services provided through publicly accountable but independent bodies — the British Broadcasting Corporation (BBC) and the Independent Broadcasting Authority (IBA)), have been widely adopted in other countries. Recently the Channel 4 model has also proved exportable, both its constitution, methods of programme commissioning and finance, and its programming concept of a television channel with a remit to provide a genuinely complementary service and for innovation and experiment in both the form and content of programmes. At present, broadcasting in the United Kingdom, as in many other countries, is undergoing a period of rapid change, due to Government initiatives and legislation, and to new technological developments, all of which will have far-reaching effects on the range and type of services available in future.

It is, perhaps, useful at this point to reflect on why and how this book came to be written. Interest in the mass media has grown enormously in recent years. The subject has gained academic respectability as an area of scholarly research, and 'communication studies' is now prominent in the curricula of universities, polytechnics and colleges. Television, in particular, has become the dominant feature in contemporary life and culture. For most people, television has now become their main source of news and information, as well as of entertainment. Over the years the IBA Library has received many enquiries from media students and researchers about the constitutional background and structure of broadcasting in the United Kingdom, which could not be answered from one single source. When I was considering a subject for a thesis for an MA in

1

Librarianship and Arts Administration at the City University in London a few years ago, the absence of such a comprehensive guide seemed a good reason for a survey of information sources in British broadcasting. Subsequently, it seemed worth revising and expanding the thesis to provide the kind of researchers' guide to the subject I would like to have had available to answer those earlier enquiries.

Dr Johnson said 'Knowledge is of two kinds. We know a subject ourselves, or we know where we can find information about it.' This book is of the second kind — intended as a guide to where to find information about British broadcasting. However, I hope it can be used in two ways: not only as a guide to sources — both institutional and documentation — of information on broadcasting in the United Kingdom; but also as a source in its own right on the history, constitutional documents, organizations and programme services. As this is primarily a reference book, to be dipped into rather than read continuously, there is inevitably some duplication of coverage in different chapters where a topic can be discussed within several categories.

The subject coverage is primarily 'broadcasting' — the broadcast radio and television services in the United Kingdom. However, related topics have also been touched on wherever relevant — 'narrow' casting (e.g. cable television, data services, hospital and student broadcasting), radio and television manufacturing, advertising, marketing and telecommunications.

The guide is intended for students (of the media, broadcasting, librarianship, information and a range of related subjects), and researchers, journalists, librarians and the general enquirer.

Chapter 1 is a narrative history of broadcasting in the UK, outlining important developments in the technology, constitutional background and programme services. Essential legislation, Government reports and constitutional documents are cited and summarized.

The structure and organizations of broadcasting in the UK is covered by Chapter 2. The inter-relationship of broadcasting, as a public service, and Parliament is detailed through debates on broadcasting policy, the scrutiny of Select Committees, and investigation by Committees of Inquiry. The evolution of the broadcasting of Parliamentary proceedings is also outlined. Other institutions include Government departments, broadcasting authorities, and such industry bodies as trade associations, trade unions and research organizations. A description of the aims, activities, constitutional documents, types of information and publications provided is given for each organization.

The primary source material of broadcasting — the operational documentation of administration, programme production and audience research — is described in Chapter 3. Also considered as primary source material is the end product of broadcasting — the radio and television programmes.

An extended annotated bibliography of print and electronic sources on broadcasting forms Chapter 4. It includes essential printed reference works, online services and databases arranged by category of material. Full bibliographical citations are given, with short descriptive annotations on the aims, coverage and contents of each work.

Chapter 5 contains brief notes of guidance on researching into broadcasting: the lines of enquiry, search strategies and source material on the subject.

A directory of the institutional sources of information in broadcasting — archives, libraries and museums — constitutes Chapter 6. The entries for each unit, compiled through questionnaires, contain details of address, contact, history, coverage, holdings, special collections, catalogues and publications. A warning — changes to the details given in these entries are bound to occur in these changing times, as the libraries and archives move or reorganize. I am grateful to all those organizations and their staff who took the trouble to complete and return the questionnaire for these entries.

I should like to thank all those who helped with the compilation of this work, unfortunately too many to name individually. However, special mention must be made of a few contributions to the project.

To Janet Rennie at the City University, who acted as my supervisor for the original MA thesis, I am grateful for her generous help and guidance.

At the IBA I have received enthusiastic encouragement from successive Controllers of Information/Public Affairs, firstly Barbara Hosking, and subsequently Colette Bowe. Other colleagues who have done me the favour of reading the manuscript, or parts of it, and making helpful suggestions have been Lesley Aston, Information Officer, Barrie Gunter, Head of Research, and the Archivist at Thames Television, Bill Parker. At the BBC, Selwyn Eagle, the Chief Librarian, and Jacquie Kavanagh, the Written Archives Officer, among many friends and former colleagues, have also helped enormously.

A special debt of gratitude must go to Stephen Murphy for generously giving up his time to a detailed reading of the manuscript; through his wise advice I have had the benefit of his extensive knowledge and experience of British broadcasting which has been invaluable to me in writing this book.

Lastly, and certainly not least, my thanks to my colleagues in the IBA Library, for their forbearance and support.

1

History of broadcasting
in the United Kingdom

This summary history covers the developments in the engineering, legislative background, manufacturing industries, organizations and programme output of broadcasting in the United Kingdom over the past ninety years since the first wireless patent was granted in 1896.

The principal constitutional documents, such as Acts of Parliament and the reports of Government Committees of Inquiry and other advisory bodies, are indicated and summarized; they are, of course, essential sources of information on the structure and services of British broadcasting.

1896

Although the origins of broadcasting in Britain may be traced further back, the granting of the first British wireless patent to Guglielmo Marconi on 2 June 1896 is a convenient starting point. After many experiments and demonstrations, Marconi transmitted the first transatlantic wireless message on 12 December 1901. His invention, 'radio telephony', was to develop far beyond the system of point-to-point communication he originally envisaged. He recognized the potential social and cultural significance of his invention, but was apprehensive about broadcasting: 'Have I done the world good or have I added a menace?'[1]

1904

With the *Wireless Telegraphy Act 1904*, the British Government anticipated the rapid development of the medium and its future strategic importance by bringing wireless telegraphy firmly under public control. It gave the State very

5

wide powers for regulation and control, by requiring every wireless operator to take out an official licence. The Post Office, the Government department then responsible for wireless telegraphy, and eventually broadcasting, was also required to operate two Government transmitting stations on an experimental basis.

1914–18

Official concern over the expansion of wireless, and the need to control the wavelengths, particularly for military and naval purposes, was heightened in 1914 by the outbreak of the First World War. For the duration of hostilities, all amateur radio activities were suspended. The war 'harnessed the new powers of wireless to the needs of separate armies, navies and intelligence services',[2] turning it into an instrument of major strategic importance and creating a large wireless manufacturing industry to meet wartime radio requirements.

1922

After the war, popular interest in radio grew rapidly, and by 1920 over twenty wireless societies had been established. Pressure from both the listening public and the wireless industry, for some central broadcasting of radio programmes, resulted in the Post Office authorizing the Marconi Company in February 1922 to provide regular programmes of speech and concerts from a transmitting station at Writtle, near Chelmsford. Later in the year, on 18 October, the British Broadcasting Company was formed by major wireless manufacturers, including Marconi and the General Electric Company. The company started daily broadcasts on 14 November from Marconi House in London, using the 2LO transmitters. John Reith was appointed the first General Manager.

1923

The British Broadcasting Company officially received its Licence from the Post Office on 18 January 1923. Although the programmes were very basic to begin with, they soon grew increasingly varied, with the first broadcast General Election results on 15 November, the first *Children's Hour* on 5 December, the first orchestral concert on 23 December, and the first religious address the next day. The boom in radio telephony, as crystal sets and earphones became cheaper, led to the fashionable pastime of 'listening in'. The *Radio Times* began publication to inform listeners of the BBC programmes. The first broadcast receiving licence cost ten shillings (50p in post-decimal value).

John Logie Baird began his experiments with television, and on 25 June took out his first patent for 'Seeing by wireless'.

In 1923 the Government set up the first of many Committees of Inquiry into broadcasting, under the Chairmanship of Sir Frederick Sykes. Its terms of reference were to consider unresolved issues of the finance, organization and control of broadcasting. The Sykes Committee received information on the use of advertising as a means of finance, and the control of the wavelengths in the United States, Canada and Australia. It decided against advertising as a source of finance for British broadcasting, and for the continuance of the existing broadcasting services operated by the British Broadcasting Company, financed by revenue from the receiving licence fee: *Broadcasting Committee Report* (Cmd 1951) London: HMSO, 1923.

1925

Baird first displayed his television equipment to the public at Selfridges department store in London's Oxford Street in March, and subsequently formed a company, Television Ltd, to develop the system. At his Soho laboratory he 'televised' the first recognizable image of a human face on 2 October, that of his office boy, William Taynton.

John Reith saw that one of the advantages of the broadcasting monopoly held by the BBC was, what he called, 'unity of control'.[3] During this period the BBC evolved into a centralized institution with a strong moral ethic and sense of social purpose. The Committee set up in 1925 under the Chairmanship of the Earl of Crawford and Balcarres, to consider the constitution, finance and future of the BBC, heard evidence from John Reith. Convinced by his advocacy of the concept of public service broadcasting and the educational value of the medium, the Committee recommended that broadcasting should be conducted by a public corporation acting in the nation's interest: *Report of the Broadcasting Committee, 1925* (Cmd 2599) London: HMSO, 1926.

1926

The Times (28 January 1926) reported the first important demonstration of television, to members of the Royal Institution and newspaper reporters at Baird's Soho laboratory. 'The image as transmitted was faint and often blurred, but substantiated a claim that through the "Televisor", . . . it is possible to transmit and reproduce instantly the details of movement, and such things as the play of expression on the face.'[4]

1927

On 1 January 1927 the British Broadcasting Company received a Royal Charter and became the British Broadcasting Corporation: *Wireless broadcasting* (Cmd 2756) London: HMSO, 1926.

The formation of the Television Society, later to become the Royal Television Society, on 7 September, with the aim to further the study and development of television, acknowledged the public interest in the new medium. *Television*, the official organ of the Society and the world's first television journal, was launched the following year.

1929

On 30 September the Baird Television Development Company began regular experimental 30-line television broadcasts from the BBC's 2LO London station. At first, with only one transmitter, sound and vision could not be broadcast simultaneously, and it was not until the new BBC station at Brookman's Park opened that dual transmission was possible.

1930

The golden age of the BBC began with the 1930s, when its reputation grew at home and abroad. The number of radio licence holders reached the 5,000,000 mark in November 1932; and by 1938, 98 per cent of the population could listen to BBC programmes. Its secure statute, and guaranteed income from the licence fee, enabled the BBC to extend the range and quality of radio broadcasts. Outside broadcasts became an important feature of programming, beginning with the first coverage of a budget speech (by Winston Churchill) and of an Armistice Day ceremony at the Cenotaph, both in 1928, and later the first Royal Christmas message (by King George V) in 1932, and broadcast of a Royal Wedding when the Duke of Kent married Princess Marina at Westminster Abbey in 1934.

Experimental television broadcasts continued with a notable first broadcast play, Luigi Pirandello's *The man with a flower in his mouth*, on 14 July. However, discouraged by the BBC's lack of enthusiasm for his invention, Baird turned his efforts to making television a public, as well as a domestic medium, by developing large-screen television for cinemas and theatres. His first demonstration was at the London Colisseum on 28 July 1930, followed in June 1932 by a live transmission of the Derby to the Metropole Cinema in London.

1932

At nine o'clock on the morning of 22 May the BBC's new London headquarters, Broadcasting House, or 'BH' as it has always been known, went into full service, and the last programme from Savoy Hill was broadcast on 14 May.

The BBC began its first public, low-definition television service, from a Baird-equipped studio in Broadcasting House, using his mechanical process, on 22 August. The BBC also encouraged Electrical and Musical Industries (EMI) to develop their rival all-electronic television system.

The BBC Empire Service began on 19 December with English language programmes beamed to Australia, India, South Africa, West Africa and Canada. It was an entirely new concept in short-wave broadcasting, and 'very quickly won a wide and scattered audience'.[5] Later, the addition of foreign language services, beginning in 1938 with the inauguration of the Arabic and Latin American Services, and European news bulletins delivered in German, French and Italian, would form the BBC External Services, a system financed through a Government grant-in-aid and not the broadcast receiving licence fee.

1934

In May, Lord Selsdon was invited to chair a Committee 'to consider the development of television', particularly the future of low-definition television, and weigh up the relative merits of the rival high-definition television systems, primarily the Baird 240-line mechanical process and the Marconi–EMI 405-line electronic system. The Committee decided that 30-line low-definition television had no future for a regular public service, and that both the Baird and Marconi–EMI systems should be developed, and used as alternate systems for the London television service until one of them proved the most satisfactory. The appointment of a Television Advisory Committee to plan and guide the development of the service was proposed: *Report of the Television Committee, 1934–5* (Cmd 4793) London: HMSO, 1935.

1936

BBC Television was officially inaugurated by the Postmaster General, Major G. C. Tryon, on 2 November 1936. Certainly it was the first regular high-definition television service in the United Kingdom. However, as Germany began a regular 180-line service the previous year, on 23 March 1935, 'the accolade of world's first regular high-definition service thus depends somewhat on the interpretation of high-definition chosen'.[6] BBC television programmes were transmitted from Alexandra Palace, with the two systems — the Baird 240-line and the Marconi–EMI 405-line — alternating each week, beginning with Baird. Finally, in February 1937, the Baird system was dropped on the advice of the Television Advisory Committee. The new service was only available to a small number of viewers within the London area. However, it was popular, especially after the coverage of the Coronation of King George VI in May 1937.

The last of the pre-war Committees of Inquiry on broadcasting, chaired by Lord Ullswater, was generally admiring of the achievements of the BBC, but recommended 'further strengthening and securing of the position' by more internal decentralization of control, especially towards the national regions, and passing the Ministerial responsibility for broadcasting from the Postmaster General to a Cabinet Minister (not to happen for another forty years): *Report of the Broadcasting Committee, 1935* (Cmd 5091) London: HMSO, 1936.

1938

John Reith, the creator of public service broadcasting in the United Kingdom, resigned after fifteen years as Director-General of the BBC on June 1938, effectively closing the first, formative chapter in the history of broadcasting in the country.

1939

On 3 September the Prime Minister, Neville Chamberlain, told listeners that Britain was at war with Germany. The television service had already closed down on 1 September, due to the imminent outbreak of war, and the possibility that the Alexandra Palace transmitter could act as a navigational aid to enemy aircraft. On radio the National and Regional Programmes were replaced by the Home Service.

1939–45

During the Second World War, broadcasting united the country and helped raise morale. The 'V for Victory' broadcasts on the BBC European Service in 1941 caught the imagination of listeners in Britain and Europe. Winston Churchill's wartime broadcasts 'mobilized the English language and sent it into battle' (to quote Ed Murrow).[7]

Over the next few years the BBC inaugurated more foreign language services to war-torn Europe, including Polish, Czech, Romanian, Greek, Turkish, Bulgarian, Swedish, Norwegian, Danish and Maltese Services. By the end of 1943 they were broadcasting in over forty-five different languages. 'Consistency was as necessary in foreign broadcasting as objectivity.'[8] Although some critics wanted the service to have the same 'planned coherence' as the German propaganda broadcasts, BBC steadfastness to the truth in war reports won universal praise.

On 7 January 1940 the Forces Programme began as an alternative to the Home Service for the British Expeditionary Forces in France. It was a 'light programme' of variety, music and news that became popular with the forces, as well as listeners at home. Memorable wartime radio programmes included Vera Lynn's *Sincerely Yours, The Brains Trust*, Tommy Handley's *ITMA, Music While You Work, Workers' Playtime*, and the *Radio Doctor* broadcasts of Dr Charles Hill (later to become Chairman of both the ITA and the BBC as Lord Hill of Luton).

William Haley, who had joined the BBC as Editor-in-Chief, became Director-General on 31 March 1944, a post he held until 1952.

The BBC team of war correspondents, including such distinguished reporters as Wynford Vaughan Thomas, Frank Gilliard and Thomas Cadett, sent back graphic reports from the war zones. From D-Day, 6 June 1944, *War Report*, introduced by John Snagge, covered the invasion of Normandy, the liberation of Paris, Brussels and The Hague by the Allies and their entry into Berlin. The voices of the BBC broadcasters became familiar both at home and throughout the world. War ended, as it had begun, with a broadcast: a monitored German announcement of the declaration of unconditional surrender on 7 May 1945.

1945

The wartime coalition Government had set up the Television Committee, under Lord Hankey as Chairman, 'to prepare plans for the restatement and development of the television service after the war'. The report concluded that 'television has come to stay'. It recommended that television should restart after the war, under the control of the BBC, and would be transmitted on the 405-line system in the London area, with plans made to extend it to six 'of the most populous provincial centres'. The appointment of another Television Advisory Committee was also recommended: *Report of the Television Committee, 1943* London: HMSO, 1945.

1946

The BBC Television service resumed on 7 June 1946, again from Alexandra Palace, with coverage of the Victory Parades in London the following day. The unenthusiastic attitude to the new service of some senior BBC staff was matched by the slow take-up by the public. Full nationwide coverage was not achieved for some years because tight Government control of capital expenditure restricted the building programme of new transmitters. Television licences numbered only 14,560 by 1947, rising slowly to 45,564 the following year, and 126,567 in 1948.

A White Paper, issued by the newly-elected post-war Labour Government, under Prime Minister Clement Attlee, stated that 'taken as a whole the achievements of British broadcasting will bear comparison with those of any other country'. It proposed the extension of the BBC's Royal Charter for another five years, and created a new £2 licence fee for radio and television. The BBC was required to broadcast daily reports of the proceedings of Parliament and to introduce a plan for a third radio service of cultural programmes for the 'serious-minded listener'. Following this recommendation, the BBC started the Third Programme on 29 September 1946, joining the Home Service and Light Programme to extend the cultural spectrum of radio programming: *Broadcasting policy* (Cmd 6852) London: HMSO, 1946.

1950

The United Kingdom was a founder member of the European Broadcasting Union (EBU), which was established on 12 February, with BBC Director-

General, Sir Ian Jacob, as the first President. From its Geneva and Brussels headquarters, the EBU initiated the Eurovision international television exchanges in 1954, and many activities concerned with the policy, technical and legal issues of broadcasting in Europe.

1951

The Government appointed a new Committee of Inquiry, under Lord Beveridge as Chairman, 'to consider the constitution, control, finance and other aspects of the sound and television broadcasting services of the United Kingdom'. The Beveridge Committee met sixty-two times over eighteen months from 27 June 1949, and received over 640,000 written and spoken words of evidence in 220 memoranda from interested bodies, including the BBC. The report argued that broadcasting should be protected from any form of competition which would bring about a degrading battle for audiences; it rejected the ideas of competing corporations, commercial advertising, sponsorship, and finance from general taxation. It wanted to see increased regional broadcasting from Scotland, Wales and Northern Ireland. By calling for greater public involvement in the decision-making of broadcasting, and a public right of access to airtime, it foreshadowed later debates in the 1970s. For the time being the BBC's monopoly was maintained, though growing support for the idea of commercial radio and television was signalled by a significant, and subsequently influential, minority report from the Conservative MP, Selwyn Lloyd: *The Report of the Broadcasting Committee, 1949* (Cmd 8116) London: HMSO, 1951.

The Beveridge Committee Report was followed on 10 July 1951 by a Government White Paper, which accepted its basic recommendations on the issues of advertising and monopoly: *Memorandum on the Report of the Broadcasting Committee, 1949* (Cmd 8291) London: HMSO, 1951.

In the next few years there was gradual acceptance by the public of television as more than just a luxury or novelty. At the same time there was the evolution of a campaign for breaking the monopoly of the BBC with the introduction of a 'commercial' television service supported by revenue from advertising.

1952

The new Conservative Government, elected in October 1951, with Winston Churchill as Prime Minister, introduced a White Paper in May 1952, which marked a slight change in broadcasting policy by proposing 'some element of competition' when feasible financially: *Memorandum on the Report of the Broadcasting Committee, 1949* (Cmd 8550) London: HMSO, 1952.

A House of Lords debate on the White Paper, on 22 May 1952, provided vigorous examples of the opposition to commercial television, notably from Lord Reith. He felt it would jeopardize a broadcasting system which 'commands the respect and admiration of the whole world', and went on to say: 'And somebody introduced smallpox, bubonic plague and the Black Death. And somebody is minded now to introduce sponsored broadcasting.'[9] However, in the House of Commons debate, on 11 June, many supporters spoke in favour of commercial television.

1953

The Conservative Government introduced a second White Paper, on 13 November 1953, which outlined their policy for the structure of the new television service. The system would give scope to private enterprise under public control, and avoid the pitfalls of direct sponsorship, while still receiving revenue from advertising: *Broadcasting policy* (Cmd 9005) London: HMSO, 1953.

The public debate on television gathered momentum with the formation of two organized pressure groups. The National Television Council, with Lady Violet Bonham Carter as Chairman and Christopher Mayhew as leading exponent, was inaugurated to oppose commercial television. The Popular Television Association, with Lord Derby as Chairman, was formed 'to awaken the national conscience to the dangers, social, political and artistic, of monopoly of the rapidly expanding field of television'.[10] It promoted the provision of alternative programme services for the public.

The popularity of BBC television grew with the coverage of the Coronation of Queen Elizabeth II on 2 June 1953, which brought a huge increase in television set ownership, and with such programmes as *1984, The Quatermass Experiment, Zoo Quest, The Good Old Days* and the beginning of *Panorama*.

The Act, establishing a new television service in the United Kingdom, received the Royal Assent on 30 July 1954. During the long Parliamentary passage, the amount spoken on the subject in Parliament had exceeded 'the number of words in the Old Testament'.[11] The Act provided for Independent Television (ITV) to be set up and supervised by a public authority responsible to Parliament, the Independent Television Authority (ITA), which would own and operate the transmitters, appoint the programme companies, supervise programme planning and control advertising. It created a unique system of private enterprise under public control: *Television Act 1954* (2 & 3 Eliz. 2 Ch. 55) London: HMSO, 1954.

Five days after the Act reached the Statute Book, on 4 August, the Independent Television Authority, with Sir Kenneth Clark as Chairman, held their first meeting. The first Director-General, Sir Robert Fraser, took up his post on 1 October. Together they designed a federal system of regional television companies contracted to the ITA for the provision of programme services in their own franchise area. By splitting the franchises between weekday and weekend, the Authority sought to accommodate four major companies in three areas, achieving an element of the competition required by the *Television Act*. On

24 August the Authority advertised for programme contractors for the London, Midlands and the North of England franchises.

1955

Independent Television began on 22 September 1955, with a live transmission from an inaugural banquet at the Guildhall in the City of London, and programmes provided by the first two programme contractors for the London area, Associated-Rediffusion and the Associated Broadcasting Company (later renamed Associated Television), together with Independent Television News.[12] The first television commercial to be seen by the British public that opening night was for 'tingling fresh' Gibbs SR Toothpaste. Full ITV coverage of the United Kingdom was not complete for seven years, when the last of the original regional companies, Wales West and North (WWN), went on air on 14 September 1962; the system by then had fifteen companies serving fourteen franchise areas. The 'network companies', the four contractors for the lucrative, heavily-populated franchise areas of London, the Midlands and the North of England (Associated-Rediffusion, Associated Television, Granada Television and ABC Television), had the responsibility for producing the principal peak-hour programming for the whole ITV network, while the smaller companies mostly concentrated on the production of local programmes for their own areas. ITV programmes appeared distinctive and innovative compared to those of the BBC, particularly in the areas of light entertainment, and news and current affairs. Independent Television News (ITN), set up by the ITV companies to provide their news service, had an especially revolutionary approach. Previously, news bulletins on BBC television had been summaries read by unseen and anonymous newsreaders over caption cards, a method thought then to be a guarantee of impartial presentation. ITN, first under Aidan Crawley, then Geoffrey Cox, presented the news pictorially, with good actuality coverage, and such personality journalist-newsreaders as Robin Day and Christopher Chataway. ITV soon found audience popularity with such programmes as *Sunday Night at the London Palladium* and *Armchair Theatre*. Financially, however, the first few years brought mixed fortunes for the ITV companies, with early heavy losses soon turning into the 'unacceptable profitability' later criticized, in 1959, by the House of Commons Committee of Public Accounts.[13]

   The new Independent Television programme companies formed their own trade association, the Television Programme Contractors' Association (successively renamed the Independent Television Companies Association and the Independent Television Association), to deal with matters of common interest, co-ordinate policy for the network, particularly in programme planning and advertising copy clearance, and to conduct trade union and inter-company negotiations.

1957

The first regular television broadcasts for schools in the United Kingdom began on 13 May, when the Associated-Rediffusion programme, *Looking and Seeing*, started the ITV schools service.

1961

The imposition of the Television Advertisement Duty, by the Chancellor of the Exchequer, Selwyn Lloyd, on 1 May, brought sharp reactions from the ITV companies and the advertising agencies, and resulted in a temporary shift of advertising expenditure from television back to the press.

1962

The Government had always emphasized that the plan for ITV was an experimental one, with the possibility of later modifications. Such an opportunity was the Committee on Broadcasting, appointed in July 1960 by the Postmaster General, Reginald Bevins. The Committee, under Sir Harry Pilkington as Chairman, had 'to consider the future of broadcasting services in the United Kingdom . . .' Prominent among the members was Richard Hoggart, author of *The uses of literacy*, and a known critic of 'commercial' television; his views influenced the Committee's dislike of ITV and the financing of broadcasting by advertising. After 78 meetings of the Committee, a further 43 of its Sub-Committee, and the receipt of 852 papers, including 636 submissions of evidence from individuals and organizations, they finally reported in June 1962. The report, highly critical of ITV, proposed an overhaul of its structure, by recommending that the ITA should take over the direct planning of programmes and sales of advertising airtime, leaving the companies merely to produce programmes for sale to the Authority for inclusion in its programme schedules. The whole emphasis of the report was on the quality and balance of programmes, and the role of the BBC and the ITA as trustees for the national interest in broadcasting. However, apart from the recommendation of an additional television service from the BBC on 625-line UHF, the report was largely rejected by the Government, though it remained an influential statement of broadcasting ideals for many years: *Report of the Committee on Broadcasting, 1960* (Cmnd 1753) London: HMSO, 1962.

The Government promptly issued a White Paper, on 4 July 1962, following the Pilkington Committee Report, which authorized the BBC to increase its hours of radio broadcasting and start a second television channel on 625-line UHF: *Broadcasting* (Cmnd 1770) London: HMSO, 1962.

The first transatlantic satellite television transmission took place on 11 July, via Telstar 1; 200 million viewers in 16 European countries saw transmissions direct from the USA.

A second Government White Paper, issued in December, rejected the proposals by the Pilkington Committee to restructure ITV, but proposed strengthening the role of the Authority with supervision of programme scheduling, ensuring high programme standards, particularly in controlling the depiction of violence on television, and a 'more formal and direct control' over advertising. Advertising magazines, or 'admags', which incorporated advertisements within a programme of appeal to consumers, were to cease from 31 March 1963: *Broadcasting* (Cmnd 1893) London: HMSO, 1962.

1963

A new Act, embodying proposals from both the two 1962 White Papers, reached the Royal Assent on 31 July 1963. It required the ITA to draw up a code for programme makers, giving guidance on rules for showing violence, and for other matters concerning standards and practice. The BBC also gave assurances that they would adhere to similar programme standards, in a letter from Lord Normanbrook, the Chairman, to the Postmaster General, dated 13 June 1964. Programme schedules would have to be drawn up in consultation with the ITA, which would have stronger powers for programme control. For the 'more formal and direct control' of advertising, the Authority should assume responsibility for the timing, amounts, distribution and standards of advertising. Provision was made for an Exchequer Levy of 'additional payments' from the companies, based on net advertising revenue in excess of £1.5 million, to replace the Television Advertisement Duty. Other matters covered included: newspaper shareholdings in ITV companies; the provision of news programmes; limiting the value of games show prizes; and audience research by the ITA: *Television Act 1963* (Ch. 50) London: HMSO, 1963.

Lord Hill of Luton, formerly Charles Hill, the BBC Radio Doctor, and a Postmaster General, took up his appointment as Chairman of the ITA on 1 July 1963 and found an Authority demoralized by the criticism of the Pilkington Committee. He determined to rebuild its morale and strengthen its role, through implementing the more formal programme control arrangements required by the *Television Act 1963*. The most pressing task for the ITA was the awarding of new ITV contracts. Despite twenty-two applications for the ITV franchises, no changes were made, and the existing contractors were all reappointed for the period 1964–7. During the year the first (and by 1988 the only) ITV company failed, when Wales West and North (WWN) ceased trading due to substantial losses; the company, and the separate franchise for North Wales, was absorbed by the neighbouring ITV company, Television Wales and West (TWW).

1964

An Act to consolidate the *Television Act 1954* and *Television Act 1963*, and to form a basic constitutional document for the ITA, was given the Royal Assent on 25 March 1964. It also made provision for a comprehensive 'ITV Code of Advertising Standards and Practice' as the basis of advertising control by the Authority: *Television Act 1964* (Ch. 21) London: HMSO, 1964.

The arrival of the second BBC television channel, BBC2, on 20 April 1964, heralded an exciting period in programme making. The subsequent explosion of talent and innovative programmes on both BBC and ITV disproved the Pilkington Committee's fears about the detrimental effect on programme standards of competition in broadcasting. Sir Hugh Greene, who had become Director-General of the BBC in 1960, encouraged the broadening of programme content on television, new standards of current affairs programmes, and the pioneering of television satire with such programmes as *That Was The Week That Was* and *Not So Much A Programme More A Way Of Life*.

Television became the dominant medium while the BBC radio services were less and less popular. A further challenge to BBC radio at this time came from the newly emergent offshore pirate radio stations. Radio Caroline had begun transmitting from a ship moored off the Essex coast on 28 March 1964, and other radio pirates soon followed. They successfully catered for the demand for continuous pop music from a large and rapidly increasing young audience, and they made considerable profits from the advertising they carried. However, these pirate radio stations were illegal; they played records continuously without paying royalties to performers or record companies, but evaded legal action by operating from just outside British territorial waters and jurisdiction.

From 30 July the Television Advertisement Duty on ITV was replaced by an Exchequer Levy on advertising revenue.

1965

Following reports from the Royal College of Physicians (*Smoking and health*) and the United States Surgeon-General on the link between smoking and cancer and heart disease, the Government announced a ban on the advertising of cigarettes and hand-rolled tobacco on television on 2 March, to take effect on 1 August 1965; it had accounted for about 7 per cent of total ITV advertising revenue.

In December the Postmaster General announced that the Television Advisory Committee had recommended the German PAL (Phase Alternation Line) colour television system for the United Kingdom, in preference to the American NTSC or French SECAM transmission systems. All Eurovision members had agreed to originate and receive on the 625-line, though transcoders were necessary to convert from the PAL and SECAM systems used in Europe.

1966

On 15 June 1966 the House of Lords voted in favour of a motion, by Lord Egremont, for the public televising of some of their proceedings for an experimental period; this led to the appointment of a Select Committee on the Televising of the Proceedings of the House of Lords. However, the House of Commons, in the first of many debates on the subject over the following twenty years, rejected an all-party motion, introduced by the Leader of the House, Richard Crossman, for a closed-circuit experiment of televising Commons proceedings.

A Government White Paper proposed a new 'University of the Air', to offer degree courses involving a combination of television, radio, and correspondence course, tutorials, and short residential courses, which would eventually start in 1971 as the Open University: *A university of the air* (Cmnd 2922) London: HMSO, 1966.

1967

The first regular colour television service in Britain began on 1 July, when BBC2 began colour transmissions, using the PAL system on UHF 625-line. It greatly contributed to the rising public awareness of BBC2 after a slow beginning.

As an attempt to stem the threat from the radio pirates, a new Act of Parliament, implementing a Council of Europe treaty, made it an offence to supply, maintain, publicize or advertise on the off-shore pirate radio stations: *Marine, &c, Broadcasting (Offences) Act 1967* (Ch. 41) London: HMSO, 1967.

From 30 September 1967 the new BBC Radio 1 service offered a popular music channel to cater for the young audience of the banned pirate stations. The BBC Light and Third Programmes, and Home Service were renamed Radios 2, 3 and 4. Later in the year, on 8 November, the BBC Local Radio experiment began when Radio Leicester went on-air.

1968

The first attempts at radio and television coverage of Parliamentary proceedings took place in 1968. In February a closed-circuit television and radio experiment in broadcasting the House of Lords was undertaken, and between 23 April and 17 May the House of Commons allowed a radio only closed-circuit experiment.

On 30 July 1968 new ITV contracts for 1968 to 1974 took effect, which included a new franchise area for Yorkshire and the dropping of the split weekday/weekend franchises, except in the London area. The new programme contractors were Thames Television (the result of an enforced merger of Rediffusion and ABC Television) and London Weekend Television for the London area, HTV (originally Harlech Television) taking over Wales and West of England from TWW, and Yorkshire Television; all other companies were reappointed.

1969

Colour television was extended to BBC1 and ITV on 625-line UHF on 15 November 1969.

The changes in broadcasting in the 1960s, particularly the intensified competition between the BBC and ITV, brought new attitudes and concerns. As the broadcasting organizations grew larger and more complex, labour relations became strained and more difficult. The principal trade unions in broadcasting (the Association of Broadcasting Staffs (ABS), the Association of Cinematograph, Television and Allied Technicians (ACTT), and the National Association of Theatrical, Television and Kine Employees (NATTKE)) became more militant, and pressed for greater participation in broadcasting policy and decision-making.

Equally vociferous were the new pressure groups. The licence that Hugh Greene allowed his broadcasters had resulted in many innovative, but controversial programmes, to the dislike of a strong lobby of mostly self-appointed guardians of the public interest. Most notable among them was Mary Whitehouse and her 'Clean Up TV Campaign', which eventually became the National Viewers and Listeners Association. Mrs Whitehouse considered Hugh Greene 'more than anyone else' responsible for the moral collapse in Britain; he described her organization as the 'lunatic fringe'.[14] Another group, the Free Communications Group, launched in 1969, campaigned, through its journal *Open Secret*, for social ownership of the means of communication, in particular for greater openness in broadcasting decision-making. It also campaigned against some of the proposals in *Broadcasting in the seventies*, the BBC's plan for network radio and non-metropolitan broadcasting.

However, the 1960s had brought many achievements in television programming that were popular with audiences and critics alike, particularly in current affairs, satire, and notably in drama, with such milestones as *Cathy Come Home*, *Z-cars* and *The Forsyte Saga*.

1971

After the June 1970 General Election, the new Conservative Government, under Prime Minister Edward Heath, implemented its election manifesto promise on local commercial radio by issuing a White Paper, in which it maintained that the new radio stations would add to the vitality of broadcasting by providing an element of competition with the BBC, and that local radio advertising would be a new and useful service for the consumer: *An alternative service of radio broadcasting* (Cmnd 4636) London: HMSO, 1971.

Open University transmissions began on 10 January 1971, and developed a service offering weekly some 70 hours of lessons on radio and television for 34 weeks of the year.

1972

The Act enabling the provision of local commercial sound broadcasting in the United Kingdom reached the Statute Book on 12 June 1972. It established Independent Local Radio, to be set up and supervised by the Independent Television Authority, to be renamed the Independent Broadcasting Authority; and set out procedures for financing, rental payments, shareholdings and local advisory committees: *Sound Broadcasting Act 1972* (Ch. 32) London: HMSO, 1972.

The future planning of broadcasting would also depend largely on the availability of channels and wavelengths. A new Television Advisory Committee, under Chairman Sir Robert Cockburn, recommended the extension of the 625-line UHF television, the phasing out of the 405-line VHF service, and proposals for cable and satellite broadcasting: Ministry of Posts and Telecommunications *Report of the Television Advisory Committee, 1972* London: HMSO, 1972.

The demand for greater accountability by the broadcasting authorities, and increased public participation and access in broadcasting, surfaced again among the recommendations of a House of Commons Select Committee report: House of Commons *Second report from the Select Committee on Nationalised Industries: Independent Broadcasting Authority* (1971–72 HC 465) London: HMSO, 1972.

1973

In April the IBA announced a new type of broadcast service, developed as a result of research into digital transmission. Teletext utilizes the unused lines of the 625-line UHF picture to transmit textual information and data to domestic TV sets via a decoder. The IBA teletext system would be known as ORACLE (Optional Reception of Announcements by Coded Line Electronics). The BBC had been working on similar research, and announced their teletext system, CEEFAX, the following year.

An Act to consolidate the *Television Act 1964* and the *Sound Broadcasting Act 1972*, and give the IBA a comprehensive constitutional document, became law on 23 May 1973: *Independent Broadcasting Authority Act 1973* (Ch. 19) London: HMSO, 1973.

The first Independent Local Radio station, London Broadcasting Company (LBC), operating the London News and Information franchise, went on-air on 8 October 1973, soon followed by Capital Radio, the London General and Entertainment franchise holder, on 16 October, and Radio Clyde in Glasgow on 31 December.

1974

Departmental responsibility for broadcasting passed to the Home Office in March 1974, when the Ministry of Posts and Telecommunications was wound up. Reflecting the increasing importance of broadcasting, the Home Secretary, one of the most senior posts in the Cabinet, would be the responsible Government Minister and senior spokesman in Parliament.

The Act changing the basis for the additional payments, an Exchequer Levy collected from the ITV companies on behalf of the Treasury by the IBA, from one on advertising revenue to one on profits derived from the business of providing programmes, reached the Royal Assent on 23 May 1974: *Independent Broadcasting Authority Act 1974* (Ch. 16) London: HMSO, 1974.

A Committee, with Sir Stewart Crawford as Chairman, was appointed to consider the question of broadcasting coverage, particularly in Scotland, Wales, Northern Ireland and rural England. The report recommended that the fourth television channel in Wales should be allotted to a separate service in which Welsh-language programmes, provided jointly by the BBC and the ITV contractor for Wales, should be given a priority, and the extension of local radio services into the rural areas of England, Northern Scotland and Northern Ireland: *Report of the Committee on Broadcasting Coverage* (Cmnd 5774) London: HMSO, 1974.

An Act extending the life of the Independent Broadcasting Authority from 31 July 1976 to 31 July 1979 was passed: *Independent Broadcasting Authority (No. 2) Act 1974* (Ch. 42) London: HMSO, 1974.

The BBC teletext service, CEEFAX, began regular transmissions on 23 September 1974.

1975

A working party, with J. W. M. Siberry as Chairman, reported on the working arrangements required to provide a fourth channel in Wales, including timing and estimates of costs for the television service: Home Office/Welsh Office *Report of the Working Party on a Fourth Television Service in Wales: Adroddiad y Gweithgor ar Bedwerydd Gwasanaeth Teledu yng Nghymru* (Cmnd 6290) Cardiff: HMSO, 1975.

1977

In April 1974 the Labour Government, which had won the General Election in February that year, had set up a Committee on the Future of Broadcasting, with Lord Annan as Chairman. After over two years of meetings — 44 of the full Committee and 28 of its specialist groups, and receiving submissions of evidence from some 750 organizations and individuals — it reported on 24 March 1977. The Committee's main objectives were: to preserve British broadcasting as a public service accountable to the public, through Parliament; to devise a new structure to enable broadcasting to expand and evolve over the following fifteen years, achieving a full diversity of services; and to keep the editorial independence of broadcasters free from political pressure or control. Its main recommendations were for a new Local Broadcasting Authority (to take over local radio services from the BBC and the IBA) and an Open Broadcasting Authority (to run the fourth television channel), neither of which was implemented. Other recommendations, however, which did eventually come to fruition were an independent Broadcasting Complaints Commission and a joint BBC/ITV system of television audience measurement: *Report of the Committee on the Future of Broadcasting* (Cmnd 6753) London: HMSO, 1977.

In September 1977 the World Administrative Radio Conference (WARC) in Geneva allocated five DBS channels to the UK which could be used for future satellite television transmissions.

1978

The first regular sound broadcasting of Parliamentary proceedings began on 3 April 1978, when the BBC and Independent Radio News started radio broadcasts of debates.

A White Paper, published on 28 July, proposed legislating on some of the Annan Committee's recommendations: the Open Broadcasting Authority, the Broadcasting Complaints Commission and supervision of Pay-TV and cable by the IBA. However, the Labour Government did not legislate on these policy proposals before losing the General Election in May 1979: *Broadcasting* (Cmnd 7294) London: HMSO, 1978.

Legislation further extended the life of the Independent Broadcasting Authority until 31 July 1981: *Independent Broadcasting Authority Act 1978* (Ch. 48) London: HMSO, 1978.

A Home Office Local Radio Working Party was set up to plan the expansion of local radio services in the United Kingdom, and to consider recommendations of areas suitable for new radio stations.

1979

Following the May 1979 General Election, the new Conservative Government announced, in the Queen's Speech to the new Parliament on 15 May, the proposal to authorize the IBA to operate the fourth television channel. The IBA had already been empowered to undertake the engineering work necessary for the new television channel: *Independent Broadcasting Authority Act 1979* (Ch. 35) London: HMSO, 1979.

The deterioration in labour relations within the broadcasting industry reached a crisis point in the summer with the longest strike in its history, when a dispute, between the ITV programme companies and the ACTT technicians' union, resulted in an eleven-week stoppage, from 10 August to 19 October, and an estimated loss of £90–100 million in advertising revenue.

By the close of the decade, British television programmes were internationally known and admired; in 1978 at the prestigious Prix Italia the United Kingdom won all three major prizes for drama, documentary and music programmes. Such award-winning series as the BBC's *Pennies from Heaven, I Claudius* and *Life on Earth*, and ITV's *The South Bank Show* achieved new standards, and popularity with viewers.

1980

The first half of the 1980s were to see rapid acceleration in the development of broadcasting, with the expansion of the existing public service broadcasting systems, and the emergence of new cable and satellite television services.

On 24 January the IBA announced the particulars of the new ITV contracts to run from 1982 to 1989, which included for the first time a possibility of a franchise for a breakfast-time television contract. By the closing date of 9 May, 43 applications had been received for the 16 franchises, and after a series of public meetings throughout the country to assess public opinion, the Authority announced the contract awards on 28 December. Two of the original ITV companies were not offered new contracts: Southern Television, to be replaced by TVS — Television South; and Westward Television to be replaced by TSW — Television South West. Associated Television (ATV) was required to restructure and firmly base itself within its franchise area of the East and West Midlands — it became Central Independent Television. All other regional ITV companies were offered new contracts. The IBA were persuaded of the viability of breakfast-time television by TV-am.

A new Act, which received the Royal Assent on 13 November, extended the life of the IBA until 1996, and redefined its duties to include the provision of the new fourth television channel in England, Scotland and Northern Ireland. However, in Wales, a fourth channel, to include a substantial proportion of programmes in the Welsh language, would be the responsibility of a new Welsh Fourth Channel Authority. The Act also set up an independent Broadcasting Complaints Commission: *Broadcasting Act 1980* (Ch. 64) London: HMSO, 1980.

1981

The Broadcasting Complaints Commission began operations on 1 June; its terms of reference are to adjudicate on complaints of unfair or unjust treatment, or unwarranted infringement of privacy, by broadcasters.

On 21 July a new joint BBC/ITV system of audience research, as recommended by the Annan Committee, became a reality with the establishment of the Broadcasters' Audience Research Board (BARB), with Sir Stewart

Crawford as Chairman. The new unified television ratings system, conducted under contract by AGB Research, began on 3 August 1981.

Satellite broadcasting came a little nearer with the publication of a Home Office study, which examined the legal, technical, financial and supervisory issues involved, outlined options and invited comments: Home Office *Direct Broadcasting by Satellite* London: HMSO, 1981.

Experimental Pay-TV was authorized in fourteen areas in the United Kingdom, and started with Rediffusion, on the Starview service, and the BBC, on Visionhire Cable.

On 29 July 1981 the largest ever television outside broadcast was mounted for the Royal Wedding of HRH The Prince of Wales and Lady Diana Spencer; it was seen by over 750 million viewers in 74 countries throughout the world.

1982

Cable television policy was formulated by two reports during the year. In February a Cabinet Office report urged an early start on DBS services distributed by cable, and to announce the broad outline of future policy: Cabinet Office: Information Technology Advisory Panel (ITAP) *Report on cable systems* London: HMSO, 1982.

The resultant independent inquiry was set up in March, with Lord Hunt of Tanworth as Chairman. It largely confirmed the findings of the ITAP report, and recommended the establishment of a Cable Authority, to award franchises and supervise cable services, which would be self-financing from rentals, subscriptions or advertising revenue: Home Office *Report of the Inquiry into Cable Expansion and Broadcasting Policy* (Cmnd 8679) London: HMSO, 1982.

On 4 March the Home Secretary, William Whitelaw, announced the allocation of two DBS channels to the BBC, with the objective to have a satellite television service in operation by 1986; United Satellites Ltd (Unisat), a joint company of British Aerospace, British Telecom and Marconi, was formed to provide the service with DBS facilities.

Channel 4, the fourth television channel, began on 2 November. Despite a mixed reception initially and disappointing early viewing figures, it found an enthusiastic audience and eventual critical acclaim. The channel was provided by the Channel Four Television Company, a wholly-owned subsidiary of the IBA. It had a remit, under the *Broadcasting Act 1980*, to provide programmes calculated to appeal to tastes not generally catered for by ITV, and to encourage innovation and experiment in the form and content of programmes. Early original, and often controversial, programmes included: The Royal Shakespeare Company production of *Nicholas Nickleby*; *Walter* (a drama about mental health); *The Friday Alternative* (alternative current affairs); *The Animal Programme* documentary; the trendy twice-weekly soap opera, *Brookside*. *Channel Four News* provided a daily, hour-long, in-depth news and current affairs programme.

For Wales a distinctive fourth television service of Welsh language programmes was provided by the Welsh Fourth Channel Authority. Sianel Pedwar Cymru (S4C) began on 1 November, with programmes supplied by the BBC in Wales, and HTV, the Welsh ITV programme contractor.

On 22 November the Government decided to adopt the C-MAC system, developed by the IBA, as the official technical transmission system for future DBS services in the UK, following a report of the Advisory Panel on Technical Transmission Standards, chaired by Sir Antony Part: Home Office and Department of Industry *Direct Broadcasting by Satellite. Report of the Advisory Panel on Technical Transmission Standards (*Cmnd 8751) London: HMSO, 1982.

1983

Breakfast-time television came to Britain in 1983. The BBC pre-empted its commercial rival by a fortnight and launched *Breakfast Time* on BBC1 on 17 January. It was a cosy and informal mixture of news and entertainment, which quickly found a large audience. On 1 February TV-am, the commercial breakfast-time television service, started. The company, formed by a group of well-known and experienced broadcasters, had convinced the IBA of the viability of breakfast-time television, with their 'mission to explain' programme philosophy. However, *Good Morning Britain* was overweighted with star presenters, and had a style of presentation which did not find favour initially with audiences or advertisers. Low viewing figures and advertising revenue brought financial crises and a classic boardroom struggle within the company. A subsequent radical change to a more informal style and greater emphasis on popular and children's items resulted in success, eventually overtaking the 'ratings' lead of the rival BBC service.

A Government White Paper was published on 27 April, taking up the Hunt Committee's recommendations on cable television, by proposing the granting of interim licences for up to twelve pilot cable systems: Home Office/ Department of Industry *The development of cable systems* (Cmnd 8866) London: HMSO, 1983.

1984

Sky Channel, the first satellite television programme channel in the United Kingdom, started on 16 January. It was owned by Rupert Murdoch, and initially was available through cable systems in Swindon, Milton Keynes and Greenwich, with wider distribution throughout the UK and Europe later.

Increased powers for the seizure of pirate or other illegal broadcasting equipment were conferred by an Act reaching the Royal Assent on 12 April, resulting in the investigation and prosecution of many pirate radio stations by the

Department of Trade and Industry: *Telecommunications Act 1984* (Ch. 12) London: HMSO, 1984

Legislation for cable television reached the Statute Book on 26 July. It provided for the establishment of a Cable Authority to appoint and supervise cable services, DBS services by the IBA, and a Satellite Broadcasting Board comprised equally of BBC and IBA members: *Cable and Broadcasting Act 1984* (Ch. 46) London: HMSO, 1984.

New Legislation required that videograms for sale or hire in the United Kingdom would need a certificate from the British Board of Film Classification, creating a dual-standard censorship, whereby videos seen in the privacy of the home could be subject to stricter controls than the public showing of films in cinemas, or television: *Video Recordings Act 1984* (Ch. 39) London: HMSO, 1984.

After a re-evaluation of the economics of the DBS project, the BBC initiated, in January 1984, a Tripartite Working Party, comprising the BBC, the IBA and the ITV companies, to investigate sharing the costs of the venture. Later, in July, with the approval of the Home Secretary, the BBC and the ITV companies were augmented by a 'Third Force' of five independent companies: Consolidated Satellite Broadcasting, Granada TV Rental, Pearson plc, Thorn–EMI and Virgin Group. This consortium, known as the 'Club of 21' worked with the Satellite Broadcasting Board, under its Chairman, Lord Thomson of Monifieth, on plans for DBS services for the UK.

1985

Televising the proceedings of the House of Lords, on an experimental basis, began on 23 January 1985, with a notable contribution from the Earl of Stockton (formerly Harold Macmillan). The experiment was pronounced a success, and extracts from televised debates are used regularly, in news programmes and the Channel 4 series, *Their Lordships' House* (later titled *The Parliament Programme*).

The Cable Authority started the task of advertising and granting franchises for new broadband cable systems and licences for the provision of cable programme services in Britain. Up to this time, about 14 per cent of households in the UK had received the public broadcast services of the BBC and the IBA through cable distribution for better reception. However, since 1981 thirteen experimental subscription cable television services (Pay-TV) had been licensed, a system the Cable Authority now further extended with new franchises. Such cable systems offer subscribers both the broadcast programme services, as well as such new cable programme channels as Sky Channel, Premiere, Music Box and Lifestyle.

On 11 July the Home Secretary announced various local radio proposals, including an investigation into the viability of community radio, a forthcoming consultation paper on the broader policy issues of radio, and the go-ahead to the BBC and the IBA for an experiment in split-frequency broadcasting (transmitting different programmes on the medium wave and VHF frequencies) on some of the local radio stations.

Satellite broadcasting, however, was postponed during the year. The new Satellite Broadcasting Board had to inform the Government in June that the 'Club of 21' had decided they could not proceed with plans for DBS services, because the requirement to buy the costly British Unisat equipment made the venture an impossible risk. The Board was formally wound up on 8 July. Satellite broadcasting would proceed only if it was judged to be commercially viable without public subsidy. However, in September, the IBA had more success when, at the request of the Home Office, it invited 'expressions of interest' from organizations who might want to provide one or more DBS television channels, this time without the Government requirement to use a costly British satellite system.

1986

The diversification of the broadcasting authorities into developing new, non-broadcast services gathered momentum in 1986. Datacast, a new BBC data transmission service, using the existing television signal, began in January. It had been developed by BBC research engineers as a spin-off from CEEFAX, the BBC teletext system. Data is supplied by such information providers as the *Financial Times* and the Stock Exchange to the BBC, where it is encrypted and transmitted to subscribers, who receive the signal deciphered through a decoder. The IBA had also been enabled by the *Cable and Broadcasting Act 1984* to provide additional teletext services for subscription charges; Air Call Teletext was contracted, as an agent of Oracle Teletext Ltd, to supply this service.

Another data transmission service, Radio Teletext, otherwise known as SCA (Subsidiary Communications Authorization), was also launched during the year. SCA, developed in the USA, uses the spare bandwidth within a VHF/FM channel. In August the IBA advertised two franchises for Radio Teletext services, to be carried on the London area transmitters used by Capital Radio and LBC, and awarded contracts for the provision of financial data services to subscribers in the investment community.

The Exchequer Levy on ITV was changed from 1 April by the introduction of a 25 per cent levy on overseas programme sales, balanced by a reduction to 45 per cent of the levy on the ITV contractors' domestic profits: *Finance Act 1986* (Ch. 41) London: HMSO, 1986.

The Report of the Committee on Financing the BBC, under Chairman Professor Alan Peacock, was published on 3 July. The terms of reference were: to assess the effects of the introduction of advertising or sponsorship on the BBC's Home Services on the BBC itself, and ITV, ILR, cable and satellite services; to identify a range of options for their introduction; and to consider any other type of income from the consumer other than the licence fee. Among its recommendations were: that the BBC should not be obliged to take advertising in current conditions, though it should have the options to privatize Radio 1 and 2 and local radio; the licence fee should be indexed annually at the general inflation rate; the ITV and DBS franchises should be put out to competitive tender, with the IBA having to justify its acceptance of lower bids; Channel Four Television Company to cease to be a subsidiary of the IBA, and to sell its own advertising time; a quota of airtime for independent producers; and the possible establishment of a Public Service Broadcasting Council and a Broadcasting Transmission Authority. In reaching its stated goal, that broadcasting policy should enlarge both the consumers' choice and the programme makers' opportunities, the Committee outlined a three-stage development leading to a multiplicity of choice of an indefinite number of channels, with differing charging systems: *Report of the Committee on Financing the BBC* (Cmnd 9824) London: HMSO, 1986.

Lord Young, the Secretary of State for Employment, announced, on 18 July, plans for a 'College of the Air', an adult training programme of vocational and other courses on using Channel 4, ITV, ILR and BBC TV, to start in 1987 (as the Open College).

Broadcasting hours were further extended in both the day and night, beginning in August with Yorkshire Television's experimental all-night programme of popular music videos from the European satellite service, Music Box, and the start of BBC Daytime television service on 27 October.

The IBA had advertised in April the three DBS channels, as authorized by the Home Secretary, under provisions in the *Cable and Broadcasting Act 1984*. The contract for the DBS channels was awarded in December to British Satellite Broadcasting (BSB), a consortium comprising the Granada Group, Anglia Television, the Virgin Group, Amstrad Electronics and Pearson plc. The BSB satellite service, due on air in 1990, will consist of two channels supported by advertising, Now (news and current affairs) and Galaxy (entertainment), and one subscription channel, Screen (new feature films).

1987

The debate on the future of radio services in the United Kingdom was back on the agenda in 1987. On 25 February a Government Green Paper outlined the opportunities presented by additional spectrum and technological developments, setting out options for the future of sound broadcasting (including national, regional, local and community radio services), and making a case for lighter regulation: Home Office *Radio choices and opportunities: a consultative document* (Cm 92) London: HMSO, 1987.

A study of the ways in which market forces might supplement, or replace, existing administrative procedures for radio spectrum management in the United Kingdom, commissioned from Communications Studies and Planning International Ltd (CSP) by the Department of Trade and Industry, recommended a large measure of deregulation in the licensing and use of frequencies: Department of Trade and Industry *Deregulation of the radio spectrum in the UK*. London: HMSO, 1987.

An amendment to the *Broadcasting Act 1981* changed the maximum period of the current contracts between the IBA and the ITV companies, from 12 to 15 years, now expiring on 31 December 1992, to give more time before the next contract round for consideration of the franchise system: *Broadcasting Act 1987* (Ch. 10) London: HMSO, 1987.

The Conservative Government, under Prime Minister Margaret Thatcher, was returned in the General Election on 11 June. Broadcasting reform had been prominent in their election manifesto, including proposals for a new Broadcasting Bill, to 'enable the broadcasters to take full advantage of the opportunities presented by technological advances and to broaden the choice of viewing and listening', to bring forward proposals for 'stronger and more effective arrangements' to reflect the public concern over the display of sex and violence on television, and to remove the exemption broadcasters had under the *Obscene Publications Act 1959*.

A study, commissioned by the Home Office from CSP International, explored the recommendations of the Peacock Committee on the Financing of the BBC on consumer payment for television services, by a detailed assessment of the technical feasibility of, and economic justification for, subscription services. The final report, published in July, recommended extra new Pay-TV services, but not as a replacement for public broadcast television channels financed by either the licence fee or revenue from advertising: Home Office *Subscription television. A study for the Home Office* London: HMSO, 1987.

In October, following up the election promise to act over public concern about violence and sex on television, the Home Secretary, Douglas Hurd, proposed the establishment of a Broadcasting Standards Council, to handle complaints from the public, monitor programme standards, publicize its findings, and initiate studies and research into the subject.

1988

The expansion of commercial radio, to include three new national radio channels and several hundred new 'community' stations, and a new Radio Authority to regulate them with a 'light touch', taking over from the Independent Broadcasting Authority, was announced by the Home Secretary on 19 January.

After over twenty years of regular debates on the matter, members of the House of Commons took a historic decision on 9 February to vote for an experiment in televising their proceedings.

On 4 July a House of Commons Select Committee recommended the establishment of a Commercial Television Authority to act as sole regulatory body for all commercial television, including cable and satellite broadcasting: House of Commons *Home Affairs Committee: Third Report: The future of broadcasting* (1987–88 HC 262-I, 262-II) London: HMSO, 1988.

References

1. Briggs, Asa. *The BBC: the first fifty years*. Oxford: Oxford University Press, 1985. p. 5.
2. Briggs, Asa. *History of broadcasting in the United Kingdom*: Volume 1: *The birth of broadcasting*. London: Oxford University Press, 1961. p. 36.
3. Reith, J. C. W. *Broadcast over Britain*. London: Hodder and Stoughton, 1924. p. 70.
4. The 'Televisor'. Successful test of new apparatus. *The Times* 28 January 1926.
5. Briggs, Asa. *History of broadcasting in the United Kingdom*: Volume 2: *The golden age of wireless*. London: Oxford University Press, 1965. p. 381.
6. Video concepts: a chronology, 1. *Screen Digest* October 1986. pp. 201-6.
7. Briggs, Asa. *History of broadcasting in the United Kingdom*: Volume 3: *The war of the words*. London: Oxford University Press, 1970. pp. 4-5.
8. Briggs, Asa. *The BBC: the first fifty years*. Oxford: Oxford University Press, 1985. pp. 181-2.
9. *Hansard: House of Lords* Volume 176, Column 1297, 22 May 1952.
10. Wilson, H. H. *Pressure group: the campaign for commercial television*. London: Secker and Warburg, 1961. p. 170.
11. *Hansard: House of Commons* Volume 529, Column 309, 22 June 1954.
12. Sendall, Bernard. *Independent Television in Britain*: Volume 1: *Origin and foundation 1946-62*. London: Macmillan, 1982. pp. 127-30.
13. ibid., p. 293.
14. Whitehouse, Mary. *Cleaning up tv: from protest to participation*. London: Blandford Press, 1967. p. 115.

2

Structure and organizations

The structure of broadcasting in the United Kingdom is a mixed system of public service, accountable to the people through Parliament, and private enterprise. Two public bodies, the British Broadcasting Corporation (BBC) and the Independent Broadcasting Authority (IBA), are responsible for the provision and broadcasting of television and radio services throughout the country. In Wales the programmes for one television channel are provided by the Welsh Fourth Channel Authority. Cable television services are licensed and supervised by the Cable Authority. These public bodies are accountable to Parliament through the Government Ministers responsible for broadcasting: the Home Secretary for broadcasting policy and regulation; and the Secretary of State for Trade and Industry for radio frequency spectrum management and licensing of telecommunications and cable services. The broadcasting authorities can be seen as the summit of a large broadcasting industry pyramid, consisting of television and radio manufacturers, television companies and radio stations, programme providers and production companies, trade associations and trade unions, professional associations, research organizations, training and educational establishments, and so on. The structure, functions and inter-relationships of this large and complex broadcasting industry will be outlined in this chapter.

2.1 Parliament

The broadcasting authorities work to terms and conditions laid down through Parliament, but otherwise have editorial and managerial independence in their provision of television and radio services. Legislation on broadcasting is often the result of a lengthy period of extra-Parliamentary activity, as well as

31

Parliamentary discussion and decision. However, most crucial to the development of broadcasting is the will of Parliament.

Parliamentary debates and proceedings

All legislation enacted by Parliament has to be extensively debated in both the House of Commons and House of Lords.

The origin of new legislation may begin with the appointment of a Committee of Inquiry to consider and report on the topic, followed by a Government Green Paper (a discussion paper setting out proposals for legislation still at a formative stage), and then a White Paper (a Government statement of policy and proposed legislation), before the drafting and publication of Parliamentary bill.

A bill is introduced into Parliament at its First Reading, and then normally passes through a Second Reading, Committee Stage, Report Stage and Third Reading in the House of Commons, and then similar stages in the House of Lords, before reaching the Royal Assent to become law. New legislation generally begins its Parliamentary passage in the House of Commons, unless an overcrowded legislative programme requires its introduction in the House of Lords, whereas consolidating legislation, drawing together various earlier statutes on the same topic into one comprehensive Act, normally starts in the Lords. The discussion in debates about measures in proposed new legislation is not only of interest in the context of that particular Act, but also as a collection of informed opinion on the subject generally. Such debates on broadcasting legislation, from the *Television Act 1954* to the *Broadcasting Act 1987*, as well as on the many White Papers and Committee of Inquiry reports, constitute an essential source of information and opinion on broadcasting.

Debates in broadcasting may also result from a decision of the official opposition party to devote an Opposition Day to the subject.

The answers to Parliamentary Questions also provide valuable statements of policy from Government Ministers, as well as information about forthcoming legislation, appointment of committees and official statistics.

Reports of the debates and proceedings are published daily by HMSO during the Parliamentary session in the House of Commons (and Lords) *Official Reports* (Hansards). Online access to Hansards is available through POLIS (Parliamentary Online Information Service).

Debates on broadcasting legislation

Television Act 1954

Commons:	Second Reading: 25 March 1954; Committee Stage: 4 & 5 May; Allocation of Time: 11 May; Allotted Days: 19, 20, 27 & 30 May, 1 June; Report Stage & Third Reading: 21 & 22 June; Lords Amendments: 27 July;
Lords:	Second Reading: 30 June, 1 July; Committee Stage: 12, 13 & 14 July; Third Reading: 22 July;
Royal Assent:	30 July 1954.

Television Act 1963

Commons:	Second Reading: 25 February 1963; Committee Stage: 7 March–9 May (20 sittings); Committee Amendments considered: 24, 25 & 27 June; Third Reading & Report Stage: 28 June; Lords Amendments considered: 30 July;
Lords:	Second Reading: 9 July; Committee Stage: 18, 22 & 23 July; Report Stage & Third Reading: 29 July;
Royal Assent:	31 July 1963.

Television Act 1964 (Consolidating Act)

Lords:	Second Reading: 28 January 1964; Third Reading: 20 February;
Commons:	Second Reading: 9 March; Committee, Report Stage & Third Reading: 17 March;
Royal Assent:	25 March 1964.

Sound Broadcasting Act 1972

Commons:	Second Reading: 11 November 1971; Committee Stage: 25 November 1971–7 March (34 sittings); Report Stage & Third Reading: 11 & 12 April;
Lords:	Second Reading: 27 April & 1 May; Committee Stage: 9 & 11 May; Report Stage & Third Reading: 5 & 12 June;
Royal Assent:	12 June 1972.

Independent Broadcasting Authority Act 1973 (Consolidating Act)

Lords:	Second Reading: 6 February 1973; Committee Stage: 12 April; Third Reading: 17 April;
Commons:	Second Reading, Committee Stage & Third Reading: 7 May;
Royal Assent:	23 May 1973.

Independent Broadcasting Authority Act 1974

Commons:	Second Reading: 31 January 1974 (interrupted by the General Election: 28 February); Second Reading: 29 March; Committee Stage: 9 & 30 April (2 sittings); Committee Amendments considered & Third Reading: 15 May;
Lords:	Second Reading: 20 May (Committee Stage negatived); Third Reading: 23 May;
Royal Assent:	23 May 1974.

Independent Broadcasting Authority Act (No. 2) 1974

Commons:	Second Reading: 2 July 1974; Committee Stage: 16 & 18 July; Third Reading: 23 July;
Lords:	Second (Committee negatived) & Third Reading: 25 July;
Royal Assent:	31 July 1974.

Independent Broadcasting Authority Act 1978

Commons: Second Reading: 6 April 1978; Committee Stage: 27 April;
                Report Stage & Third Reading: 19 May; Lords Amendments
                considered: 21 July;
Lords: Second Reading: 13 June; Committee Stage: 30 June; Report
                Stage: 12 July; Third Reading: 19 July;
Royal Assent: 31 July 1978.

Independent Broadcasting Authority 1979

Commons: Second Reading: 6 March 1979; Committee Stage: 29 March;
                Report Stage & Third Reading: 29 March;
Lords: Second Reading: 2 April; Third Reading: 3 April;
Royal Assent: 4 April 1979.

Broadcasting Act 1980

Commons: Second Reading: 18 February 1980; Committee Stage: 11
                March–24 April (12 sittings); Third Reading: 24 June; Lords
                Amendments considered: 10 November;
Lords: Second Reading: 24 July; Committee Stage: 8, 15 & 20 Octo-
                ber; Report Stage: 3 November; Third Reading: 6 November;
Royal Assent: 13 November 1980.

Broadcasting Act 1981 (Consolidating Act)

Lords: Second Reading: 25 June 1981; Committee & Report Stage:
                8 October; Third Reading: 15 October;
Commons: Second Reading, Committee & Third Reading: 23 October;
Royal Assent: 30 October 1981.

Cable and Broadcasting Act 1984

Lords: Second Reading: 19 December 1983; Committee Stage: 23 &
                26 January, 2 February 1984; Report Stage: 27 February,
                1 March; Third Reading: 13 March;
Commons: Second Reading: 8 May; Committee Stage: 22 May–26 June
                (10 sittings); Report Stage & Third Reading: 9 July;
Royal Assent: 26 July 1984.

Broadcasting Act 1987

Lords: Second Reading: 4 December 1986; Committee & Report
                Stage: 22 January 1987; Third Reading: 2 February;
Commons: Second Reading: 16 February; Committee Stage: 24 February–
                3 March (3 sittings); Third Reading: 26 March;
Royal Assent: 9 April 1987.

Standing Committees

The Committee Stage of legislation consists of detailed, clause-by-clause examination of a new bill. In the House of Commons this stage is usually undertaken by a Standing Committee, whereas in the Lords a new bill is often considered by a Committee of the whole House.

Despite their name, Standing Committee are reconstituted whenever a new bill is assigned to the House of Commons for the Committee Stage. Membership consists of MPs selected from the Government and Opposition parties in proportion to their numbers in the House.

Most major legislation on broadcasting has had detailed examination by Standing Committee. Official reports, often together with minutes of proceedings and evidence, are published by HMSO.

Select Committees

These Parliamentary Committees are appointed to examine the expenditure, administration and policy of the principal government departments and associated public bodies. They form part of the process of Parliamentary scrutiny. They have the right to summon witnesses, and call for papers and records. Members are nominated by the Committee of Selection, and are drawn primarily from the backbenches of the Government and Opposition parties; they serve for the life of a Parliament, unless they are promoted to be a Minister of the Crown or an Opposition Front Bench Spokesman. Select Committees of the House of Commons were reformed in 1979 to provide a new system of fourteen 'departmental' Committees, in addition to such existing ones as the Committee of Public Accounts. The House of Lords have a few Select Committees to consider such topics as sound broadcasting or European Communities.

The reports from the Select Committees are often debated in Parliament. Select Committee reports to Parliament, together with the minutes of evidence and proceedings, are published by HMSO.

Aspects of broadcasting in the UK have been examined by various Select Committees. Evidence given to the Committees, often by such senior broadcasting figures as the Chairmen and Directors-General of the BBC and the IBA, together with the Committee's findings, provide valuable information. The reports of the Select Committees have often proved influential in the continuing debate on broadcasting.

Committee of Public Accounts

One of the most important of the Select Committees is the Public Accounts Committee, which examines financial control by Government departments and public bodies. The response to reports of the Public Accounts Committee, either from the Government, as Treasury Minutes, or from the organizations examined, is often published as well.

The accounts of the BBC and the ITA/IBA have been examined by the Committee on many occasions since the Second World War.

Subject: BBC: Annual report and accounts, 1945–46
Date examined: 25 March 1947
Report: *Third report from the Committee of Public Accounts together with the proceedings of the Committee, minutes of evidence and index* (Session 1946–47: HC 139–I) London: HMSO, 1947.

Subject: BBC: Annual report and accounts, 1946–47
Date examined: 18 March 1948
Report: *Second report from the Committee of Public Accounts, together with the proceedings of the Committee, minutes of evidence and index* (Session 1947–48: HC 199–I) London: HMSO, 1948.

Subject: BBC: Annual report and accounts, 1949–50
Date examined: 1 March 1951
Report: *First, second, third and fourth reports from the Committee of Public Accounts, together with the proceedings of the Committee, minutes of evidence, appendices and index* (Session 1950–51: HC 100–I, 183–I, 184–I, 241–I) London: HMSO, 1951.

Subject: BBC: Annual report and accounts, 1952–53
Date examined: 16 February 1954
Report: *Special report and first, second and third reports from the Committee of Public Accounts, together with proceedings of the Committee, minutes of evidence and index* (Session 1953–54: HC 67–I, 101–I, 183–I, 231–I) London: HMSO, 1954.

Subject: BBC: Annual report and accounts, 1954–55
Date examined: 1 March 1956
Report: *Sixth report of the Committee of Public Accounts* (Session 1955–56: HC 348) London: HMSO, 1956.

Subject: BBC: Annual report and accounts, 1955–56; ITA: Annual report and accounts, 1955–56
Dates examined: 14 February 1957; 12 March 1957
Report: *Special report and first, second and third reports from the Committee of Public Accounts* (Session 1956–57: HC 75–I, 93–I, 190–I, 243–I) London: HMSO, 1957.

Subject: ITA: Annual report and accounts, 1957–58
Date examined: 10 March 1959
Reports: *Special report and first, second and third reports from the Committee of Public Accounts* (Session 1958–59: HC 76–I, 93–I, 201–I, 248–I); *Special report from the Committee of Public Accounts together with proceedings of the Committee* (Session 1959–60: HC 51) London: HMSO, 1959.

Subject: IBA: Additional payments by programme contractors
Date examined: 22 June 1977
Report: *Tenth report from the Committee of Public Accounts* (Session 1976–77: HC 536) London: HMSO, 1977.

Subject: IBA: Additional payments by programme contractors
Date examined: 12 November 1979
Report: *Fifth report from the Committee of Public Accounts* (Session 1979–80: HC 445) London: HMSO, 1980.

Subject: IBA: Additional payments by programme contractors
Date examined: 15 May 1985
Report: *Twenty-ninth report from the Committee of Public Accounts* (Session 1984–85: HC 400) London: HMSO, 1985.

Subject: Control of the Broadcast Receiving Licence Revenue
Date examined: 15 May 1985.
Report: *Twenty-seventh report from the Committee of Public Accounts* (Session 1984–85: HC 401) London: HMSO, 1985.

Subject: BBC External Services: financial control and accountability to Parliament
Date examined: 21 January and 9 November 1987
Report: *Seventh report from the Committee of Public Accounts* (Session 1987–88: HC 131) London: HMSO, 1987.

Subject: IBA: Additional payments by programme contractors
Date examined: 10 February 1988
Report: *Committee of Public Accounts. Minutes of evidence. Independent Broadcasting Authority: additional payments by programme contractors. Home Office, Independent Broadcasting Authority* (Session 1987–89: HC 317–i) London: HMSO, 1988.

Committee on Scottish Affairs

The House of Commons Select Committee appointed to consider matters affecting Scotland has examined the BBC in Scotland.

Subject: BBC cuts in Scotland
Date examined: 2 April 1980
Report: *Committee of Scottish Affairs. The BBC cuts in Scotland. Minutes of evidence, together with appendices; British Broadcasting Corporation* (Session 1979–80: HC 539) London: HMSO, 1980.

Committee on Welsh Affairs

Broadcasting in Wales has been considered by both the Welsh Grand Committee and the Committee on Welsh Affairs.

Subject: Radio and television in Wales
Date examined: 14 June 1972
Report: *Welsh Grand Committee. Minutes of proceedings on consideration of the matter of radio and television in Wales* (Session 1971–72: HC 311) London: HMSO, 1972.

Subject: Broadcasting in the Welsh language
Date examined: 29 October 1980–6 May 1981
Report: *Second report from the Committee on Welsh Affairs, together with proceedings of the Committee thereon, the minutes of evidence and appendices. Broadcasting in the Welsh language and the implications for Welsh and non-Welsh speaking viewers and listeners* (Session 1980–81: HC 448–I, HC 448–II) London: HMSO, 1981.

Defence Committee

House of Commons Select Committee appointed to examine the expenditure, administration and policy of the Ministry of Defence, and defence matters. It has covered the relationship with broadcasters.

Subject: The D-Notice system of voluntary self-censorship by the press and broadcasters in reporting defence matters
Dates examined: 11 June–22 July 1980
Report: *Third report from the Defence Committee, together with the minutes of proceedings of the Committee relating to the Report; part of the minutes of evidence . . . and appendices. The D-Notice system* (Session 1979–80: HC 773, 640–I–v) London: HMSO, 1980.

Subject: Media coverage of the Falklands conflict
Dates examined: 21 July–10 November 1982
Report: *First report from the Defence Committee. The handling of press and public information during the Falklands conflict* (Session 1982–83: HC 17) London: HMSO, 1982.

Estimates Committee

Broadcasting finances have also been examined by the House of Commons Estimates Committee. Observations on the reports by the responsible Government Minister or the public body examined are also published.

Subject: BBC
Date examined: 17 April 1946
Report: *First report from the Select Committee on Estimates, together with the minutes of evidence taken before Sub-Committee D on 17th April* (Session 1945–46: HC 158) London: HMSO, 1946.

Subject: BBC: Overseas broadcasting
Dates examined: 22 April–1 July 1952
Report: *Ninth report from the Select Committee on Estimates, together with the minutes of evidence taken before Sub-Committee F on 22nd April and subsequent days, and appendices. Overseas broadcasting* (Session 1951–52: HC 287) London: HMSO, 1952.

Subject: BBC
Dates examined: 27 January–11 June 1969
Report: *Third report from the Estimates Committee together with part of the minutes of evidence taken before Sub-Committee D on 27th January 1969 and following days, appendices and index* (Session 1968–69: HC 387) London: HMSO, 1969.

Select Committee on European Legislation

House of Commons Committee formed to consider draft proposals for legislation from the Commission of the European Communities, and documents for submission to the European Parliament/Council of Ministers.

Subject: A Common Market for broadcasting — EEC Green Paper: *Television without frontiers*
Date examined: 12 December 1984
Report: *Fourth report from the Select Committee on European Legislation, together with the proceedings of the Committee* (Session 1984–85: HC 5–iv) London: HMSO, 1984.

Subject: Transmission standards for direct broadcasting via satellite
Date examined: 23 October 1985
Report: *Thirtieth report from the Select Committee on European Legislation, together with the proceedings of the Committee* (Session 1984–85: HC 5–xxx) London: HMSO, 1985.

Subject: Transmission standards for direct broadcasting via satellite
Date examined: 26 March 1986
Report: *Fifteenth report from the Select Committee on European Legislation, together with the proceedings of the Committee* (Session 1985–86: HC 21–xv) London: HMSO, 1986.

Subject: Proposed harmonization of legislation affecting broadcasting in Member States
Date examined: 2 July 1986
Report: *Twenty-fourth report from the Select Committee on European Legislation, together with the proceedings of the Committee* (Session 1985–86: HC 21–xxiv) London: HMSO, 1986.

Select Committee on the European Communities

A House of Lords Select Committee appointed to consider Community proposals, in draft or otherwise, make reports on those which raise important questions of policy or principle, and report to the House.

Subject: Protection of consumers and traders from misleading advertising in the media; and systems of advertising control, including the IBA
Dates examined: 5 April–3 May 1978
Report: *Select Committee on the European Communities. Misleading advertising. Draft directive concerning unfair and misleading advertising, with minutes of evidence* (Session 1977–78: HL 230) London: HMSO, 1978.

Subject: EEC Green Paper: *Television without frontiers*
Dates examined: 21 March–18 July 1985
Report: *Select Committee on the European Communities. 4th report. Television without frontiers. With evidence* (Session 1985–86: HL 43) London: HMSO, 1985.

Subject: European Commission draft directive (6739/86 COR 1 COM(86) 146), to co-ordinate the various broadcasting activities of Member States
Dates examined: 16 October 1986–15 January 1987
Report: *Select Committee on the European Communities. 4th*

report. European broadcasting (Session 1986–87: HL 67) London: HMSO, 1987.

Select Committee on Nationalised Industries

The Select Committee appointed 'to examine the Report and Accounts of the Nationalised Industries established by Statute whose controlling Boards are appointed by Ministers of the Crown and whose annual receipts are not wholly or mainly derived from moneys provided by Parliament or advanced by the Exchequer' (*Special report from the Select Committee on Nationalised Industries. The Committee's order of reference* (Session 1967–68: HC 298) London: HMSO, 1972).

The Committee, whose remit covered the Post Office, Cable and Wireless Ltd and the IBA, was first set up in 1956, and eventually abolished in 1979 when the new 'departmental' Select Committees were introduced. Both considerations of the IBA by the SCNI have produced important and influential recommendations. Observations on SCNI recommendations by the responsible Minister of the Crown and the public body examined are also published.

Subject:	Independent Broadcasting Authority
Dates examined:	8 December 1971–26 April 1972
Report:	*Second report from the Select Committee on Nationalised Industries, together with minutes of proceedings of the Committee, minutes of evidence, appendices and index* (Session 1971–72: HC 465) London: HMSO, 1972.
Response:	*Second report from the Select Committee on Nationalised Industries. Independent Broadcasting Authority. Observations by the Minister of Posts and Telecommunications and the Independent Broadcasting Authority* (Cmnd 5244) London: HMSO, 1973.

Subject:	Independent Broadcasting Authority
Dates examined:	1 March–5 July 1978
Report:	*Tenth report from the Select Committee on Nationalised Industries, together with the proceedings of the Committee, minutes of evidence . . . and appendices* (Session 1977–78: HC 637–I, 637–II) London: HMSO, 1978.
Response:	*Tenth report from the Select Committee on Nationalised Industries. Independent Broadcasting Authority. Observations by the Home Secretary and the Independent Broadcasting Authority* (Cmnd 7791) London: HMSO, 1979.

Broadcasting the proceedings of Parliament

Reports of events in Parliament have long been a feature of broadcasting and, indeed, it is a requirement, in the Licence and Agreement, that the BBC shall broadcast an impartial account day by day of proceedings of both Houses of Parliament. However, live broadcast coverage of Parliamentary debates and proceedings has taken a long time to find approval from members.

The case in favour of broadcasting Parliamentary proceedings largely centres on the importance in a democracy of allowing the electorate to know what is going on in Parliament. The arguments against broadcasting are partly technical and partly fears that it would alter the character of Parliament. Objections have been raised over the technical problems and interruption resulting from allowing cameras and lights into the Chambers of the Houses of Parliament. However, more understandable is the apprehension of members that broadcasting (particularly television) would trivialize the proceedings and concentrate mainly on 'newsworthy' events, such as Prime Minister's Question Time in the House of Commons, rather than the basic and valuable routine work of Parliament.

When the suggestion of broadcasting debates was first made in Parliament, in 1923, the Prime Minister, Andrew Bonar Law, had declared it 'undesirable'. A proposal by John Reith for the BBC to broadcast the King's Speech at the State Opening of Parliament was declined that year, and on several subsequent occasions. Pressure for the broadcasting of debates did not build up until after the Second World War. In 1959 the House of Commons debated the broadcasting of proceedings, when Aneurin Bevan, the Deputy Leader of the Labour Party, suggested a separate Parliamentary television channel. By the early 1960s, Iain Macleod and other influential MPs were supporting the idea of broadcasting proceedings as a point of democratic principle.

Official enquiry into the possibility of sound broadcasting of Parliamentary proceedings was first begun by a House of Commons Select Committee in 1965. Eventually, on 11 December 1967, the Commons voted in favour of a closed-circuit radio experiment for MPs only, which took place from 23 April to 17 May 1968. After further consideration by Select Committee in 1968, and several debates in the House of Commons, a public experiment in sound broadcasting was authorized on 24 February 1975, and took place in June and July that year. The experiment was considered a success by the Select Committee in 1976, and a subsequent full Commons vote, on 16 March 1976. Regular sound broadcasting of proceedings began on 3 April 1978.

Live radio coverage of Question Time and major debates was supplemented by recorded extracts in news bulletins and current affairs programmes, and edited résumés in the *Today/Yesterday in Parliament* programmes on BBC Radio 4.

Television cameras entered Parliament for the first time to record the State Opening — from the House of Lords in October 1958, and from the House of

Commons in April 1966. However, full television coverage of debates and committee hearings has taken far longer.

The House of Lords has shown more enthusiasm for televising its proceedings than the lower house. They first voted in favour of televising debates on 15 June 1966, with a resulting closed-circuit experiment taking place in February 1968. A subsequent recommendation of a House of Lords Select Committee of a one-year experiment in public television coverage by the BBC and ITA was debated (though not implemented) on 20 March 1969. Television coverage of House of Lords debates eventually began on 23 January 1985. Their Lordships' approval of the television coverage of its proceedings, expressed in debates on 22 July 1985 and 12 May 1986, seems to ensure its continuance.

As shown in Table 1, the question of full television coverage of the proceedings of the House of Commons has been debated on numerous occasions since 1965, with MPs finally voting decisively in its favour in 1988.

Table 1.   Debates on televising the proceedings of the House of Commons

Debate	Proposer	For	Against	Majority
28.5.1965	T. Iremonger	Withdrawn without a vote		
24.11.1966	R. Crossman	130	131	1
21.11.1969	R. Sheldon	75	32	Invalid
19.10.1972	R. Carr	165	191	26
30.1.1974	D. Leonard	164	189	25
24.2.1975	E. Short	263	275	12
4.7.1978	J. Farr	161	181	20
30.1.1980	A. Mitchell	201	201	0
15.12.1981	J. Ashley	158	176	18
13.4.1983	A. Mitchell	153	138	15*
2.11.1983	A. Mitchell	164	159	Invalid
20.11.1985	J. Fookes	263	275	12
9.2.1988	A. Nelson	318	264	54

*Televising of Select Committees Bill: Second Reading only.

Select Committees on the broadcasting of Parliament

The possibility of broadcasting Parliamentary proceedings has been considered by various Select Committees of both Houses of Parliament on many occasions since 1965.

Subject:	To investigate the broadcasting of the proceedings of the House of Commons; recommended a separate Select Committee to continue the enquiry
Dates examined:	25 May–2 August 1965
Report:	*Special report from the Select Committee on Publications and Debates Reports, together with the proceedings of the Committee. The broadcasting of proceedings in the House*

of Commons (Session 1964–65: HC 304) London: HMSO, 1965.

Subject:	Continuation of the enquiry into the broadcasting of the proceedings of the House of Commons
Dates examined:	1 February–1 March 1966
Report:	*Special report from the Select Committee on the Broadcasting of Proceedings in the House of Commons, together with the proceedings of the Committee* (Session 1965–66: HC 111) London: HMSO, 1966.

Subject:	Enquiry into broadcasting, photographing and filming the proceedings of the House of Commons; concluded that continuous live broadcasting of all proceedings was impractical and undesirable, but recommended a closed-circuit experiment in sound and vision for MPs
Dates examined:	17 June 1965–27 July 1966
Report:	*First report from the Select Committee on Broadcasting &c., of Proceedings in the House of Commons* (Session 1965–66: HC 146) London: HMSO, 1966.

Subject:	Consideration of the resolution of the House of Lords on 15 June 1966, in favour of televising some of its proceedings for an experimental period; recommended a three-day closed-circuit television experiment to be held in 1968, and a widening of the Committee's terms of reference to cover sound broadcasting
Dates examined:	4 August 1966–14 February 1967
Report:	*First report by the Select Committee on Televising the Proceedings of the House of Lords, together with the proceedings of the Committee and minutes of evidence* (Session 1966–67: HL 190) London: HMSO, 1967.

Subject:	Consideration of the experiment in closed-circuit television, and sound broadcasting of House of Lords proceedings.
Dates examined:	21 March–27 June 1967
Report:	*Second report by the Select Committee on Televising the Proceedings of the House of Lords, together with the proceedings of the Committee, minutes of evidence and appendices* (Session 1966–67: HL 284) London: HMSO, 1967.

Subject:	Consideration of the manner in which proceedings of the

House of Lords can be publicly broadcast for an experimental period, with a timetable and details of closed-circuit
experiment to be held in February 1968

Dates examined: 7 November–4 December 1967

Report: *First report by the Select Committee on Broadcasting the
Proceedings of the House of Lords, together with the pro
eedings of the Committee and minutes of evidence* (Session
1967–68: HL 27) London: HMSO, 1967.

Subject: Consideration, in conjunction with the BBC, of the
arrangements necessary for the sound broadcasting experiment in the House of Commons from 23 April to 17 May
1968

Dates examined: 14 & 22 February 1968

Report: *Second report from the Select Committee on House of
Commons (Services). The experiment in radio broadcasting*
(Session 1967–68: HC 152) London: HMSO, 1968.

Subject: Consideration of the manner in which proceedings of the
House of Lords could best be publicly broadcast in the light
of the February 1968 experiment; recommended a one-year
broadcasting experiment by the BBC and the ITA

Dates examined: 22 February–27 June 1968

Report: *Second report by the Select Committee on Broadcasting the
Proceedings of the House of Lords, together with the proceedings of the Committee and minutes of evidence* (Session 1967–68: HL 159) London: HMSO, 1968.

Subject: The experiment in radio broadcasting of the House of Commons in April/May 1968; recommended permission be
granted for edited sound recordings only of Commons
debates to be broadcast

Date examined: 22 February–2 July 1968

Report: *Ninth report from the Select Committee on House of Commons (Services), together with the minutes of evidence
taken before the Broadcasting Sub-Committee on 2 July
1968. The experiment in radio broadcasting* (Session 1967–
68: HC 448) London: HMSO, 1968.

Subject: Consideration of the costs of radio coverage; recommended further consultations with the BBC on a less costly
scheme before granting permission

Date examined: 10 December 1968

Report: *First report from the Select Committee on House of Commons (Services). Broadcasting of the proceedings of the House* (Session 1968–69: HC 48) London: HMSO, 1968.

Subject: The live radio coverage of the debates on the entry of the UK into the EEC; not approved
Dates examined: 6 & 13 July 1971
Report: *Seventh report from the Select Committee on House of Commons (Services). Broadcasting of debates on Great Britain and the EEC* (Session 1970–71: HC 510, HC 510–i) London: HMSO, 1971.

Subject: Broadcasting the proceedings of the House of Commons Expenditure Committee public hearings
Date examined: 14 December 1972
Report: *Second special report from the Expenditure Committee. Broadcasting of proceedings* (Session 1972–73: HC 61) London: HMSO, 1972.

Subject: Radio coverage experiment by the BBC and IBA following a House of Commons resolution, on 24 February 1975, in favour of the sound broadcasting of proceedings
Date examined: 16 April 1975
Report: *Second report from the Select Committee on House of Commons (Services). The experiment in public sound broadcasting* (Session 1974–75: HC 325, HC 325–i) London: HMSO, 1975.

Subject: Advertising commercials and scheduled Parliamentary broadcasts; recommended a relaxation of the suggested embargo on advertising within ten minutes either side of Parliamentary broadcasts on Independent Local Radio
Date examined: Representation by the IBA
Report: *Third report from the Select Committee on House of Commons (Services). The experiment in public sound broadcasting (No 2)* (Session 1974–75: HC 382) London: HMSO, 1975.

Subject: The four-week experiment, in June/July 1975, of the public sound broadcasting of the proceedings of the House of Commons and some of its Committees was considered successful, and should be arranged on a permanent basis
Dates examined: 14 October 1975–27 January 1976
Report: *First report from the Select Committee on House of*

Commons (Services), together with the proceedings of the Committee and the minutes of evidence taken before the Broadcasting Sub-Committee and appendices. The experiment in public sound broadcasting (Session 1975–76: HC 142) London: HMSO, 1976.

Subject: Implementation of the resolutions of both Houses of Parliament in favour of a permanent system of sound broadcasting of their proceedings

Dates examined: 23 March–29 April 1976

Report: *First special report from the Joint Committee on Sound Broadcasting* (Session 1975–76: HL 198, HC 453) London: HMSO, 1976.

Subject: The provision of facilities for broadcasters in the Chambers of both Houses; recommended the construction of commentary boxes in the Lords Press Gallery, and the Commons South West Corner

Dates examined: 19 & 26 May 1976

Report: *First report from the Joint Committee on Sound Broadcasting. Minutes of evidence taken before the Joint Committee* (Session 1975–76: HL 214, HL 214-I; HC 494, HC 494-I) London: HMSO, 1976.

Subject: Further consideration of the arrangements for permanent sound broadcasting in the Commons and the Lords; recommended the establishment of an identical Joint Committee in the following session to conclude the enquiry

Dates examined: 4 May–15 November 1976

Report: *Second special report from the Joint Committee on Sound Broadcasting, together with the minutes of proceedings of the Committee* (Session 1975–76: HL 387, HC 723) London: HMSO, 1976.

Subject: Permanent accommodation for broadcasting staff involved in the sound broadcasting of both Houses of Parliament within the Palace of Westminster.

Dates examined: 25 November 1976–18 January 1977

Report: *First report from the Joint Committee on Sound Broadcasting* (Session 1976–77: HL 48, HC 136) London: HMSO, 1977.

Subject: Detailed arrangements for the sound coverage of Parliamentary proceedings planned to commence in 1977

Dates examined: 19 January–28 March 1977

Report: *Second report from the Joint Committee on Sound Broad-*
                   casting, together with the minutes of proceedings of the
                   Committee, the minutes of evidence taken before the Com-
                   mittee, and the Joint Committee on Sound Broadcasting in
                   Session 1975–76 (Session 1976–77: HL 123, HC 284)
                   London: HMSO, 1977.

Subject: The safeguards necessary to prevent broadcasting of secret
                   sittings or adjournment debates in the House of Commons
                   Chamber
Dates examined: 22 March–14 June 1978
Report: *Minutes of the proceedings of the Select Committee on*
                   Sound Broadcasting (Session 1977–78: HC 691) London:
                   HMSO, 1979

Subject: Permission for CBC and CBS to receive a 'clean feed' of
                   proceedings; and the Foreign & Commonwealth Office to
                   monitor how overseas broadcasting organizations, who
                   receive the clean feed, use the material
Dates examined: 7 December 1978–29 March 1979
Report: *First special report from the Select Committee on Sound*
                   Broadcasting, together with the minutes of proceedings of
                   the Committee (Session 1978–79: HC 332) London:
                   HMSO, 1979.

Subject: Interruptions from the Strangers' Gallery; recommended
                   not to be broadcast as they are not part of proceedings
Dates examined: 9 December 1980–13 January 1981
Report: *Select Committee on Sound Broadcasting. Minutes of pro-*
                   ceedings (Session 1980–81: HC 498) London: HMSO, 1981.

Subject: Broadcasters to have absolute privilege for defamatory
                   words spoken in either House, and immunity from Con-
                   tempt of Court proceedings
Dates examined: 23 March–18 May 1982
Report: *First report from the Select Committee on Sound Broad-*
                   casting, together with the proceedings of the Committee,
                   minutes of evidence and appendices (Session 1981–82: HC
                   376) London: HMSO, 1982.

Subject: Clean feed of proceedings to be granted to National Public
                   Radio (USA), and radio stations affiliated to the National
                   Association of Hospital Broadcasting Organizations
Dates examined: 23 March–20 July 1982

Report: *Select Committee on Sound Broadcasting. Minutes of proceedings* (Session 1981–82: HC 541) London: HMSO, 1982.

Subject: Scandinavian Broadcasting, Voice of America, and Falkland Islands Broadcasting to receive the clean feed, and for BBC Transcription Service to use recorded extracts of proceedings

Dates examined: 30 November 1982–24 March 1983

Report: *Select Committee on Sound Broadcasting. Minutes of proceedings* (Session 1982–83: HC 376) London: HMSO, 1983.

Subject: Consideration of whether the changes in the format of the BBC Radio programme *Yesterday in Parliament*, and its inclusion as an item in the *Today* programme, contravene Clause 13(2) in the BBC's Licence and Agreement, obliging it to broadcast daily impartial accounts of the proceedings of Parliament

Report: *Report by the Select Committee of the House of Lords on Sound Broadcasting, together with the minutes of evidence. 'Yesterday in Parliament'* (Session 1982–83: HL 98) London: HMSO, 1983.

Subject: The introduction of a Bill to vest copyright for the clean feed of the proceedings of the House, or its Committees, in the House itself (or an appropriate holder on its behalf); and for the broadcasters to insert a time delay in live broadcasts in order to delete any defamatory statements from the Gallery, etc (which is outside the protection of Parliamentary privilege)

Date examined: 17 March 1983

Report: *First report from the Select Committee on Sound Broadcasting, together with the proceedings of the Committee* (Session 1982–83: HC 270) London: HMSO, 1983.

Subject: Implementation of the endorsement by the House of Lords, on 8 December 1983, of an earlier motion (June 15 1966), in favour of an experimental public televising of their debates; recommended permission for the BBC and the IBA to record material for broadcasting for a six-month experiment in January 1985

Dates examined: 7 March–26 June 1984

Report: *First report by the Select Committee of the House of Lords on Sound Broadcasting, together with the minutes of evidence. Televising the House of Lords* (Session 1983–84: HL 299) London: HMSO, 1984.

Subject:　　　　　　Associated Press Ltd, the Cable News Network (USA), IBS News Ltd, Radio Television Hong Kong, Radio Basildon, and Departments of State to receive the clean feed of proceedings

Dates examined:　　18 January–15 May 1984

Report:　　　　　　*Select Committee on Sound Broadcasting. Minutes of proceedings* (Session 1983–84: HC 641) London: HMSO, 1984.

Subject:　　　　　　London Broadcasting Company (LBC) to supply broadcast proceedings to newspapers in the UK; Israel Broadcasting Authority, Norddeutscher Rundfunk and Westdeutscher Rundfunk to receive the proceedings; archive tapes to be transferred from the Parliamentary Sound Archives to the National Sound Archive

Dates examined:　　12 December 1984–12 June 1985

Report:　　　　　　*Select Committee on Sound Broadcasting. Minutes of proceedings* (Session 1984–85: HC 616) London: HMSO, 1985.

Subject:　　　　　　Japan Broadcasting Corporation to receive the broadcast proceedings, and for the Central Office of Information to receive a feed of proceedings of Standing Committees and public sessions of the Select Committees

Dates examined:　　5 December 1985–1 May 1986

Report:　　　　　　*Select Committee on Sound Broadcasting. Minutes of proceedings* (Session 1985–86: HC 625) London: HMSO, 1986.

Subject:　　　　　　The experimental public televising of the proceedings of the House of Lords from 23 January to 31 July 1985. The experiment had been useful; it was for the House to decide whether to continue televising proceedings (it was clear from the vote on 22 July that the majority of the House of Lords were sufficiently satisfied to see it continue on the same basis)

Dates examined:　　15 October–4 March 1986

Report:　　　　　　*Report by the Select Committee of the House of Lords on Televising the proceedings of the House, with evidence* (Session 1985–86: HL 102) London: HMSO, 1986.

Subject:　　　　　　Sound recordings to be transferred to the National Sound Archive for permanent preservation

Date examined:　　18 March 1987

Report:　　　　　　*First report by the Select Committee of the House of Lords on Broadcasting. Sound archives* (Session 1986–87: HL 95) London: HMSO, 1987.

Subject: The introduction of a public subscriber telephone service, supplied by British Telecom, to provide live broadcasts of Parliamentary proceedings without the filter of broadcasters' editorial judgements, or expenditure of public funds

Date examined: 23 March 1987

Report: *First report from the Select committee on Sound Broadcasting. A telephone broadcast service of proceedings in the Chamber of the House of Commons. Report, appendices and proceedings of the Committee* (Session 1986–87: HC 281) London: HMSO, 1987.

Subject: Transfer of older material from the Parliamentary Sound Archive to the National Sound Archive

Date examined: 23 March 1987

Report: *Second report from the Select Committee on Sound Broadcasting. Permanent preservation of the sound archive. Report, appendices and proceedings of the Committee* (Session 1986–87: HC 282) London: HMSO, 1987.

Committees of Inquiry

Committees of Inquiry, or Departmental Committees, are ad hoc advisory committees appointed by Ministers of the Crown. Membership consists of Members of Parliament and lay members, with notable figures from public life as Chairman. They are appointed to investigate areas of public interest and make recommendations for the future.

The reports, often with minutes of evidence received and appendices, form valuable sources of information and informed opinion. Ideas generated by the major Committees of Inquiry are often current for a long time after the publication of the report, and inform the continuing debate for quite a while.

Title: The Broadcasting Committee [1923]

Chairman: Sir Frederick Sykes

Terms: a. Broadcasting in all its aspects
b. The contracts and licences which have been or may be granted
c. The action which should be taken upon determination of the existing licence of the Broadcasting Company
d. Uses to which broadcasting may be put
e. The restrictions which may need to be placed upon its uses or development

Report: *The Broadcasting Committee: Report* (Cmd 1951) London: HMSO, 1923.

Title: The Broadcasting Committee, 1925
Chairman: The Earl of Crawford and Balcarres
Terms: To advise as to the proper scope of the Broadcasting service and as to the management, control and finance thereof after the expiry of the existing licence on 31 December 1926. The Committee will indicate what changes in the law, if any, are desirable in the interests of Broadcasting
Report: *Report of the Broadcasting Committee, 1925* (Cmd 2599) London: HMSO, 1926.

Title: The Television Committee [1934]
Chairman: Lord Selsdon
Terms: To consider the development of Television and to advise the Postmaster General on the relative merits of the several systems and on the conditions under which any public service of Television should be provided
Report: *Report of the Television Committee* (Cmd 4793) London: HMSO, 1935.

Title: The Broadcasting Committee, 1935
Chairman: Viscount Ullswater
Terms: To consider the constitution, control and finance of the broadcasting service in this country and advise generally on the conditions under which the service, including broadcasting to the Empire, television broadcasting, and the system of wireless exchanges, should be conducted after 31 December 1936
Report: *Report of the Broadcasting Committee, 1935* (Cmd 5091) London: HMSO, 1936.

Title: The Television Committee, 1943
Chairman: Lord Hankey
Terms: To prepare plans for the reinstatement and development of the television service after the war with special consideration of
                a. the preparation of a plan for the provision of a service to at any rate the larger centres of population within a reasonable period after the war
                b. the provision to be made for research & development
                c. the guidance to be given to manufacturers, with a view especially to the development of the export trade
Report: *Report of the Television Committee 1943* London: HMSO, 1945.

Title: The Broadcasting Committee, 1949
Chairman: Lord Beveridge
Terms: To consider the constitution, control, finance and other

general aspects of the sound and television services of the United Kingdom (excluding those aspects of the overseas services for which the BBC are not responsible) and to advise on the conditions under which these services and wire broadcasting should be conducted after 31 December 1951

Report: *Report of the Broadcasting Committee, 1949* (Cmd 8116); *Appendix H: Memoranda submitted to the Committee* (Cmd 8117) London: HMSO, 1951.

Title: The Committee on Broadcasting, 1960

Chairman: Sir Harry Pilkington

Terms: To consider the future of the broadcasting services in the United Kingdom, the dissemination by wire of broadcasting and other programmes, and the possibility of television for public showing; to advise on the services which should in future be provided in the United Kingdom by the BBC and the ITA; to recommend whether additional services should be provided by any other organization; and to propose what financial and other conditions should apply to the conduct of all these services

Report: *Report of the Committee on Broadcasting, 1960* (Cmnd 1753) London: HMSO, 1962.

Title: The Committee on Broadcasting Coverage [1973]

Chairman: Sir Stewart Crawford

Terms: Taking account of the Report of the Television Advisory Committee and the Government's intention to consider separately whether the frequencies available for a fourth television channel should be allocated, to examine the Broadcasting Authorities' plans for the coverage of television and sound broadcasting services in Scotland, Wales, Northern Ireland and rural England

Report: *Report of the Committee on Broadcasting Coverage* (Cmnd 5774) London: HMSO, 1974.

Title   The Committee on the Future of Broadcasting [1974]

Chairman: Lord Annan

Terms: To consider the future of broadcasting in the United Kingdom, including the dissemination by wire of broadcast and other programmes and of television for public showing; to consider the implications for the present of any recommended additional services of new techniques; and to propose what constitutional, organizational and financial arrangements and what conditions should apply to the conduct of all these services

Report: *Report of the Committee on the Future of Broadcasting* (Cmnd 6753); *Appendices E–I: Research papers commissioned by the Committee* (Cmnd 6753–I) London: HMSO, 1977.

Title: The Working Party on a Fourth Television Service in Wales
            [1975]
Chairman: J. W. M. Siberry
Terms: On the basis of the Report of the Crawford Committee on Broad-
            casting Coverage, to work out arrangements required to provide
            a fourth television service in Wales, including timing and esti-
            mates of cost
Report: Home Office/Welsh Office *Report of the Working Party on a
            Fourth Television Service in Wales/Adroddiad y Gweithgor ar
            Bedwerydd Gwasanaeth Teledu yng Nghymru* (Cmnd 6290)
            Cardiff: HMSO, 1975.

Title: The Inquiry into Cable Expansion and Broadcasting Policy
            [1982]
Chairman: Lord Hunt of Tanworth
Terms: To take as its frame of reference the Government's wish to secure
            the benefits for the United Kingdom which cable technology can
            offer and its willingness to consider an expansion of cable sys-
            tems which would permit cable to carry a wider range of enter-
            tainment and other services (including when available services of
            direct broadcasting by satellite), . . . to consider the questions
            affecting broadcasting policy which would arise from such
            expansion, including in particular the supervisory framework
Report: *Report of the Inquiry into Cable Expansion and Broadcasting
            Policy* (Cmnd 8679) London: HMSO, 1982.

Title: Advisory Panel on Technical Transmission Standards [1982]
Chairman: Sir Antony Part
Terms: To consider what technical transmission standards should be
            adopted for United Kingdom services of direct broadcasting by
            satellite
Report: Home Office/Department of Trade and Industry *Direct broad-
            casting by satellite. Report of the Advisory Panel on Technical
            Transmission Standards* (Cmnd 8751) London: HMSO, 1982.

Title: The Committee on Financing the BBC [1985]
Chairman: Professor Alan Peacock
Terms: i. To assess the effects of the introduction of advertising or spon-
            sorship on the BBC's Home Services, either as an alternative or a
            supplement to the income now received through the licence fee,
            including
                a. the financial and other consequences for the BBC, for
            independent television and independent local radio, for the

prospective services of cable, independent national radio and direct broadcasting by satellite, for the press and the advertising industry and for the Exchequer; and

    b. the impact on the range and quality of existing broadcasting services; and

    ii. to identify a range of options for the introduction, in varying amounts and on different conditions of advertising and sponsorship on some or all of the BBC's Home Services; with an assessment of the advantages and disadvantages of each option, and

    iii. to consider any proposals for securing income from the consumer other than through the licence fee

Report: *Report of the Committee on Financing the BBC* (Cmnd 9824) London: HMSO, 1986.

2.2 Government departments

Government responsibility for broadcasting in the United Kingdom has been vested successively in the Post Office, until 1969, the Ministry of Posts and Telecommunications, from 1969 to 1974, and, since 1974, the Home Office, for broad policy issues, and the Department of Trade and Industry for radio frequency and telecommunications matters.

THE POST OFFICE
33 Grosvenor Place, London SW1X 1PX; 01-235 8000
The first Government department to have responsibility for broadcasting services in the United Kingdom was the Post Office, with the Postmaster General (PMG) as the Minister answerable to Parliament.

    The Post Office was first constituted as a public mail service, under Royal monopoly, in 1635, and then brought under Parliamentary and Government control by Oliver Cromwell's *Post Office Act 1657*. In the nineteenth century it gradually acquired control of the newly developing telegraph and telephone services, and by the time Marconi came to Britain in 1896 to demonstrate his invention of radio telephony, it was the responsibility of the General Post Office to examine and licence developments in communications. Under the *Wireless Telegraphy Acts* the Post Office was responsible for the licensing of all wireless telegraph stations and installations, the examination and testing of new wireless equipment, and the regulation of the wavelengths.

    In the area of broadcasting services, the Postmaster General exercised the 'ultimate control' of Parliament over the broadcasting authorities. In the case of the BBC, the PMG nominated the Governors for appointment by the Queen in Council, and granted the Licence and Agreement authorizing the provision of a range of broadcasting services. For Independent Television, the PMG appointed the Members of the Independent Television Authority, and controlled broadasting hours and areas of transmission. For both authorities the Postmaster General could require them either to broadcast official announcements or refrain from broadcasting specified programmes or material.

The Post Office ceased to be a Government department, and responsible for broadcasting services, when the *Post Office Act 1969* abolished the post of Postmaster General, transferring the powers conferred by the *Wireless Telegraphy Act 1949* and the *Television Act 1964* to a newly created Minister of Posts and Telecommunications, and reconstituted the Post Office as a public corporation.

Postmasters General, 1900–69

1900	The Duke of Norfolk	1931	Clement Attlee
1900	Marquis of Londonderry	1931	William Ormsby-Gore
1902	Austen Chamberlain	1931	Kingsley Wood
1903	Lord Stanley	1935	George Tryon
1905	Sydney Buxton	1940	William Morrison
1910	Herbert Samuel	1942	Harry Crookshank
1914	Charles Hobhouse	1945	Earl of Listowel
1915	Herbert Samuel	1947	Wilfred Paling
1916	Joseph Pease	1950	Ness Edwards
1916	Albert Illingworth	1951	Earl De La Warr
1921	Frederick Kellaway	1955	Charles Hill (later Lord Hill
1922	Neville Chamberlain		of Luton
1923	William Joynson-Hicks	1957	Ernest Marples
1923	Laming Worthington-Evans	1959	Reginald Bevins
1924	Vernon Hartshorn	1964	Tony Wedgwood Benn
1924	William Mitchell-Thomson	1966	Edward Short
	(later Lord Selsdon)	1968	Roy Mason
1929	Hastings Lees-Smith	1968	John Stonehouse

Ministers of Posts and Telecommunications, 1969–74

1969	John Stonehouse	1972	Sir John Eden
1970	Christopher Chataway	1974	Tony Wedgwood Benn

The office of Minister of Posts and Telecommunications was wound up in March 1974, and Government responsibilities for broadcasting were divided between the Home Office and the Department of Industry (later merged with Department of Trade in 1983).

The Post Office is still responsible for the collection of the broadcast receiving licence fee through its branch offices.

Publications: *Post Office Prospects* (later *Post Office Report and Accounts*).

Archives: Post Office records and papers are available at the Post Office Archives (q.v.) and the Public Record Office (q.v.).

HOME OFFICE
50 Queen Anne's Gate, London SW1H 9AT; 01-213 3000
The Home Office is an historic Department of State, dating from 1782, concerned with internal affairs for England and Wales, and domestic policy over a

wide range of issues. Regarded as the 'law and order' department, it is responsible for the administration of justice, criminal law, the prison service, the police, immigration and nationality, community relations, and broad questions of national broadcasting policy.

Although it had been suggested as early as 1935, in the *Report of the Broadcasting Committee*, chaired by Viscount Ullswater, that Government responsibility for broadcasting should be transferred from the Postmaster General to a more senior ranking Cabinet Minister, this did not happen until 1974 when the Home Secretary took over broadcasting policy on the dissolution of the Ministry of Posts and Telecommunications.

The Home Secretary nominates for appointment by the Queen in Council the Governors of the BBC, appoints the Members of the IBA and the Cable Authority. Under the terms of the *Broadcasting Act 1981*, and the Licence and Agreement with the BBC, the Home Secretary has control of hours of broadcasting and areas of transmission coverage, the right to require the IBA and the BBC to broadcast official announcements, and reserve powers (which could give the Government a power of veto over programmes) to require the broadcasting authorities to refrain from broadcasting specified material.

Home Secretaries, 1974–

1974	Roy Jenkins	1983	Leon Brittan
1976	Merlyn Rees	1985	Douglas Hurd
1979	William Whitelaw		

The Broadcasting Department of the Home Office is concerned with the structure and development of broadcasting services, and advises on the form and content of broadcasting legislation. It liaises with the BBC and the IBA on the provision of public broadcasting services, and matters of finance and technical policy and planning.

Publications: No annual report on the work of the Home Office generally, or of the Broadcasting Department is published. *Home Office* (Sectional List No. 26) (London: HMSO, 1987) lists Home Office originated publications on broadcasting in-print and available from HMSO Books.

Archives: Home Office records and papers relating to broadcasting, selected for permanent preservation, are transferred to the Public Record Office (q.v.) for public inspection after thirty years.

DEPARTMENT OF TRADE AND INDUSTRY
1 Victoria Street, London SW1H OET; 01-215 7877
Radiocommunications Division: Waterloo Bridge House, Waterloo Road, London SE1 8UA; 01-275 3000
The Department of Trade and Industry (DTI) is the Government Department with overall responsibility for the electronics industry, telecommunications services, in particular British Telecom and the Post Office, and the regulation of radio frequencies. Technical requirements for cable systems, and their

installation, come under the DTI, working in partnership with the Cable Authority and the Office of Telecommunications (OFTEL).

The Radiocommunications Division, formerly the Radio Regulatory Division, has as its prime concern the use and management of the radio frequency spectrum. Particular responsibilities are: planning to ensure the continuance of spectrum availability in the future; the safeguarding of UK interests internationally; prevention of the pollution of the UK radio environment; and the deregulation of radio wherever possible. The Division operates under provisions in the *Wireless Telegraphy Act 1949* (and 1967) and the *Telecommunications Act 1984*. The Radio Investigatory Service carries out enforcement under the Acts, which includes campaigns against licence evasion for citizens band radio and unlicensed land-based pirate broadcasters.

Publications: *Annual report* (1985/86–); *United Kingdom table of radio frequency allocations* London: HMSO, 1985; *Independent Review of the Radio Spectrum: Interim report* (Cmnd 8666) London: HMSO, 1982; *Report of the Independent Review of the Radio Spectrum* (Cmnd 9000) London: HMSO, 1984; various codes of practice and information sheets.

Archives: Public Record Office (q.v.) when available.

2.3 Broadcasting authorities and public bodies

Broadcasting services in the United Kingdom are provided by public bodies established by Royal Charter or legislation. The broadcasting bodies are accountable to Parliament, through the relevant Government Minister, for overall policy, but are otherwise independent in their day-to-day operation. Other statutory public bodies involved in broadcasting are included in this section. They are the layer of public control over a largely private enterprise system.

BRITISH BROADCASTING CORPORATION (BBC)
BBC Radio: Broadcasting House, London W1A 1AA; 01-580 4468
BBC Television: Television Centre, Wood Lane, London W12 7RJ; 01-743 8000
BBC External Services: Bush House, Strand, London WC2B 4PH; 01-240 3456
BBC Enterprises: Woodlands, 80 Wood Lane, London W12 OTT; 01-743 5588
The BBC is a public corporation whose principal object is to provide public broadcasting services in the United Kingdom and overseas.

The BBC was originally formed in 1922 as a private company, the British Broadcasting Company, by a group of wireless manufacturers at the invitation of the Postmaster General. It was incorporated on 15 December 1922, and received its first Licence to broadcast on 18 January 1923. John Reith (later Lord Reith), the first General Manager, was convinced that broadcasting was a medium of great potential for information, education and entertainment, and that it should operate as a public service to high standards and with a strong sense of social responsibility. In 1923 a Broadcasting Committee, with Sir Frederick Sykes as Chairman, appointed to consider broadcasting and the licence of the BBC, recommended that such a potential power over the public should be a national service and under State control. In 1925 a further Broadcasting Committee, under the Earl of Crawford and Balcarres, recommended that broadcasting should be conducted by a public corporation of independent status acting in the national interest. As a result, broadcasting became a monopoly, financed by a broadcast receiving licence fee, and provided by an independent public body. A Royal Charter was granted to enable the BBC to operate as the British Broadcasting Corporation from 1 January 1927.

The BBC has two basic constitutional documents: the Royal Charter; and the Licence and Agreement.

The Royal Charter, the latest of which came into force on 1 August 1981 for a period of fifteen years to 31 December 1996, defines the constitution, objects, powers and responsibilities of the BBC in providing domestic and overseas broadcasting services. It provides for: the term of operation and constitution of the Corporation, including the appointment of a Board of Governors; the appointment of advisory bodies, including a General Advisory Council, and National Broadcasting Councils for Scotland, Wales and Northern Ireland; staffing and finance; and an annual report and statement of accounts for presentation to Parliament. Supplemental Royal Charters extending the life of the Corporation and its borrowing powers are also issued. The full text of the Royal Charters are published as Command Papers by HMSO; the latest are reprinted in the current edition of the *BBC annual report and acounts*.

Terms	*Royal Charters*
1927–36	(Cmd 2756) HMSO, 1926
1937–46	(Cmd 5329) HMSO, 1936
1947–51	(Cmd 6974) HMSO, 1946
1951–52	(Cmd 8416) HMSO, 1951
1952–62	(Cmd 8605) HMSO, 1952
1962–64	(Cmnd 1724) HMSO, 1962
1964–76	(Cmnd 2385) HMSO, 1964
	(Cmnd 4194) HMSO, 1969
	(Cmnd 5721) HMSO, 1974
1976–79	(Cmnd 6581) HMSO, 1976
1979–81	(Cmnd 7568) HMSO, 1979
1981–96	(Cmnd 8313) HMSO, 1981
	(Cmnd 9013) HMSO, 1983

The Licence and Agreement, issued by the Home Secretary, is a statement of the terms and conditions under which the BBC operates. According to provisions in the *Wireless Telegraphy Acts*, it authorizes the Corporation to operate transmitting stations and apparatus for broadcasting programmes in the British Isles and overseas for a specified period. It also confers on the Home Secretary certain reserve powers in relation to programmes, in particular the right to require the BBC to broadcast official announcements, or to refrain from broadcasting specified programmes. The latter power of veto over programmes has virtually never been invoked, even in times of war, the Suez crisis or the Falklands conflict, or over controversial matters such as major industrial disputes. The BBC's programmes and editorial judgements have often been under attack, but its independence from Government control on editorial or management matters has not been compromised. Another significant obligation outlined in the Licence restrains the BBC from expressing its own opinions on current affairs or areas of public policy, marking a major difference between broadcasting and the press in the United Kingdom; newspapers can promote their own views through editorials, whereas broadcasters cannot. The full text of the Licences and Agreements are published as Command Papers by HMSO; the latest are reprinted in the current edition of the *BBC annual report and accounts.*

Terms	Licences and Agreements
1927–36	(Cmd 2756) HMSO, 1926
1937–46	(Cmd 5329) HMSO, 1936
1947–51	(Cmd 6975) HMSO, 1946
1952–62	(Cmd 8579) HMSO, 1952
	(Cmd 9196) HMSO, 1954
	(Cmnd 80) HMSO, 1957
	(Cmnd 1016) HMSO, 1960
1962–64	(Cmnd 1537) HMSO, 1961
1964–76	(Cmnd 2236) HMSO, 1963
	(Cmnd 4095) HMSO, 1969
1976–79	(Cmnd 6468) HMSO, 1976
1979–81	(Cmnd 7508) HMSO, 1979
1981–96	(Cmnd 8233) HMSO, 1981

The Board of Governors, including a Chairman, Vice-Chairman and National Governors for Scotland, Wales and Northern Ireland, are appointed by the Queen in Council, on the nomination of the Home Secretary. The powers, responsibilities and obligations laid upon the Corporation are vested in the Board of Governors. The Governors normally serve for a term of five years. The BBC's chief executive officer is the Director-General.

Chairmen	Directors-General
1927 Earl of Clarendon	1927 Sir John Reith
1930 John Whitley	1938 Frederick Ogilvie
1935 Viscount Bridgeman	1942 Cecil Graves & Robert Foot
1935 Ronald Norman	1943 Robert Foot
1939 Sir Allan Powell	1944 William Haley
1947 Lord Inman	1952 Basil Nicholls (acting)
1947 Lord Simon	1952 Sir Ian Jacob
1952 Sir Alexander Cadogan	1959 Hugh Carleton Greene
1957 Sir Arthur fforde	1968 Charles Curran
1964 Sir James Duff (acting)	1977 Ian Trethowan

1964 Lord Normanbrook
1967 Lord Hill of Luton
1973 Sir Michael Swann
1980 George Howard
1983 Stuart Young
1986 Marmaduke Hussey

1982 Alasdair Milne
1987 Michael Checkland

Publications: *Annual report and accounts* (1927–. London: BBC); *BBC handbook* (1928–87. Annual. London: BBC); *Radio Times* (1923–. Weekly. London: BBC); *The Listener* (1929–. Weekly. London: BBC); *World Broadcasting Information* (Weekly. Caversham Park, Reading: BBC Monitoring Service); press releases and programme publicity. BBC Enterprises produce a wide range of programme-related books, records and videos.

Archives: BBC Written Archives (q.v.); Radio Programme Index (q.v.), Radio Drama Information Centre (q.v.) and Television Script Unit (q.v.) hold scripts; BBC Film and Videotape Library (q.v.) and BBC Sound Archives (q.v.) contain selected programmes.

INDEPENDENT BROADCASTING AUTHORITY (IBA)
70 Brompton Road, London SW3 1EY; 01-584 7011
Engineering Headquarters: Crawley Court, Winchester, Hants SO21 2QA; 0962 823434
The IBA is a corporate body, established by legislation, to provide public television and sound broadcasting services for the United Kingdom and the Channel Islands additional to those of the BBC.

The Independent Television Authority was established on 4 August 1954, under provisions of the *Television Act 1954*, to set up, control and regulate Independent Television (ITV). ITV began on 22 September 1955, in the London area, and by 1962 covered virtually the whole United Kingdom. The *Sound Broadcasting Act 1972* extended the Authority's responsibilities to include local sound broadcasting, and renamed it the Independent Broadcasting Authority. Independent Local Radio began in 1973. A further extension of the IBA's remit, under the provisions of the *Broadcasting Act 1980*, was the establishment of the fourth television channel, which opened as Channel 4 in 1982. The IBA was enabled to provide satellite television services (DBS) by the *Cable and Broadcasting Act 1984*.

The IBA has two basic constitutional documents: the current *Broadcasting Act*; and the Licence granted by the Home Secretary.

The *Broadcasting Act* establishes the functions and duties of the Authority in its provision of television and radio services. The principal functions of the IBA laid down by the Act are: selection and appointment of the programme companies; supervision of programme planning; control of advertising; and the transmission of programmes through transmitting stations built, owned and operated by the Authority. It provides for: the term of operation; the appointment of a Chairman, Deputy Chairman and Members by the Home Secretary;

the establishment of transmitting stations; and provisions as to programmes, advertisements, appointment of advisory committees, programme contractors, finances, audited accounts and an annual report. The public service broadcasting ethic is spelt out for the IBA more precisely in the Act than it is for the BBC in their Royal Charter, and the detailed programme remit for the IBA services codifies the largely unwritten programming principles of the BBC. Another basic difference is that the BBC can expand its range of services unless specifically prohibited by the Charter, whereas the IBA can only provide services prescribed in the Act, and requires new legislation to enable it to extend its remit. The IBA is both the *broadcaster* and the *regulator* of Independent Broadcasting services.

The full text of Acts of Parliament governing the IBA are published by HMSO. Details of provisions and commencement dates in the Acts are enacted by Statutory Instruments from HMSO.

Terms	Acts of Parliament
1954–64	Television Act 1954
1964–76	Television Act 1963
	Television Act 1964
	Sound Broadcasting Act 1972
	Independent Broadcasting Authority Act 1973
	Independent Broadcasting Authority Act 1974
1976–79	Independent Broadcasting Authority (No 2) Act 1974
1979–81	Independent Broadcasting Authority 1978
	Independent Broadcasting Authority Act 1979
1981–96	Broadcasting Act 1980
	Broadcasting Act 1981
1996–2001	Cable and Broadcasting Act 1984
2001–2005	Broadcasting Act 1987

The Licence granted to the IBA by the Home Secretary, under the terms of the *Wireless Telegraphy Act 1949*, authorizes it to use transmitting stations for broadcasting television and sound services.

Terms	Licences
1954–64	Broadcasting (Cmd 9451) HMSO, 1955
1964–76	Broadcasting (Cmnd 2424) HMSO, 1964
	Broadcasting (Cmnd 4193) HMSO, 1969
	Broadcasting (Cmnd 5413) HMSO, 1973
1976–79	Broadcasting (Cmnd 6541) HMSO, 1976
1979–81	Broadcasting (Cmnd 7616) HMSO, 1979
1981–96	Broadcasting (Cmnd 8467) HMSO, 1982

The *Broadcasting Act* provides for an Authority consisting of a Chairman and Deputy Chairman and ten other Members, appointed by the Home Secretary. The Authority Members are the equivalent of the BBC Board of Governors. The chief executive is the Director-General.

Chairmen	*Directors-General*
1954 Sir Kenneth Clark	1954 Sir Robert Fraser
1957 Sir Ivone Kirkpatrick	1970 Sir Brian Young
1962 Sir John Carmichael (acting)	1982 John Whitney
1963 Lord Hill of Luton	
1967 Lord Aylestone	
1975 Lady Plowden	
1981 Lord Thomson of Monifieth	

In the selection and appointment of the programme companies, the IBA determines the franchises to be offered, issues a document giving particulars or specifications of each contract, advertises the terms and details, holds open meetings and conducts research within the franchise areas to ascertain the views of the public, and interviews the various applicant groups, before announcing the award of the contracts. The ITV and ILR companies are contracted to the IBA to provide programme services within their franchise area for a specified period. Each company pays the IBA a rental for the use of the transmitters to meet the Authority's administrative and operating costs. In addition, the fifteen regional ITV companies pay the IBA a subscription to meet the costs of Channel 4 and S4C, for which in return they sell the advertising time within their area.

For the supervision of programme planning, the IBA is in consultation with the companies over their forward planning and scheduling of programmes; the Authority may require changes to the content, or time of scheduling, of programmes before they are approved for transmission. The *Television Programme Guidelines* are drawn up as a codification of good working standards and practice, based partly on an interpretation of the *Broadcasting Act*, and partly on IBA and agreed IBA/ITV company policy. They are in part mandatory, otherwise merely advisory.

The control of advertising by the IBA, on both ITV, Channel 4 and Independent Radio, involves the drawing up of a *Code of advertising standards and practice*, in accordance with the Act, to cover the frequency, amount and nature of commercials. Television commercials themselves have to be cleared by the IBA at script stage and on completion, to ensure compliance with the code, before they can be shown.

The IBA builds, owns and operates the transmitters, and transmits the programmes supplied by the contractors. It establishes technical standards for transmission, reception and broadcasting quality control, and undertakes research and development in the field of broadcast engineering and telecommunications.

The IBA maintains a London administrative headquarters, an engineering establishment at Crawley Court in Hampshire, regional offices in the major franchise regions, regional operations centres, and transmitter stations throughout the UK.

Publications: *The IBA annual report and accounts* (1954–. London: HMSO/IBA); *Television and radio* (1963–88). Annual. London: Independent Television Publications); *Television programme guidelines*; *Code of advertising standards and practice*; *Independent Television and Radio: a pocket guide*; various leaflets.

Archives: Library (q.v.).

WELSH FOURTH CHANNEL AUTHORITY (WFCA)
Clos Sophia, Caerdydd (Cardiff) CF1 9XY; 0222 43421
The WFCA is a public body established by the *Broadcasting Act 1980* to provide television programmes for broadcasting by the IBA on the fourth channel in Wales.

The Chairman and Members of the Authority were appointed on 22 January 1981, and it held its first meeting on 31 January 1981. It provides the Sianel Pedwar Cymru (S4C) service in Wales, which began transmission on 2 November 1982.

The principal constitutional document is the *Broadcasting Act 1981*, consolidating the *Broadcasting Act 1980* and earlier broadcasting legislation. The Act provides for an Authority to consist of a Chairman and four other Members, and provisions for the programmes, advertisements and finances of the Welsh fourth television channel. It stipulates that a substantial proportion of the programmes shall be in the Welsh language, particularly during the peak-hour viewing period between 6.30pm and 10.00pm. The sources of programmes for the channel would be the BBC and the IBA programme contractor for Wales. Although it is a public body like the BBC and the IBA, and entrusted with the provision of programme services, it is not a *broadcaster*, as they are, but a programme provider. The programmes supplied by the WFCA are broadcast by the IBA through its network of transmitters to over 97 per cent of homes in Wales.

The Chairman and Members are appointed by the Home Secretary, and a headquarters staff is led by the Director.

Chairmen	Director
1981 Sir Goronwy Daniel	1981 Owen Edwards
1986 John Howard Davies	

Although the Act did not specify the total hours of Welsh language programmes to be broadcast, an overall target of 22 hours a week was indicated by the Home Secretary in the debate on the Second Reading of the bill in the House of Commons on 18 February 1980. Since S4C began, the total hours of Welsh programmes has steadily exceeded that amount to approximately 25 hours a week — 10 hours supplied by BBC Wales, 9 hours from HTV, the IBA programme contractor for Wales, and an increasing amount from independent producers. At other times, S4C shows the majority of Channel 4 programmes.

The Authority is financed from a portion of the Fourth Channel subscriptions paid to the IBA by the ITV programme contractors.

Publications: *WalesS4Cymru: Sianel Pedwar Cymru: annual report and accounts* (1981–. Caerdydd: WFCA); *Teledu yng Nghymru — y Diwydiant Newydd/Television in Wales — the new industry* (S4C 1982–87) (Caerdydd: WFCA, 1987); *TVTimes* supplement *Sbec* (1968–. Weekly. London: Independent Television Publications) contains details of Welsh language programmes on Sianel Pedwar Cymru.

CABLE AUTHORITY
Gillingham House, 38–44 Gillingham Street, London SW1V 1HU; 01-821 6161
The Authority is a statutory corporate body established to provide cable programme services in the United Kingdom.

The Authority came into existence on 1 December 1984, and assumed its full statutory powers on 1 January 1985.

The constitutional document for the Authority is the *Cable and Broadcasting Act 1984*, which provides for the following functions: the granting of franchises for the installation and operation of large-scale broadband systems; the licensing of cable programme services; the licensing of the provision of television for public showing; the regulation of the content of programme services, including the drawing up of codes on programme standards, advertising practice and sponsorship; and the promotion of cable services, especially those on the new broadband systems. The Act also provides for: a Chairman, Deputy Chairman and Members of the Authority; an annual report and accounts to be laid before Parliament; and financial arrangements. No specified term of operation for the Authority is laid down by the Act; it is open-ended.

The Chairman and Members of the Authority are appointed by the Home Secretary for a term of not more than five years. The small London headquarters staff is headed by the Director-General.

Chairman	*Director-General*
1984 Richard H. Burton	1985 Jon Davey

In November 1983, before the Cable Authority came into existence, the Government announced the award of interim franchises for pilot projects in eleven areas and, since the Authority was established, it has awarded further franchises for new broadband cable systems. By the end of 1987, twelve of these new systems — Swindon, Aberdeen, Coventry, Croydon, Glasgow, Westminster, Windsor, Ealing, Luton and South Bedfordshire, East London, Camden in London, and Guildford — were all operational, with over 250,000 homes connected to cable television systems in the United Kingdom.

The Cable Authority is financed from the licence and application fees paid by cable operators, and receives no public money, except for initial loans from the Home Secretary, to be repaid when it is practicable to be self-supporting.

Publications: *Annual report and accounts* (1985/86–. London: Cable Authority); various codes and promotional leaflets.

THE BROADCASTING COMPLAINTS COMMISSION
Grosvenor Gardens House, 35 & 37 Grosvenor Gardens, London SW1W OBS; 01-630 1966
The Commission is a statutory body established by the *Broadcasting Act 1980* to adjudicate upon complaints of unfair treatment, or infringement of privacy by broadcasters.

The Commission's functions derive from the *Broadcasting Act 1981* (re-enacting the *Broadcasting Act 1980*) and the *Cable and Broadcasting Act 1984*. It replaced the independent Programmes Complaints Commission set up by the BBC in October 1971. It is financed by contributions from the BBC, the IBA and the Cable Authority.

The Commission's duty is to consider and adjudicate upon complaints of unjust or unfair treatment in sound and television programmes broadcast by the BBC or the IBA on or after 1 June 1981; or included in a licensed cable programme service on or after 1 June 1985; or unwarranted infringement of privacy in, or in connection with the obtaining of material included in such programmes. This extends to all sound, television and cable programmes, including advertisements and teletext transmissions, and programmes broadcast by the BBC's External Services. Complaints must be made in writing, by the person or body affected, to the Commission, who can demand from the broadcasting organization a tape or transcript of the relevant programme, and any accompanying correspondence with the complainant. The Commission is required to publish reports of its adjudications in its annual report and elsewhere, including the *Radio Times* and the *TVTimes* as appropriate, and to broadcast the findings on-air.

The Act provides for the appointment by the Home Secretary of not less than three Members, including a Chairman:

Chairmen
1981 Baroness Pike of Melton
1985 Sir Thomas Skyrme
1987 Lady Anglesey

Due to the Commission's rather narrow terms of reference, many of the complaints received fall outside of its jurisdiction. In 1986–87, for example, only 48 out of 222 complaints received came within its remit, and of the 76 considered (including 28 already before the Commission at the beginning of the year) only 53 were considered and 21 given full adjudications, of which 12 were upheld and 9 rejected.

Publication: *Report of the Broadcasting Complaints Commission* (1982–. Annual. London: HMSO).

OFFICE OF TELECOMMUNICATIONS (OFTEL)
Atlantic House, Holborn Viaduct, London EC1N 2HQ; 01-822 1690
OFTEL is an independent regulatory body set up to monitor and enforce licences granted to public telecommunications operators.

The principal constitutional document of OFTEL is the *Telecommunications Act 1984*. Its expenditure is provided by Parliament, though its costs are largely met by the income from the licences. As a non-ministerial Government Department, its Director-General of Telecommunications is independent of ministerial control, though he is required to consult with advisory bodies on telecommunications (for England, Scotland, Wales and Northern Ireland), as well as two further advisory committees (Advisory Committee on Telecommunications for Disabled and Elderly People, and the Advisory Committee on Telecommunications for Small Businesses), all appointed by the Secretary of State for Trade and Industry. OFTEL has the sole responsibility for the monitoring and enforcing of licences granted by the Secretary of State to operators of public telecommunications systems — British Telecom and Mercury Communications. Also, it promotes the interests of the consumer, and effective competition, through the enforcement of the competition legislation in telecommunications, and ensuring that the services meet reasonable demands placed on them. It grants licences to cable operators, telecommunications systems, and suppliers of apparatus and equipment, and provides information and advice to consumers. Registers of licences, approved contractors and approved apparatus are available.

Publications: *Report of the Director-General of Telecommunications* (1984–. Annual. London: HMSO); *A guide to the Office of Telecommunications*; *OFTEL News* (quarterly); *Telecommunications Code*.

Further reading

Briggs, Asa. *Governing the BBC*. London: BBC, 1979.
Briggs, Asa and Spicer, Joanna. *The franchise affair*. London: Century Hutchinson, 1986.
Burns, Tom. *The BBC: public institution and private world*. London: Macmillan, 1977.
Central Office of Information. *Britain: an official handbook*. 1946–. Annual. London: HMSO.
Sendall, Bernard. *Independent Television in Britain*. London: Macmillan, 2 vols, 1982–83.

2.4 Advisory councils and committees

Official councils and committees established by either the Government or the broadcasting authorities to advise them on matters of broadcasting policy and practice.

Television Advisory Committee

From time to time the Government has appointed advisory committees to consider and advise on future development of services and technical matters.

The first Television Advisory Committee, as proposed by Lord Selsdon's Television Committee, was established on 31 January 1935, and ceased to meet after February 1940 as the BBC Television service had closed down at the outbreak of war.

In 1945, as a result of a recommendation in the *Report of the Television Committee 1943*, a second Television Advisory Committee was set up. Between 1946 and 1949 it reported to the Postmaster General on the development of the post-war television service, including the standards to be adopted.

A third Television Advisory Committee was reconstituted in October 1952, 'to advise the Postmaster General on the development of television and sound broadcasting at frequencies above 30 megacycles per second, and related matters, including competitive television services . . .'. In its various reports, published between 1952 and 1972, the Committee considered such technical issues as broadcasting frequencies, television line definition and standards, colour television systems, satellite broadcasting, and wired (cable) distribution. A Technical Sub-Committee undertook detailed studies and investigations, and its reports were included with the full Television Advisory Committee reports:

General Post Office *First report of the Television Advisory Committee, 1952.* London: HMSO, 1953.
General Post Office *Second report of the Television Advisory Committee, 1952.* London: HMSO, 1954.
General Post Office *Report of the Television Advisory Committee, 1960.* London: HMSO, 1960.
General Post Office *Report of the Television Advisory Committee, 1967.* London: HMSO, 1968.
Ministry of Posts and Telecommunications *Report of the Television Advisory Committee, 1972.* London: HMSO, 1972.

The constitutional documents for both the BBC and the IBA contain provisions for the appointment of advisory councils and committees.

Under the Royal Charter, the BBC is required to appoint: a General Advisory Council to advise the Corporation on a wide range of broadcasting issues; three National Broadcasting Councils for Scotland, Wales and Northern Ireland; Regional Advisory Councils for England; Local Radio Advisory Councils; and other specialist advisory bodies with regard to broadcasting services, such as the Central Music Advisory Committee, the Asian Programmes Advisory Committee, and the Engineering Advisory Committee.

The IBA, under the terms of the *Broadcasting Act*, may appoint: a General Advisory Council; Advisory Committees for Scotland, Wales and Northern Ireland; Local Advisory Committees for the localities served by Independent Local Radio stations; and specialist committees to advise on advertising (Advertising Advisory Committee, the Medical Advisory Panel, and the Advertising Liaison Committee), educational broadcasting (Educational Advisory Council), and religious broadcasting (Panel of Religious Advisers).

Three particular advisory bodies have broader responsibilities.

Central Appeals Advisory Committee

This Committee advises both the BBC and the IBA, normally in separate sessions, on policy issues connected with charitable appeals on radio and television, and considers applications from the charities for broadcast appeals.

Central Religious Advisory Committee (CRAC)

CRAC advises both the BBC and the IBA on religious broadcasting policy. The members, widely drawn to reflect organized religious opinion in the UK, include the Chairmen of the BBC Religious Advisory Committees and members of the IBA Panel of Religious Advisers. The Committee meets twice a year, both separately with BBC and the IBA representatives, and in a joint session with both bodies and the ITV Association on matters of common interest and selected major topics.

School Broadcasting Councils

The School Broadcasting Council for the United Kingdom, and for the National Regions of Scotland, Wales and Northern Ireland are not only advisory, but work in partnership with the BBC on educational programmes. The SBC was established in 1926. It consists of members representative of government departments, local authorities, and the major professional and educational associations, nominated by educational bodies, including the teaching unions, and the BBC. The function of the Councils is to guide the BBC in its provision of educational broadcasts on radio and television to schools, and the support services and materials associated with the programmes.

2.5 Programme services and companies

The programmes seen and heard on television and radio in the United Kingdom are broadcast, though not necessarily produced, by the national broadcasting organizations, the BBC and the IBA, or relayed by the cable services licensed by the Cable Authority.

The BBC provides two national television services, national, regional and local radio services, and overseas services. The IBA broadcasts a network of regional television services of programmes supplied by area programme contractors, a national television channel of programmes provided by the Channel Four Television Company and the Welsh Fourth Channel Authority, and local radio services. The Cable Authority presides over a system of cable television services relaying broadcast channels and special cable programme channels.

BBC Radio and Television

The constitution of the BBC, described more fully in a previous chapter of this book, enables the Corporation to provide public sound and television services in the United Kingdom and overseas. The 'Home Services', the domestic radio and television channels, are financed primarily from the income derived from the television licence fee, supplemented by profits from such trading activities as television programme exports and the sale of programme-related publications and recordings (See Table 2). Over 65 per cent of the BBC's expenditure on domestic services is spent on the television services (BBC1, BBC2 and regional television), compared to around 25 per cent on radio (Radios 1, 2, 3 and 4, regional and local radio stations). The 'External Services' are financed by a grant-in-aid from the Foreign and Commonwealth Office.

Table 2.   Broadcasting   receiving   licences   (1922–87)   and   BBC   income (1927–87)*

Year	Radio†	Radio & TV	Colour TV	BBC income‡
1922	35,755			
1923	595,496			
1924	1,129,578			
1925	1,645,207			
1926	2,178,259			
1927	2,263,894			800,959
1928	2,470,639			871,763
1929	2,717,367			944,300
1930	3,075,828			1,043,023
1931	3,626,418			1,179,031
1932	4,590,292			1,306,000
1933	5,461,367			1,460,352
1934	6,220,429			1,710,286
1935	6,969,885			2,038,262
1936	7,572,442			2,509,750
1937	8,081,161			2,875,044
1938	8,538,946			3,534,104
1939	8,915,717			
1940	8,897,618			4,744,769
1941	8,701,899			4,854,802
1942	8,635,642			6,700,000
1943	9,193,641			8,400,000
1944	9,506,714			8,400,000
1945	9,663,369			8,300,000
1946	10,347,831			8,300,000
1947	10,713,298	14,560		10,405,230
1948	11,081,977	45,564		8,927,363
1949	11,567,227	126,567		9,444,472
1950	11,819,190	343,882		9,938,917
1951	11,546,925	763,941		12,094,198
1952	11,244,141	1,449,260		12,267,386
1953	10,688,684	2,142,452		11,694,833
1954	10,125,512	3,248,892		12,963,451
1955	9,414,224	4,503,766		18,943,844
1956	8,459,213	5,739,593		21,202,109
1957	7,496,390	6,966,256		23,790,208
1958	6,494,960	8,090,003		25,297,527

Table 2. Continued

Year	Radio†	Radio & TV	Colour TV	BBC income‡
1959	5,423,207	9,255,422		27,323,115
1960	4,480,300	10,469,753		31,286,153
1961	3,858,132	11,267,741		33,522,816
1962	3,491,725	11,833,712		36,731,867
1963	3,212,814	12,442,806		37,972,143
1964	2,959,011	12,885,331		46,758,301
1965	2,759,203	13,253,045		52,698,444
1966	2,579,567	13,567,090		64,314,769
1967	2,476,272	14,267,271		71,573,170
1968	2,529,750	15,068,079	20,428	74,746,943
1969	2,438,906	15,396,642	99,419	80,626,464
1970	2,279,017	15,609,131	273,397	93,877,912
1971	——	15,333,221	609,969	95,630,363
1972	——	15,023,691	1,634,760	113,284,000
1973	——	13,792,623	3,331,996	125,942,000
1974	——	11,766,424	5,558,146	136,939,000
1975	——	10,120,493	7,580,322	146,372,000
1976	——	9,148,732	8,639,252	212,862,000
1977	——	8,098,386	9,957,672	226,989,000
1978	——	7,099,726	11,049,192	261,826,000
1979	——	6,249,716	12,131,445	312,279,000
1980	——	5,383,125	12,901,740	394,700,000
1981	——	4,887,663	13,779,548	502,300,000
1982	——	4,293,668	14,260,552	563,700,000
1983	——	3,795,587	14,698,648	683,200,000
1984	——	3,261,272	15,370,481	702,000,000
1985	——	2,896,263	15,819,674	723,100,000
1986	——	2,679,396	16,025,336	922,900,000
1987	——	2,414,000	16,539,000	960,700,000

*Figures for licences and BBC income are for years ending 31 March.
†Not including free licences issued to the blind (1927–70).
‡In £s. Net income from licence fee only (not including income from sales of programmes and publications, etc.); 1940–46 wartime income a Government grant-in-aid.
Sources: Post Office/National Television Licence Records Office; BBC.

BBC Radio

BBC Radio services officially began on 14 November 1922, transmitting a National Programme first from the 2LO London station and then from regional stations in Birmingham, Manchester, Newcastle upon Tyne, Cardiff, Glasgow and Belfast by 1924. In 1930 the Regional Programme began an alternative pro-gramme service to the national service for London, North, Scotland, and West of England and Wales regions.

At the outbreak of the Second World War in 1939, these were replaced by the Home Service and then, in January 1940, a Forces Programme, as a second ser-vice of entertainment for British troops in the war.

After the end of the war, two new radio channels joined the Home Service: the

Light Programme, which replaced the wartime Forces Programme; and the Third Programme, consisting of music and the spoken word. Regional Home Services also restarted in 1945.

The challenge to the BBC from the pirate radio stations in the 1960s was met by the introduction in 1967 of a new popular music network, Radio 1. The existing channels were renamed — Radio 2 (Light Programme), Radio 3 (Third Programme) and Radio 4 (Home Service). These services were the basis for a new pattern of 'generic' broadcasting in 1970, when Radio 3 became primarily a serious music channel with Radio 4 concentrating on news, current affairs and features, Radio 2 on light music and entertainment, and Radio 1 on pop music.

BBC Local Radio began on an experimental basis in 1967, and had over thirty stations by 1987 serving England and the Channel Islands:

1967	Radio Leicester	1971	Radio Humberside
	Radio Sheffield		Radio Lancashire
	Radio Merseyside		Radio Newcastle
1968	Radio Durham (–1972)	1975	Radio Cumbria
	Radio Leeds	1980	Radio Lincolnshire
	Radio Nottingham		Radio Norfolk
	Radio Stoke-on-Trent	1982	Radio Cambridgeshire
	Radio Brighton		Radio Furness
1970	Radio Bristol		Radio Guernsey
	Radio Cleveland		Radio Jersey
	Radio Kent		Radio Northampton
	Radio London	1983	Radio Cornwall
	Radio Manchester		Radio Devon
	Radio Oxford		Radio York
	Radio Solent	1985	Radio Shropshire
	Radio WM (West Midlands)		Radio Bedfordshire
1971	Radio Derby	1986	Radio Essex

The national regions became independent services in 1978, operating as Radio Scotland, Radio Wales/Radio Cymru, and Radio Ulster.

Community and area stations in Scotland, Wales and Northern Ireland opt out from the Regional Radio service for part of each weekday with local programming: Radios Aberdeen, Highland, nan Gaidheal, Orkney, Shetland, Solway and Tweed in Scotland; Radios Clwyd and Gwent in Wales; and Radio Foyle in Ulster.

A new pattern of regional broadcasting for England was introduced in 1987; five large regions were created — North West, North East, Midlands, South and West, and South and East — each with an integrated broadcasting structure (of television, regional and local radio services within the area) and a large degree of autonomy.

BBC Television

The BBC began a full public television service on 2 November 1936, after several years of experimental broadcasts. The high-definition service, on

405-line television, was transmitted from Alexandra Palace and was only available to viewers in the London area. The coverage of King George VI's Coronation procession caught the public interest and, together with improved reception and range of programmes, brought increased sales of television sets and viewer appreciation before the service closed down at the outbreak of the Second World War on 1 September 1939.

The television service resumed after the war on 7 June 1946, again from Alexandra Palace, with coverage the following day of the Victory parades in London. The service was slowly extended to the regions with the opening of transmitters for the Midlands in 1949, the North in 1951, Scotland and Wales and the West of England in 1952, by which time over 80 per cent of the population could receive television, and over a million combined radio and television licences were sold. Again coverage of a Coronation — this time of Queen Elizabeth II on 2 June 1953 — brought an enormous increase in the awareness of television.

A second BBC television service, BBC2, began on 20 April 1964, on 625-line UHF. Slow acceptance of the new channel can be attributed to several reasons — a disastrous opening night, blacked-out by a power failure, followed by unpopular scheduling and timing of programmes; the need for viewers to have new or converted sets to receive the UHF transmissions; and the incomplete transmitter coverage of the country.

Colour television was first transmitted in the United Kingdom on BBC2 in 1967, the full service beginning on 2 December. It was extended to BBC1 (and ITV) on 15 November 1969. With the increasing popularity of colour television and the easing of the credit squeeze in 1971, the sales of colour sets soon leapt, resulting in the percentage of the population having colour television rising from 4 per cent in 1970 to 18 per cent in 1972.

BBC External Services

The overseas services of the BBC began on 19 December 1932, with the Empire Service broadcasts in the English language to Australia, India, South Africa, West Africa and Canada. Foreign language broadcasts first began in 1938, with the start of the Arabic and Latin American Services, and the European news bulletins delivered in French, German and Italian. During the war the BBC's vernacular language broadcasts to countries throughout the world increased considerably. Today, BBC External Services broadcast in English, on the World Service, and in 37 other languages to a world audience of over 120 million.

Independent Broadcasting

The Independent Broadcasting system consists of Independent Television, two television channels (ITV and Channel 4), Independent Radio, a network of local radio stations (Independent Local Radio), and DBS satellite television services. The system is supervised and regulated by the Independent Broadcasting Authority (q.v.).

Independent Television was set up, according to provisions in the *Television*

Act 1954, by the Independent Television Authority. The *Sound Broadcasting Act 1972* provided for local radio services to be provided by the ITA, and renamed it the Independent Broadcasting Authority. The system was further extended by the addition of a fourth television channel, under the *Broadcasting Act 1980*, and DBS services by the *Cable and Broadcasting Act 1984*.

Independent Broadcasting services are financed largely through the sale of advertising air-time; no income comes from the licence fee or public funds. The ITV programme companies are contracted to the IBA for the provision of programme services for a specified franchise area, and they finance their operations with the revenue from the sale of spot advertising on ITV and Channel 4 in their area. The radio companies' revenue also comes from the sale of air-time. The frequency, amount and nature of the advertising is laid down by the IBA, in accordance with the *Broadcasting Act*, though the rates charged to advertisers for advertising time is determined by each company, and varies in each franchise area according to the composition and size of the audience. The IBA receives its income from the television and radio companies in the form of an annual rental for the use of the transmitters, which finances the Authority's operations (see Table 3).

Table 3.   Finances of Independent Broadcasting services

Year	ITV revenue	ILR revenue	ITA/IBA income	Levy
1955			55,000*	
1956	13,024,000		500,000*	
1957	31,986,000		1,702,152	
1958	48,671,000		2,284,086	
1959	58,359,000		2,871,293	
1960	76,960,000		3,756,572	
1961	93,276,000		4,212,517	
1962	99,794,000		4,693,161	
1963	62,931,783		5,463,524	
1964	74,433,162		5,622,899	
1965	82,840,106		7,245,653	8,350,326
1966	91,776,136		8,380,678	21,186,258
1967	91,776,136		8,697,081	22,855,044
1968	98,758,870		8,697,081	24,811,159
1969	97,539,737		7,555,851	25,779,281
1970	94,742,399		6,936,069	26,101,957
1971	108,633,692		7,793,002	24,893,223
1972	134,221,157		11,247,881	10,839,006
1973	160,830,730		13,054,000	18,243,451
1974	149,244,563		13,641,000	22,762,512
1975	176,532,201	8,534,997	14,897,000	19,162,774
1976	230,806,620	14,700,000	15,614,000	22,161,661
1977	299,886,549	23,100,000	17,876,000	48,878,061
1978	363,004,836	29,845,000	21,304,000	62,073,841
1979	346,795,589	44,587,000	22,317,000	68,982,502

Table 3. Continued

Year	ITV revenue	ILR revenue	ITA/IBA income	Levy
1980	529,311,243	44,858,000	24,443,000	42,307,517
1981	611,222,523	50,824,000	30,243,000	52,028,672
1982	697,169,612	60,748,000	36,441,000	57,512,767
1983	824,417,275	70,800,000	53,769,000	38,495,332
1984	912,265,807	75,700,000	58,253,000	23,293,841
1985	982,603,315	72,100,000	62,595,000	40,440,000
1986	1,183,000,000	79,006,000	65,331,000	20,202,624
1987	1,325,870,555	99,404,939	68,052,000	75,170,000

Figures are in £s.
*ITA income 1954–6 a repayable loan from the Postmaster General. ITV/ILR revenue figures are by calendar year ending 31 December; ITA/IBA income from programme company rentals and the Exchequer Levy by financial year ending 31 March.
Sources: ITV: Independent Television Association; ILR: Association of Independent Radio Contractors; IBA: *IBA annual report and accounts*. 1955–. London: HMSO; Exchequer Levy: *Independent Broadcasting Authority: Additional payments by programme contractors*. 1965–. Annual. London: HMSO.

The Government has received revenue from Independent Broadcasting in the form of normal taxation on the companies and a special levy, collected by the IBA but passed through to the Treasury. The levy was originally a Television Advertisement Duty (TAD), from 1961 to 1964, then replaced by an Exchequer Levy, or 'additional payments', on company turnover, from 1964 to 1974, and changed to one calculated on operating profits in 1974. The Exchequer Levy was extended by the *Finance Act 1986* to cover profits from overseas sales of programmes.

ITV

The ITV service is provided by 16 television companies — 15 regional companies contracted to the IBA to provide programme services within specified franchise areas, and a national breakfast-time television contractor (see Table 4). Fourteen ITV franchise areas cover the United Kingdom, each with its own programme contractor, except London with two programme contractors for separate weekday and weekend services.

Table 4. Current Independent Television companies (1982–92)

Franchise area	Company	Address & phone no.
The Borders	Border Television	Television Centre, Carlisle CA1 3NT; 0228 25101
Central Scotland	Scottish Television	Cowcaddens, Glasgow GG 3PR; 041-332 9999
Channel Islands	Channel Television	The Television Centre, St Helier, Jersey; 0534 73999

Table 4.   Continued

Franchise area	Company	Address & phone no.
East and West Midlands	Central Independent Television	Central House, Broad Street, Birmingham B1 2JP; 021–643 9898
East of England	Anglia Television	Anglia House, Norwich NR1 3JG; 0603 615151
London (Weekday)	Thames Television	Thames Television House, 306–316 Euston Road, London NW1 3BB; 01–387 9494
London (Weekend)	London Weekend Television	South Bank TV Centre, London SE1 9LT; 01–261 3434
North Scotland	Grampian Television	Queen's Cross, Aberdeen AB9 2XJ; 0224 646464
North-East England	Tyne Tees Television	Television Centre, City Road, Newcastle upon Tyne NE1 2AL; 091–261 0181
North-West England	Granada Television	Granada TV Centre, Manchester M6O 9EA; 061–832 7211
Northern Ireland	Ulster Television	Havelock House, Ormeau Road, Belfast BT7 1EB; 0232 328122
South and South-East England	TVS Television	Television Centre, Southampton SO9 5HZ; 0703 634211
South-West England	TSW—Television South West	Derry's Cross, Plymouth PL1 2SP; 0752 663322
Wales and the West of England	HTV	Television Centre, Culverhouse Cross, Cardiff CF5 6XJ; 0222 590590
Yorkshire	Yorkshire Television	Television Centre, Leeds LS3 1JS; 0532 438283

The first companies to be appointed were Associated-Rediffusion and Associated Television (ATV), contracted for the London weekday and weekend services; they inaugurated ITV on 22 September 1955. The ITV service was only available in the London area at first; transmitter coverage was not complete for the whole country until 1962, when Channel Television, for the Channel Islands, and Wales (West and North) went on-air. Since then the ITV franchises have been fully reviewed on three occasions, for contract periods from 1964 (when all contractors were reappointed), 1968 and 1982 (see Table 5). *The Broadcasting Act 1987* provides for the 1982 contracts to expire on 31 December 1992.

Table 5. Independent Television companies (1955–)

On-air	Off-air	Programme company	Franchise area
22.9.1955	29.7.1968	Associated-Rediffusion	London (Weekday)
24.9.1955	28.7.1968	Associated Television (ATV)	London (Weekend)
17.2.1956	31.12.1981	Associated Television (ATV)	Midlands (Weekday)
18.2.1956	28.7.1968	ABC Television	Midlands (Weekend)
3.5.1956		Granada Television	North of England (Weekday)
5.5.1956	28.7.1968	ABC Television	North of England (Weekend)
31.8.1957		Scottish Television	Central Scotland
14.1.1958	3.3.1968	TWW	Wales and West of England
30.8.1958	31.12.1981	Southern Television	South of England
15.1.1959		Tyne Tees Television	North-East England
27.10.1959		Anglia Television	East of England
31.10.1959		Ulster Television	Northern Ireland
29.4.1961	11.8.1981	Westward Television	South-West England
1.9.1961		Border Television	The Borders
30.9.1961		Grampian Television	North Scotland
1.9.1962		Channel Television	Channel Islands
14.9.1962	26.1.1964	Wales (West and North)	West and North Wales
4.3.1968		HTV	Wales and the West of England
29.7.1968		Thames Television*	London (Weekday)
29.7.1968		Yorkshire Television	Yorkshire
2.8.1968		London Weekend Television	London (Weekend)
12.8.1981		TSW—Television South-West	South-West England
1.1.1982		TVS Television	South and South-East England
1.1.1982		Central Independent Television†	East and West Midlands
1.2.1983		TV-am	(Breakfast-time)

*Merger of ABC Television and Rediffusion.
†A restructured ATV.

Each ITV company has close links and identification with its franchise area. They have local representation on the board and among the shareholders. Each has contractual obligations to make a specified quota of local programmes for viewers within their own franchise area.

The network system, the distinctive feature of ITV, guarantees an agreed supply of approximately 42 hours a week of programming for the national network from the five major contractors for the largest franchise areas — London, Midlands, North-West England and Yorkshire, determined by their share of the Net Advertising Revenue. The smaller regional companies pay for network programmes through the Live Network Agreement, and can also supply programmes to the network at a fixed price. This mix of local and net-worked programmes gives ITV a unique character that is both national and strongly regional.

INDEPENDENT TELEVISION NEWS (ITN)
ITN House, 48 Wells Street, London W1P 4DE; 01-6372424
The company providing national and international news for ITV and Channel 4, ITN is not a contractor of the IBA, but jointly owned by the ITV companies. Suggestions of a stock market floatation as a public company may lead to a change of status for the company.

Basic information about the franchise and the contractual obligations appears in the 'Particulars of Contract', issued by the IBA, and about the company from its franchise application document.

Publications: The ITV companies produce an annual report and accounts, for deposit at the Companies Registration Office, and also for publication. Other publications include press releases, programme publicity, programme schedules, rate cards and marketing guides.

INDEPENDENT TELEVISION PUBLICATIONS (ITP)
247 Tottenham Court Road, London W1P OAU; 01-323 3222
ITP is jointly owned by the ITV companies, and publishes *TV Times* (the programme journal for ITV and Channel 4), *Look-in* (a programme magazine for children and young people) and various programme books.

Archives: The contracts between the ITV companies and the IBA provide for the preservation of archives. Some of the companies maintain programme documentation archives (q.v.) and film libraries (q.v.), though no overall policy for their organization and public access has yet been established. Selected ITV programmes are available for viewing at the National Film Archive (q.v.).

Channel 4

Independent Broadcasting's second television service, Channel 4, was launched on 2 November 1982. The IBA was authorized by the *Broadcasting Act 1980* to establish a fourth television channel designed to be a distinctive service comple-mentary to that of ITV. It is a national service for the whole of the United Kingdom, except Wales, which has its own Sianel Pedwar Cymru (S4C) service operated by the Welsh Fourth Channel Authority (q.v.).

Channel 4 is financed by subscriptions paid to the IBA by the ITV companies, based on their share of the Net Advertising Revenue (NAR), which in return entitles them to sell the advertising time on the channel within their franchise area. The IBA transfers appropriate portions of the fourth channel subscrip-tions to the Channel Four Television Company and the Welsh Fourth Channel Authority.

CHANNEL FOUR TELEVISION COMPANY

60 Charlotte Street, London W1P 2AX; 01-631 4444

The Channel Four Television Company was set up by the IBA, as a wholly-owned subsidiary, to provide the programmes for the fourth television service in England, Scotland and Northern Ireland. The company began operating on 1 January 1981.

The Chairman and the Board of Directors of the company are appointed by the IBA. The Chief Executive, Managing Director, Controller of Programmes and Commissioning Editors head the executive.

Chairmen	*Chief Executives*
1981 Edmund Dell	1981 Jeremy Isaacs
1987 Sir Richard Attenborough	1988 Michael Grade

Channel 4 programmes are not produced by the company itself, apart from presentation, continuity links and the viewers' answerback programme, *Right to Reply*. They are acquired through commission from the ITV companies and independent producers, or purchased from foreign broadcasting organizations and companies. Programmes are commissioned by the Channel 4 Commissioning Editors, often on the basis of programme ideas and proposals, or completed scripts received. In the case of independent productions, they often contribute some advance financing to enable the producer to go ahead with the production. The channel has a remit, from the *Broadcasting Act 1980*, to innovate in the form and content of programmes, and in particular to appeal to audience tastes and interests not catered for by ITV. As a complementary service, it is designed to offer programmes for special interests and concerns not provided by ITV, in particular programmes for ethnic, cultural and occupational minority groups. It also has to ensure that a suitable proportion of programmes are of an educational nature or of a recognizably religious aim.

Publications: Channel Four Television Company annual report and accounts; *See4* (a thrice-yearly journal); weekly programme press packs; publicity and promotional material; programme support leaflets and books. Programme details are listed in *TV Times*.

Archives: Channel Four Television Company records are archived by arrangement with the British Film Institute (q.v.). Selected Channel 4 programmes are available at the National Film Archive (q.v.).

Independent Radio

Independent Radio was set up in 1973, under provisions in the *Sound Broadcasting Act 1972*, which provided for local sound broadcasting supported by the revenue from the sale of advertising air-time.

Independent Local Radio stations provide local radio services to over 85 per cent of the population throughout the United Kingdom (see Table 6).

Table 6.   Independent Radio stations (1973–)

On-air	Off-air	Station	Franchise area
8.10.73		LBC	London News & Information
16.10.73		Capital Radio	London General & Entertainment
31.12.73		Radio Clyde	Glasgow
19.2.74		BRMB Radio	Birmingham
2.4.74		Piccadilly Radio	Manchester
15.7.74		Metro Radio	Tyne & Wear
30.9.74		Swansea Sound	Swansea
1.10.74		Radio Hallam	Sheffield/Rotherham (*later also* Barnsley/Doncaster)
21.10.74		Radio City	Liverpool
22.1.75		Radio Forth	Edinburgh
19.5.75		Plymouth Sound	Plymouth
24.6.75		Radio Tees	Teeside
3.7.75		Radio Trent	Nottingham (*later also* Derby)
16.9.75		Pennine Radio	Bradford (*later also* Huddersfield/Halifax)
14.10.75	28.6.86	Radio Victory	Portsmouth
28.10.75		Radio Orwell	Ipswich
8.3.76		Radio 210	Reading (*later also* Basingstoke/Andover)
16.3.76		Downtown Radio	Belfast (*later also* Londonderry)
12.4.76		Beacon Radio	Wolverhampton (*later also* Shrewsbury/Telford)
11.4.80		CBC (*later as* Red Dragon Radio)	Cardiff (*later also* Newport)
23.5.80		Mercia Sound	Coventry
10.7.80		Hereward Radio	Peterborough
15.9.80		Two Counties Radio	Bournemouth
17.10.80		Radio Tay	Dundee/Perth
23.10.80		Severn Sound	Gloucester/Cheltenham
7.11.80		DevonAir Radio	Exeter/Torbay
27.7.81		NorthSound Radio	Aberdeen
1.9.81		Radio Aire	Leeds
7.9.81	6.10.83	Centre Radio	Leicester
12.9.81		Essex Radio	Southend/Chelmsford
15.10.81		Chiltern Radio	Luton/Bedford
16.10.81		West Sound	Ayr
27.10.81		Radio West (*later as* GWR)	Bristol (*later also* Bath)
23.2.82		Moray Firth Radio	Inverness
4.10.82		Radio Wyvern	Hereford/Worcester
5.10.82		Red Rose Radio	Preston/Blackpool
12.10.82		Wiltshire Radio (*later as* GWR)	Swindon/West Wiltshire
6.11.82		Saxon Radio	Bury St Edmunds
4.4.83		County Sound	Guildford
13.6.83	24.4.85	Gwent Broadcasting	Newport
29.8.83		Southern Sound	Brighton (*later also* Newhaven/Eastbourne/Hastings)

Table 6. continued

On-air	Off-air	Station	Franchise area
5.9.83		Marcher Sound	Wrexham/Deeside
5.9.83		Signal Sound	Stoke-on-Trent
17.4.84		Viking Radio	Humberside
7.9.84		Leicester Sound	Leicester
1.10.84		Invicta Radio	Maidstone/Medway/East Kent
1.10.84		Radio Broadland	Great Yarmouth/Norwich
20.10.84		Radio Mercury	Reigate/Crawley
12.10.86		Ocean Sound	Portsmouth/Southampton (*later also* Winchester)
30.11.86		Northants 96	Northampton

Areas for local radio services have been designated by the Home Office Local Radio Working Party. The IBA selects from the designated areas those it wishes to proceed with, or proposes new areas, and submits them for approval by the Home Office. Selection is based on the population coverage of the area, reception of other radio stations, and local pressure for a service. The IBA then advertises the franchises, issues contract specifications and appoints the contractors. Each contractor must meet the requirements of the *Broadcasting Act* with regard to programme quality, balance, political impartiality and the provision of items of specifically local appeal. In each ILR area the IBA appoints a Local Advisory Committee, chosen to represent, as far as is possible, the tastes and interests of the local community. Local radio can play an important part in community life by broadcasting local news, weather and coverage of local events.

The ILR companies finance the initial cost of setting up a station from money raised through shareholders, though they fund their operating costs from the income from the sale of spot advertising time in their own areas. The companies are constituted separately and are responsible to their shareholders. Financial difficulties have recently resulted in a greater concentration in commercial radio with the merger of several ILR companies forming larger groups.

Basic information about the franchise can be found in the 'Contract Specifications', issued by the IBA, and about the radio companies from their franchise application documents.

News bulletins and features are provided for the ILR stations by Independent Radio News (IRN), a subsidiary of LBC, which acts as a news agency for the system.

The establishment of Independent National Radio (INR) was provided for in the *Cable and Broadcasting Act 1984*, and national commercial radio services were recommended by the Peacock Committee.

Publications: ILR company annual reports and accounts, some published, but all available through the Companies Registration Office; promotional and publicity material. There is no national programme journal for ILR; however, programmes are listed in the local press within each radio station area.

Archives: A selection of ILR programme output is available at the National Sound Archive (q.v.).

Cable television

Cable services in the United Kingdom have their origins as far back as 1924, when relay services began as a way of providing radio broadcasts to areas of poor reception, where the airwaves were impeded by local topography or high buildings. These relay services were not a method of broadcasting, but of receiving broadcast programmes. Originally community aerials, or master receivers, sited in advantageous positions, would amplify the signal received from the transmitters and relay it to linked-up subscriber homes. Later, in the 1930s, radio broadcasts were also relayed by wired distribution through underground cable networks. By 1949, when the Relay Services Association of Great Britain gave evidence to Lord Beveridge's Broadcasting Committee, relay services were available to one-third of the population and were used by 900,000 homes. They operated under licence from the Postmaster General and were subject to the control of local authorities.

'Wired' television began in the 1950s, when the relay operators started carrying television, via their cable systems, offering an improved reception quality to subscribers. Eventually about 14 per cent of homes in the UK received their television pictures through small, localized narrowband cable systems.

Cables have the potential to offer more programme services than the broadcast channels on the overcrowded airwaves. Interest in using cable systems for special pay-TV channels or for community and educational purposes led to various experiments. A community cable television service in Greenwich was licensed by the Minister of Posts and Telecommunications in 1972, with similar experiments following in Bristol, Swindon, Sheffield and Wellingborough. In these the cable operator provided a few hours of local interest programmes each week and was allowed to take local advertising. However, apart from Greenwich, where the programmes were provided by enthusiasts, the community cable services were not successful because they did not attract sufficient new subscribers or advertising. In 1981 an experiment in subscription TV was authorized when the Home Secretary licensed thirteen pilot schemes, with the aim to investigate the market for additional programme services.

The development of cable services was given new impetus in the 1980s, beginning in 1982 with the report of the Information Technology Advisory Panel, *Report on cable systems* (London: HMSO, 1982). The report regarded the relay of BBC and ITV services, previously the mainstay of cable operations, no longer a base for future activities as the broadcasting authorities had considerably improved the signal reception for all but the smallest communities. It recommended the speedy introduction of modern cable systems, based on the wider bandwidth coaxial cables or optical fibres, with their potential to carry up to thirty channels and provide many new telecommunications-based services to homes and businesses. The report believed that the new broadband systems could stimulate the development of DBS services, to be distributed through cable, and bring benefit to the British telecommunications, consumer electronics and service industries.

The resulting inquiry, with Lord Hunt of Tanworth as Chairman, in its *Report of the Inquiry into Cable Expansion and Broadcasting Policy* ((Cmnd 8679) London: HMSO, 1982), also urged the rapid 'wiring up' of the UK, and recommended a regulatory structure to develop and supervise the new broadband cable services.

The following year a Government White Paper, *The development of cable systems* ((Cmnd 8866) London: HMSO, 1983), took up the Hunt Committee recommendations and proposed the granting of interim licences for up to twelve cable systems. The legislation for this general expansion of cable services, under the control of a new public authority, was provided by the *Cable and Broadcasting Act 1984*.

The advantages of widespread multi-channel cable systems were thought to be a greater choice of entertainment and home-based interactive services for the consumer, as well as considerable benefits to the British electronics industries. However, critics maintained that more choice did not mean better programmes and that cabling is expensive, resulting in costly services and a discriminatory distribution largely in the more affluent urban areas.

The new broadband cable services were intended to be entirely financed by private enterprise, though the Government provided £5 million to the cable television industry to encourage the development of advanced interactive services such as home banking and shopping, to be carried by the new cable systems, in addition to the special programme channels and the broadcast services.

The Cable Authority (q.v.) was set up in 1984 as the new public body with responsibility to oversee the development of the new broadband cable systems, by granting franchises to cable operators, regulating cable programmes and generally promoting the industry.

Cable television consists of two elements: the cable system, provided in a particular franchise area by the cable operator; and the cable programme services or channels offered by the system.

Cable operators are granted a franchise by the Cable Authority (under the *Cable and Broadcasting Act 1984*) and a Telecommunications Licence (under the *Telecommunications Act 1984*) by OFTEL (q.v.).

The franchise from the Cable Authority, which lasts for fifteen years for the first term, is not exclusive, though it is not Authority policy in the foreseeable future to issue more than one franchise for an area unless, perhaps, it has an older relay system to be replaced by new broadband cables. The franchise process includes: ascertaining from applicants details of company composition and shareholders, finance, technical plans, and planned provision of programme and interactive services; consulting both the public and the local authorities in the area to be cabled; and consulting with OFTEL.

The Telecommunications Licence, issued by OFTEL (acting for the Department of Trade and Industry), allows a cable operator to act a telecommunications service, and as a Public Telecommunications Operator, digging up the highways to lay cables in its franchise area.

By May 1988 25 franchises for new broadband cable systems had been awarded, including those granted by the Government in November 1983, of which 12 had started operations (see Table 7). The operator is granted a franchise for the installation and operation of a cable system, and a full licence on commencement of the service.

Table 7.   Broadband cable operators

Start	Operator	Address & phone no.	Franchise area
15.9.84	Swindon Cable	Newcombe Drive, Hawkesworth Estate, Swindon SN2 1TU; 0793 615601	Swindon
3.5.85	Aberdeen Cable Services	303 King Street, Aberdeen AB2 3AP; 0224 649444	Aberdeen
9.9.85	Coventry Cable Television	London Road, Coventry CV3 4HE; 0203 505345	City of Coventry
17.9.85	Croydon Cable Television	Communications House, Blue Riband Estate, Roman Way, Croydon CR9 3RA; 01–760 0222	London Borough of Croydon
9.10.85	Clyde Cablevision	40 Anderston Quay, Glasgow G3 8DA; 041–221 7040	Glasgow
15.10.85	Westminster Cable Company	87–89 Baker Street, London W1M 1AH; 01–935 6699	City of Westminster
2.12.85	Windsor Television	21 Victoria Street, Windsor SL4 1YE; 0753 856345	Windsor/Slough/ Maidenhead/ Staines/ Heathrow Airport
1.11.86	Cabletel Communications	Fieldway, Bristol Road, Greenford UB8 8UN; 01–575 9000	London Borough of Ealing
17.11.86	Cablevision Bedfordshire	Camp Drive, Hougton Regis, Dunstable LU5 5HE; 0582 865095	Luton & South Bedfordshire (Pilot scheme)
12.3.87	Cable Camden	13 Hawley Crescent, London NW1 8NP; 01–485 4121	London Borough of Camden (Pilot scheme)

Table 7.   Continued

Start	Operator	Address & phone no.	Franchise area
6.4.87	Eastside Cable (East London Telecommu- nications)	2 Millharbour Lane, London E14 9TE; 01–538 4838	London Boroughs of Newham & Tower Hamlets
1.7.87	British Cable Services	187 Coombe Lane West, Kingston upon Thames KT2 7DJ; 0483 505200	Guildford, West Surrey & East Hampshire

It will be some time before any of these new broadband systems are completely constructed to cover the whole of their franchise area. At present most cable viewers still receive their programmes through the old narrowband cable relay systems throughout the country. Audience research figures released by JICCAR (q.v.), in January 1988, showed 254,508 homes were receiving cable programmes, a penetration of some 18.7 per cent of the households actually 'passed' by cable systems.

The cable programme services offered by the cable operators are provided by separate companies usually known as programme providers. Each programme channel is made available to the cable operators, either delivered via satellite or on videotape. The cable operators then assemble them in packages at various prices for subscribers. Cable viewers are able to subscribe to a range of channels offering entertainment, education, information, overseas, ethnic and local programmes (see Table 8). Most cable systems carry the principal programme channels.

Table 8.   Cable programme channels

Start	Channel	Address & phone no.	Programming
16.1.84	Sky Channel	Satellite Television, 31–36 Foley Street, London W1P 7LB; 01–637 4077	General entertainment
30.3.84	Screensport	W. H. Smith Television, The Quadrangle, 180 Wardour Street, London W1V 4AE; 01–439 1177	Sports Programmes
1.6.84	The Children's Channel	44–46 Whitfield Street, London W1P 5RF; 01–580 6611	Children's entertainment
1.9.84	Premiere	6–7 D'Arblay Street, London W1A 2AD; 01–434 0611	Feature films

Table 8.   Continued

Start	Channel	Address & phone no.	Programming
1.9.85	Bravo	Communications House, Blue Riband Estate, Roman Way, Croydon CR9 3RA; 01–680 1444	Feature films
1.9.85	Home Video Channel	6–7 D'Arblay Street, London W1A 2AD; 01–434 0611	Feature films
27.9.85	The Arts Channel	PO Box 7, Ebbw Vale, Gwent NP3 5YP; 0495 306995	Ballet, drama, opera, music
31.10.85	Lifestyle	W. H. Smith Television, The Quadrangle, 180 Wardour Street, London W1V 4AE; 01–439 1177	Daytime programming
29.1.87	Super Channel	19–21 Rathbone Place, London W1P 1DF; 01–636 7888	ITV/BBC entertainment and news

In addition to these programme services cable subscribers can also receive such foreign channels as the French TV5 or Music TV Europe, ethnic programming from Indra Dhnush (in Ealing and Windsor) or the Arabic Channel (in Westminster), and some locally-produced programmes (in Coventry, Croydon, Glasgow, Aberdeen and Swindon).

Publications: Cable Authority *Annual report and accounts*; Cable operators' and cable programme providers' annual reports and accounts; *National Cable & Satellite Guide* (programme journal); *British Cable TV Programme Guide* (monthly programme journal).

Satellite television

The era of satellite television began on 12 August 1960, when the world's first successful communications satellite, Echo 1, was launched from Cape Canaveral in Florida. It was followed less than two years later by Telstar 1, the first satellite with an 'active' transponder specially designed to relay telephony and television, which began transmitting 'live' television relays across the Atlantic on 11 July 1962.

Communications satellites are really relay stations in space, receiving and transmitting signals from and to ground stations on Earth, without the blockages or interference experienced by terrestrial transmissions. The earliest artificial earth satellites had low-altitude elliptical orbits around the planet, giving varied periods of mutual visibility from orbit to orbit, resulting in limited length of programme exchange. Later communications satellites were launched on to geostationary, or 'synchronous', orbits some 22,300 miles above the

Equator, where they move in a circular orbit equal to the rotation of the Earth, therefore appearing to be stationary and from where they can cover a broad area of the Earth's surface. To enable satellite transmissions, which travel in straight lines, to cover the curve of the planet, a chain of satellites, encircling the Earth, relay the signals from one to another. The transponders in communications satellites are powered from the Sun through large arrays of solar cells mounted on the surface of the satellite.

Satellites make available thousands of communications channels at a time, for telephony, telex and television. The ability to transmit coverage of events from one side of the world to the other, as they are happening, has revolutionized news gathering, and in particular television news. However, satellite relay of television pictures from one country to another is problematic as the television systems throughout the world operate on different 'line' standards and at varying frames per second, so that when television broadcasts are exchanged they require conversion. A digital field-rate converter called DICE (Digital Intercontinental Conversion Equipment), developed by IBA engineers, changes the television picture into digital form at tremendous speed, using a computer-type binary code, and can convert from, say, the US standard (525 lines) to the UK standard (625 lines). DICE was first used for the coverage of the American presidential election in November 1972, and installed at ITN the following year.

Originally communications satellites acted only as a 'relay' to earth stations linked to transmitting stations. However, they can now provide distribution of television programme channels to head stations of cable networks, or direct broadcasting from satellite (DBS) services, transmitted at a higher power, for reception directly by television sets in the home, through small individual dish aerials and decoding equipment — a TVRO (television receive only) installation.

The relay of colour television pictures via DBS requires a technical transmission to enhance the picture quality of the different colour systems (NTSC, PAL or SECAM). The MAC (Multiplexed Analogue Components) transmission format, also developed by IBA engineers, uses separate time-sequence compressed signals for luminance and colour difference to improve picture quality, and also has the capacity to carry high-definition (HDTV), wide-screen pictures and enhanced data services with a conventional picture, both with stereo sound. The C-MAC version was officially adopted by the Government for the UK on 22 November 1982, following the recommendation of an advisory panel, under Chairman Sir Anthony Part: Home Office and Department of Industry *Direct broadcasting by satellite. Report of the Advisory Panel on Technical Transmission Standards* ((Cmnd 8251) London: HMSO, 1982). The European Broadcasting Union (EBU) adopted C-MAC as the recommended standard for direct broadcasting by satellite in Europe, and the MAC family of standards was finally given the seal of approval by the EEC Council of Ministers in 1986, preparing the way for a genuinely Europe-wide cable and satellite broadcasting system.

In 1977 the World Administrative Radio Conference (WARC) in Geneva produced a world agreement on satellite broadcasting services, and a plan for the allocation of a number of frequency channels at one or more specified orbital positions for each country. The plan came into effect on 1 January 1979 and is valid for fifteen years, until 31 December 1993. The United Kingdom was allocated five channels and an orbital position of 31° longitude West above the South Atlantic for DBS broadcasts to the British Isles.

Interest in the possibility of DBS services in the United Kingdom was stimulated by the prospects of a significant increase in broadcasting outlets and the resulting opportunities for a number of industries, including the aerospace and electronics industries, programme makers and advertisers. The technical, legal, financial and supervisory implications of satellite television services in the United Kingdom were examined in a study from the Home Office: *Direct broadcasting by satellite* (London: HMSO, 1981).

The Home Secretary awarded 2 of the 5 UK DBS channels to the BBC on 4 March 1982, and United Satellites Ltd (Unisat) was formed, by a consortium comprising British Aerospace, British Telecom and Marconi, to provide the BBC with satellite facilities. Later the IBA, following a submission to the Home Secretary in March 1983, was enabled to provide DBS services by the *Cable and Broadcasting Act 1984*, which also established the Satellite Broadcasting Board to provide DBS services for the United Kingdom.

In 1982 the United Kingdom was one of the hosts to Eurikon, the first experimental pan-European satellite television service. Launched on 24 May 1982, under the auspices of the EBU and using the European Space Agency's Orbital Test Satellite (OTS), Eurikon had a series of week-long trials, co-ordinated by the broadcasting services of the United Kingdom (IBA), Italy (RAI), Austria (ORF), the Netherlands (NOS) and the Federal Republic of Germany (ARD), to test the feasibility of a full-scale European service. Subsequently the Europa satellite television channel was set up in 1984, without British participation, by the national broadcasting services of the Federal Republic of Germany, Ireland, Italy, the Netherlands and Portugal. The Europa programme service of sports and general interest programmes reached over four million homes in Europe, but failed to attract advertisers, and finally closed down in November 1986.

On investigation of the finances of DBS services, the BBC found the venture too costly to consider alone and initiated a Tripartite Working Party with the IBA and the ITV companies to explore a joint approach. In July 1984, with approval from the Home Secretary, they were joined by a 'Third Force' of independent companies: Consolidated Satellite Broadcasting; Granada TV Rental; Pearson plc; Thorn — EMI; and the Virgin Group. This consortium, known as the 'Club of 21', worked with the Satellite Broadcasting Board on plans for DBS services. However, by June 1985 the Board had to inform the Government that the consortium had decided that they could not proceed with plans for DBS, because the Government requirement to use a costly British-made satellite from Unisat made the project a financial risk and unviable. The Satellite Broadcasting Board was wound up on 8 July 1985.

A further attempt to stimulate the development of satellite broadcasting was initiated by the Home Secretary in July 1985, when he asked the IBA to 'invite expressions of interest' from organizations in providing one or more DBS channels, this time without the requirement to use the costly British satellite system. The IBA was able to report by January 1986 an encouraging response, indicating strong interest in a project freed from the constraints of satellite supply, with the guarantee of a longer statutory period of operation.

The Home Secretary authorized the IBA to advertise in April 1986 a contract for the provision of three DBS programme channels, under Sections 37–41 of the *Cable and Broadcasting Act 1984*, aiming to start in 1990, and to be the world's first national, privately-funded DBS service. Applicants were invited to apply for a 15-year contract to provide all 3 channels, funded either by advertising or subscription (or both), and a DBS teletext service. The contractor would have a free choice of the satellite to be used, providing it fulfilled the IBA's spacecraft specifications. The Government announced that broadcasting on the remaining two DBS channels would remain in reserve and not begin until the new service had been in operation for at least 3 years, giving the contractor a reasonable time to establish the service before facing any further competition and, given the 15-year contract, a longer period in which to recoup the considerable costs involved. By the closing date in August 1986 the IBA had received 5 major applications to run all 3 services, with 2 single-channel proposals. On 11 December 1986 the IBA announced the appointment of British Satellite Broadcasting (BSB) as the DBS contractor.

BRITISH SATELLITE BROADCASTING (BSB)

Marco Polo House, 346 Queenstown Road, London SW8 4NP; 01-622 2465
The BSB Group was a consortium originally comprising Amstrad Consumer Electronics, Anglia Television Group, The Granada Group plc, Pearson plc and the Virgin Group Ltd. Subsequent changes to the group have included the departure of Amstrad and the addition of several substantial new shareholders, including the Bond Corporation of Australia, Chargeurs SA (a French transport company), Reed International, the Next Group and London Merchant Securities.

Chairman	*Chief Executive*
1987 Sir Trevor Holdsworth	1987 Anthony Simonds-Gooding

The programme plans for the three DBS services were: Now, a 24-hour news and current affairs channel; Galaxy, an entertainment channel; Zig Zag, a children's channel; and Screen, a feature film channel. The children's channel, in the afternoons, and Screen, in the evenings, will share one channel. Screen will be a subscription channel, the others funded by advertising.

The BSB services will be transmitted from two high-power satellites from the Hughes Aircraft Company, launched in 1989 by a McDonnell Douglas Delta rocket. The D-MAC version of the IBA-developed MAC transmission standard will be used.

Competition for BSB will come from Astra, the sixteen channel satellite television service covering France, Germany, Benelux countries, Scandinavia and the United Kingdom. The Luxembourg-based company, Société Européenne des Satellites, includes among its shareholders Thames Television and British Telecom. The launch of the Astra satellite by the French Ariane rocket will be in 1988.

Independent programme production

An increasing number of television programmes shown in the United Kingdom now originate from independent production companies and not from the broadcasting companies' own production facilities. These private companies are often small, specialized production companies making both films for theatrical release and television programmes.

Since Channel 4 began in 1982, it has stimulated the growth of the independent sector through acquiring or commissioning programmes from a wide range of production sources. The independent producers now provide a substantial share of Channel 4 programme output, with over 350 companies providing some 25 per cent of the hours of programmes transmitted. Since the Peacock Committee recommendation of a quota for independently produced programmes for the BBC, there has been increased Government support for the encouragement of the independent sector.

Examples of independent producers are Brook Productions (*A Week in Politics*), Brookside Productions (*Brookside*), Diverse Productions (*Diverse Reports*), Goldcrest (*The Far Pavilions*), Limehouse Productions (*The Business Programme*) and Primetime Television (*Nicholas Nickleby*). Some ITV contractors have formed subsidiary companies to make feature films or film series. Euston Films, the Thames Television film drama subsidiary which made the *Minder* and *Widows* series, is one such company. However, while they remain wholly-owned subsidiaries of the ITV contractors they cannot qualify as independent producers able to supply the entire television industry.

Information about the independent production companies can be found in their annual reports, filed at the Companies Registration Office; lists of them can be found in the *Independent Producers Handbook* (q.v.) and various directories for the television industry.

Hospital broadcasting

There are over 400 hospital broadcasting stations in the United Kingdom providing closed-circuit radio and, in some cases, television services for an estimated audience of 250,000 patients and staff. These services are manned largely by teams of volunteer staff, with occasional assistance from professional broadcasters, and financed through grants from hospital trustees or fundraising. The programmes are essentially local with patients' requests on disc jockey music programmes attracting a large audience, closely followed by local news, special features, interviews and discussions, plays and arts reviews. Programmes are relayed via cable from a small studio to bedside headphones for patients. The system is supported through administrative and technical advice by the National Association of Hospital Broadcasting Organizations (NAHBO) (q.v.).

Student broadcasting

Over twenty universities, polytechnics and colleges in the United Kingdom have their own closed-circuit broadcasting stations. These campus radio stations have studios and equipment provided by the university or college, and are run by teams of enthusiastic students with some professional advice and training from the local radio stations. Most accept commercial advertising to help support the services. Programmes are often quite broad and ambitious, offering a mix of popular music, campus and national news, features, phone-ins, quiz shows, talks and arts reviews. Some of these stations broadcast over 80 hours a week of programming to student audiences on and off the campus. Most stations belong to the National Association of Student Broadcasting (NASB).

2.6 Trade and employers' associations

Most areas of industry and commerce have their own trade and employers' associations to act on their behalf in such matters of common interest as industrial relations and trade union negotiations, training, promotion and marketing. In broadcasting and related industries, the ITV and ILR companies, the cable and satellite operators and programme providers, the independent programme producers, radio and television manufacturers, and the advertisers all have trade associations. Trade associations are often a useful and unique source of information, statistics and research material.

ADVERTISING ASSOCIATION
Abford House, 15 Wilton Road, London SW1V 1NJ; 01-828 2771
The Association, founded in 1926, is a federation of trade associations in advertising, representing advertisers, agencies and the media, as well as marketing and research organizations.

The Association promotes the interests of the advertising industry through monitoring proposals for legislation, lobbying and consultation with Parliament and Government, both in the United Kingdom and the EC. It organizes a biennial conference, seminars and courses, provides statistics, research, information and a library service (q.v.).

Publications: *Advertising statistics yearbook* (annual); *European advertising and media forecast* (annual); *Marketing pocket book*; *International journal of advertising* (quarterly); annual report and accounts; newsletter (quarterly); monographs; pamphlets and student briefs.

ASSOCIATION OF INDEPENDENT PRODUCERS (AIP)
17 Great Pulteney Street, London W1R 3DG; 01-434 0181
The AIP, formed in 1976, acts as a pressure group for creating a better climate for British independent television production and encouraging a broader base of finance and exhibition outside of the BBC and ITV system. Activities include political and Government lobbying, monitoring and public campaigns. Services to members include information, library services, research, seminars, marketing, workshops and training through the Independent Producers Course.
Publications: *Independent production handbook*; *Producer* (quarterly).

ASSOCIATION OF INDEPENDENT RADIO CONTRACTORS (AIRC)
Regina House, 259-69 Old Marylebone Road, London NW1 5RA; 01-262 6681
The AIRC, established in 1973, is the trade association for the Independent Radio companies, representing them to the Government, the IBA, trade unions, copyright organizations and other relevant bodies.
The Association provides a range of services for its members, including meetings, research and legal advice. It handles relations with the advertisers, agencies and other media organizations, co-ordinates industry initiatives and operates a programme exchange scheme between the radio stations. Liaison with Government departments and the lobbying of Parliament is undertaken on behalf of members. In 1985 the AIRC established, jointly with the NUJ, a Joint Advisory Committee for Radio Journalism, to issue guidelines for colleges on courses and training for radio journalists.
Publications: Press releases; publicity; JICRAR reports (q.v.).

BRITISH FILM AND TELEVISION PRODUCERS' ASSOCIATION (BFTPA)
Paramount House, Wardour Street, London W1V 4LA; 01-437 7700
The BFTPA, originally formed in 1941 as the British Film Producers' Association, is an employers' association for the major production companies, film and television studios, facilities houses and specialized producers. Industrial relations are an important part of the work of the BFTPA; it negotiates with the film and television unions on behalf of members; and runs, jointly with the Independent Programme Producers Association, an Industrial Relations Service to give advice and information on union agreements, training and the employment of overseas nationals. It also organizes export promotion, specialist committees and lobbying of Government and Parliament.
Publication: Annual report.

BRITISH RADIO AND ELECTRONIC MANUFACTURERS' ASSOCIATION (BREMA)

Landseer House, 19 Charing Cross Road, London WC2H 0ES; 01-930 3206

The trade association for the radio and television manufacturing industry in the United Kingdom originated as the Radio Manufacturers' Association in 1926, and was replaced in 1944 by BREMA.

It organizes meetings, exhibitions, trade promotions, liaises with the BBC and IBA, and represents its members on such bodies as the British Standards Institute and National Electronics Council. BREMA collects regular statistical information from members on production, imports, sales and stocks of a full range of television and audio products, which are processed by the Economics and Statistics Department for publication.

Publications: *Deliveries of selected video and audio products to the UK market* (quarterly); *The UK market for domestic television receivers and video recorders* (annual); *The UK market for domestic audio equipment* (annual).

BRITISH VIDEOGRAM ASSOCIATION (BVA)

10 Maddox Street, London W1R 9PN; 01-499 3131

The BVA was formed in 1980 to represent the producers and distributors of pre-recorded video cassettes and video discs. It organizes meetings, export promotion and copyright negotiating facilities.

Publications: Newsletter (monthly); list of members.

CABLE PROGRAMME PROVIDERS GROUP (CPPG)

34 Grand Avenue, London N10 3BP; 01-883 7229

Represents UK satellite-delivered programme services — Children's Channel, Lifestyle, Premiere, Screensport and Super Channel. The group is working with the IBA and BSB to promote the MAC transmission package with the satellite television receiver manufacturers.

CABLE TELEVISION ASSOCIATION (CTA)

50 Frith Street, London W1V 5TE; 01-437 0549/0983

Originally founded in 1932 as The Relay Services Association of Great Britain to represent the relay service operators. The CTA now encompasses the interests of both the older narrowband cable relay systems and the newer broadband cable operators, as well as the cable programme channels, telecom and equipment suppliers.

It promotes the development of the cable television industry in Britain, through lobbying Parliament, liaising with Government and the Cable Authority, and organizing conventions, exhibitions and meetings.

Publications: *Cable compendium* (members only); *Cablegram* (quarterly).

INCORPORATED SOCIETY OF BRITISH ADVERTISERS (ISBA)

44 Hertford Street, London W1Y 8AE; 01-499 7502

ISBA was formed in 1900 and is the trade association for the protection of advertisers' interests in all matters relating to advertising.

The work of the Society includes: liaison with Government departments, the EC, the press and other media; promotion of high standards of advertising practice by the observance of (and adherence to) the various codes governing advertising; the provision of conferences and exhibitions; and statistics and information.

Publications: Annual report; newsletter (members only); research reports and booklets.

INDEPENDENT PROGRAMME PRODUCERS ASSOCIATION (IPPA)
50–51 Berwick Street, London W1V 3RA; 01-439 7034
The IPPA, established in 1981, is the trade association for the independent production sector. It is recognized by the trade unions and Channel 4 as the negotiating body for the independent producers. It runs the Industrial Relations Service jointly with the British Film and Television Producers' Association. It also provides a wide range of services for members, including advice, conferences, meetings and exhibitions. In common with other trade associations, it acts as an effective lobbying body with the broadcasters, Government and Parliament.

Publication: *IPPA bulletin* (bi-monthly).

INDEPENDENT TELEVISION ASSOCIATION
Knighton House, 56 Mortimer Street, London W1A 8AN; 01-636 6866
The trade association for the ITV companies. It was originally established in 1955, as the Television Programme Contractors' Association, changing its name to the Independent Television Companies Association (ITCA) in 1958, and then to the Independent Television Association in 1987.

It provides a central secretariat to facilitate a co-ordinated and centralized approach to matters of common interest for the ITV companies. It is incorporated as a limited company. The governing body, comprising the Managing Directors from the ITV companies, is the Council, which determines joint policy over a wide range of industry matters, including programme planning, industrial relations, marketing and advertising copy clearance. A Programme Planning Secretariat centralizes programme planning for the ITV network and assists in the planning of networking arrangements in liaison with the IBA. The Industrial Relations Secretariat conducts, on behalf of the companies, the annual pay negotiations with the seven trade unions involved in broadcasting, resolves disputes at national level, and provides legal advice on the interpretation of national agreements. The Copy Clearance Department deals with the examination and approval of all television and radio commercials at script stage, and on completion, to ensure that they meet the requirements of the IBA *Code of advertising standards and practice* and the relevant legislation. The Association offers advice to member companies on staff training, and information to the public on careers in Independent Television. The Engineering Department co-ordinates technical research.

Its headquarters also accommodate the Broadcasters' Audience Research Board (q.v.) and the Television Consumer Unit.

Publications: *An introduction to Independent Television*; *Careers in Independent Television*; *The Viewer* (quarterly).

Archives: Library (q.v.) of documentation, and television commercials. The archives are also administered by the Library.

NATIONAL ASSOCIATION OF HOSPITAL BROADCASTING ORGANISATIONS (NAHBO)
107 Bare Lane, Morecambe, Lancs. LA4 6RP; 0524 415809
NAHBO was formed in 1970 to promote the provision and extension of hospital broadcasting. Its members are from the 400 or so hospital broadcasting stations in the United Kingdom. It provides conferences, meetings, competitions, information, statistics and a tape library for member organizations.

Publications: *Hospital radio news* (quarterly); list of members.

RADIO, ELECTRONIC & TELEVISION RETAILERS' ASSOCIATION (RETRA)
RETRA House, 57–61 Newington Causeway, London SE1 6BE; 01-403 1463
RETRA, formed in 1942, is the trade association for the retailers of radio, television, audio and electrical equipment. It provides conferences and meetings, training courses and information for members.

Publications: Yearbook; *RETRA dealer* (formerly *Electrical & electronic dealer*) (monthly).

VIDEO TRADE ASSOCIATION (VTA)
54D High Street, Northwood, Middlesex HA6 1BL; 09274 29122
The VTA was founded in 1981 to represent independent video retailers, and improve trading standards and customer service. It provides advice, conferences, exhibitions, statistics and information.

Publication: *Network* (monthly).

VIDEOTEX INDUSTRY ASSOCIATION (VIA)
176 Temple Chambers, London EC4Y 0DT; 01-583 0113
Trade association for teletext receiver manufacturers, systems suppliers and operators, information providers and retailers. It organizes conferences, exhibitions, export promotion and information.

Publications: *A guide to choosing viewdata systems*; *Videotex information providers code of practice*: *World videotex news* (monthly).

Further reading

Henderson, G. P. and Henderson, S. P. A. (eds.) *Directory of British associations*. Beckenham, Kent: CBD Research Ltd, 8th edn, 1986.

Millard, Patricia. (ed.) *Trade associations and professional bodies of the United Kingdom*. Oxford: Pergamon Press, 8th edn, 1986.

2.7 Trade unions and employees' associations

Broadcasting is the result of a collaboration between workers from a very wide range of professions and skills, for whom there are several representative trade unions.

Until recently the larger, and dominant, trade unions in broadcasting were the Association of Cinematograph, Television and Allied Technicians (ACTT) and the Association of Broadcasting Staffs (ABS), two unions born out of very different circumstances, the first from the pre-war film industry and the latter evolving from the BBC Staff Association. Rivalry between these two unions in the 1970s, and subsequent unsuccessful merger talks between them, eventually resulted in the ABS seeking amalgamation with another union in the entertainment industry, the National Association of Theatrical, Television and Kine Employees (NATTKE), and the formation of the Broadcasting and Entertainment Trades Alliance (BETA) in 1984. Another attempt at a merger, to create a single union for production workers in the electronic media, was approved at the 1988 annual conference of both the ACTT and BETA. Other trade unions in broadcasting are: British Actors' Equity Association; the Electrical, Electronic, Telecommunications and Plumbing Union (EETPU); the Musicians' Union; the National Union of Journalists; and the Writers' Guild of Great Britain.

ASSOCIATION OF CINEMATOGRAPH, TELEVISION AND ALLIED
TECHNICIANS (ACTT)
2 Soho Square, London W1V 6DD; 01-437 8506
The ACTT was originally formed in 1933 as the Association of Cine Technicians, with the present title adopted in 1956 to embrace the membership of television technicians. ACTT members work mostly in BBC Television, ITV, film production and professional film processing. ACTT membership has been virtually a condition of employment, and accepted as proof of professional status in some areas.

The union has an administrative General Council, and is divided into branches representing film production, television, laboratory and educational technology. Policy making is by the membership at the Annual Conference. The ACTT negotiates pay, conditions of service, manning levels and other measures on behalf of its members in ITV, the BBC and independent production with the Independent Television Association, BBC, IPPA and BFTPA.

Traditionally the ACTT is one of the most vigorous and militant unions in television. In 1979 the union's dispute with ITV over pay, conditions and the introduction of new technology led to an eleven-week stoppage, from August to October, the longest strike in the history of broadcasting. It has actively campaigned against bias in reporting trade union matters in the media, and for cutting back on imported foreign television programmes and sustaining the quota to encourage home production, among other matters.

Publications: *Action: fifty years in the life of a union* (1983); *Film and television technician* (monthly).

BROADCASTING AND ENTERTAINMENT TRADES ALLIANCE (BETA)
181–185 Wardour Street, London W1V 4BE; 01-439 7585
An alliance formed in 1984 of two older unions, the Association of Broadcasting and Allied Staffs (ABS) and the National Association of Theatrical, Television and Kinematograph Employees (NATTKE). It is now the largest trade union in broadcasting, with over 45,000 members in the BBC, the IBA, local radio, film production, cinemas and theatres.

The Association of Broadcasting and Allied Staffs (ABS) had its origins in the BBC Staff (Wartime) Association, formed in 1940, which amalgamated with the Association of BBC Engineers in 1945 to form the BBC Staff Association. It was re-registered in 1956 as the Association of Broadcasting Staff, and given its final name in 1974 in recognition of members working in cable and closed-circuit television. It was recognized by the BBC and the IBA for representation of all categories of staff. It affiliated with the Trades Union Congress in 1963. The Conference was the supreme policy-making body, and the union had a National Executive Council with Divisions representing the main areas of membership — the BBC, the IBA, Independent Local Radio stations and freelance workers. News and conference decisions appeared in the bi-monthly members' journal *ABStract*.

The National Association of Theatrical, Television and Kine Employees (NATTKE) dated back to 1890, when the UK Theatrical and Music Hall Operatives' Union was formed, following a stagehands' dispute at the Adelphi Theatre in London. Later, it became the National Association of Theatrical Employees and was recognized officially for collective bargaining in 1907. Cinema and film studio workers were absorbed into the union in the 1930s, and television workers after the war. The supreme policy-making body was the biennial National Delegate Conference; it had a National Executive Council, with membership sections representing theatres, film studios, cinemas and broadcasting. The members' journal was the *NATTKE newsletter*.

In 1985, following the amalgamation of these two unions, the BETA Conference adopted a set of common rules, and re-affirmed their primary purposes as: collective bargaining; and the defending, consolidating and, where possible, improving the job opportunities, pay and conditions of service of its members. It has a commitment to defend the cultural values which have shaped the organizations in which members work, in particular the principle of public service broadcasting. A National Executive Council is directly elected from the ten trade group divisions.

Publication: *BETA news* (bi-monthly).

ELECTRICAL, ELECTRONIC, TELECOMMUNICATIONS AND PLUMBING
UNION (EETPU)
Hayes Court, West Common Road, Bromley BR2 7AU; 01-462 7755
The EETPU was formed in 1968 from an amalgamation of the Electrical Trades
Union, originally founded in 1889, and the Plumbing Trades Union, estab-
lished in 1865. The union was originally for skilled craftsmen, but now covers
all grades — administrative, technical, supervisory and managerial employees
— in a wide range of industries, including film and television. The Executive
Council manages the union's affairs under direction from the Biennial Delegate
Conference.
  Publication: *Contact* (bi-monthly).

EQUITY (BRITISH ACTORS' EQUITY ASSOCIATION)
8 Harley Street, London W1N 2AB; 01-636 6367
The actors' union, popularly known as Equity, was formed originally in 1930
after the demise of the Actors' Association and the Stage Guild. The Variety
Artistes' Federation was incorporated in 1967. It represents all performers in
the theatre, films, radio and television, except the musicians. It negotiates on
members' behalf with broadcasting companies, film and independent production companies, and theatre managements. The Equity Council is elected from
the membership, and the union has regional branches around the country.
  Publications: *Equity journal* (quarterly); Annual report.

MUSICIANS' UNION (MU)
60–62 Clapham Road, London SW9 0JJ; 01-582 5566
Trade union formed in 1921 for the whole of the music profession, including
broadcasting orchestras, and has collective agreements with major employers
of musicians, the BBC and the ITV companies incuded.
  Publication: *The Musician* (quarterly).

NATIONAL UNION OF JOURNALISTS (NUJ)
314 Grays Inn Road, London WC1X 8DP; 01-278 7916
The NUJ represents over 4,000 journalists working in broadcasting, particularly in news, current affairs, sport and features, and has agreements with the
BBC and other broadcasting employers. It has drawn up guidelines on radio
journalism training with the Association of Independent Radio Contractors.
Though generally non-political, the NUJ has actively lobbied for press and
broadcasting freedom.
  Publications: *NUJ freelance directory*; *The Journalist* (monthly).

WRITERS' GUILD OF GREAT BRITAIN
430 Edgware Road, London W2 1EH; 01-723 8074
Trade union, originally formed in 1959 as the Screenwriters' Guild, representing writers' interests in film, television, radio and publishing. It has

collective agreements with the major employers of writers, including the BBC and the ITV companies. The Writers' Guild has campaigned for a reduction in imported television programmes.

Publications: *The writers' newsletter* (monthly).

Further reading

Eaton, Jack and Gill, Colin. *The trade union directory*. London: Pluto Press, 1981.
Marsh, Arthur. *Trade union handbook*. Aldershot: Gower Press, 4th edn, 1988.
Seglow, Peter. *Trade unionism in television*. Farnborough: Saxon House, 1978.

2.8 Professional associations

Professional associations are concerned with promoting knowledge and expertise in their fields of endeavour. They exist to further the professional interests of members, and to advance the art and technique of the profession, through education, training, examinations and qualifications, conferring membership, meetings, information and publications. Published journals and monographs of such bodies are of a recognized scholarly and professional level, and are regarded as a primary source of information.

Perhaps because broadcasting is the result of the collaboration of workers from a wide range of professional backgrounds there are only a few general professional associations for broadcasters, though many more representing the individual skills and professions involved.

BRITISH ACADEMY OF FILM AND TELEVISION ARTS (BAFTA)
195 Piccadilly, London W1V 9LG; 01-734 0022
BAFTA was originally formed in 1946 as the Society of Film and Television Arts. Its aims are to promote and advance original and creative work among those engaged in film and television, and encourage experiment and research in the arts, sciences and techniques of film and television production. Membership is restricted to those who have made a creative contribution to the industry. BAFTA holds screenings of films and television programmes, discussions, lectures and meetings. It advises Government departments and makes representations to Committees of Inquiry (such as the Peacock Committee) and other committees. The annual British Academy Awards ceremony for film and television is a celebrated event within the industry and popular with the public through television coverage.

Publication: Newsletter.

BRITISH KINEMATOGRAPH, SOUND AND TELEVISION SOCIETY (BKSTS)
Victoria House, Vernon Place, London WC1B 4DJ: 01-242 8400
The Society was formed in 1931 by film technicians as a means to keep up to date with major technical developments. It organizes a biennial International Film and Technology Conference and Exhibition, and a programme of lectures

and seminars for discussions, and demonstrations of new equipment and techniques.

Publications: *Dictionary of audio visual terms*; *Education and training for film and television*; *Image technology (Journal of the BKSTS)* (monthly); directory of members; conference papers; training manuals.

DIRECTORS' GUILD OF GREAT BRITAIN (DGGB)
Lyndhurst Hall, Lyndhurst Road, London NW3 5NG; 01-431 1800
The Guild was established in 1982, and amalgamated with the Association of Directors and Producers in 1984. It represents directors and producers in television, film, radio and the theatre. It organizes conferences, meetings, lobbying and training courses.

Publications: Directory of members; *Direct* (monthly).

GUILD OF BRITISH CAMERA TECHNICIANS
303–315 Cricklewood Broadway, London NW2 6PQ; 01-450 3821
The Guild was formed to further the professional interests of technicians working with motion picture cameras, through establishing minimum standards of skill, and providing a forum for the dissemination of information about new equipment and techniques. Members must be working directly in the area, have membership of the appropriate trade union, and be able to demonstrate competence in their field of work.

Publication: *Eyepiece* (bi-monthly).

GUILD OF TELEVISION CAMERAMEN
72 St Augustine's Avenue, Wembley Park, Middlesex HA9 7NX
The Guild was formed in 1972 with the aim 'to improve the art and craft of television cameramen for broadcast television', and ensure the professional status of cameramen through establishing standards of qualification. It organizes conferences, meetings and gives awards.

Publications: *Zerb* (bi-annual); newsletter.

INSTITUTE OF BROADCAST SOUND (IBS)
27 Old Gloucester Street, London WC1N 3XX; 01-878 3118
Founded in 1977 as a professional body for sound engineers in radio and television. It organizes regular meetings, seminars and training.

Publication: *Line Up* (members' journal).

INSTITUTE OF PRACTITIONERS IN ADVERTISING (IPA)
44 Belgrave Square, London SW1X 8QS; 01-235 7020
The IPA has been serving the interests of advertising agencies and agency personnel, both as a professional and trade association, since 1929. It acts on members' behalf in lobbying other media bodies and Government departments, and as a negotiating body with trade unions. A Secretariat of specialists covers

research, employee relations, the law, agency finance, television production and public relations. Members' services include advice, meetings, training and information.

Publications: Annual report; monographs and pamphlets.

INSTITUTION OF ELECTRICAL ENGINEERS (IEE)
Savoy Place, London WC2R OBL; 01-240 1871
The Institution was founded in 1871, originally as the Society of Telegraph Engineers, and assumed its present name in 1880. It is the major professional association in the United Kingdom for electrical engineers. Its aims are: to promote the general advancement of electrical science and engineering; to facilitate the exchange of information and ideas; and to give financial assistance to the promotion of invention and research. It acts both as a professional body for electrical and electronic engineers, by conferring membership and qualifications, and requiring members to observe a code of conduct, and as a learned society for the dissemination of the knowledge of electrical and electronic science. Other activities include: educational work; advising Government and education authorities; preparation of technical regulations for electrical equipment, and the harmonization of European wiring regulations; and the organizing of conferences, seminars, meetings, courses and exhibitions. INSPEC (Information Services for the Physics and Engineering Communities) provides a wide range of abstracting and indexing services from a large-scale database, including broadcast and telecommunications engineering.

Publications: *IEE yearbook and list of members*; *IEE proceedings* (bi-monthly); *IEE newsletter* (monthly); *Electrical and electronics abstracts* (INSPEC abstracting bulletin) (monthly); many other journals, conference papers, reports, books, etc.

INSTITUTION OF ELECTRONIC AND RADIO ENGINEERS (IERE)
99 Gower Street, London WC1E 6AZ; 01-388 3071
Professional and learned society, established in 1925, for electronic and radio engineers. It provides conferences, meetings, publications and information.

Publication: *Radio & Electronic Engineer* (monthly).

RADIO ACADEMY
2nd Floor, 30 Whiteladies Road, Bristol BS8 2LG; 0272 237485
The Academy was formed in 1984 as a non-profit-making professional institution. Its aims are to bring together all those working in radio broadcasting in the United Kingdom and to stimulate interest in, and an appreciation of, radio among the general public. It organizes training support, research, conferences, seminars, lectures, and an annual Radio Festival and radio awards.

Individual membership is open to anyone working in radio currently or in the past — journalists, engineers, critics, presenters and freelance broadcasters;

institutional members include the broadcasting organizations, manufacturers and trade unions.

Publications: *Radio research: a comprehensive guide, 1975–85*; *Radio Academy News* (quarterly).

THE ROYAL TELEVISION SOCIETY (RTS)
Tavistock House East, Tavistock Square, London WC1H 9HE; 01-387 1970
Formed as the Television Society in 1927, following a lecture to a British Association meeting at Leeds University by John Logie Baird and demonstration of 'Noctovision'. It was granted the title 'Royal' in 1966, in recognition of its contribution to television. The RTS is concerned with furthering the art and science of the medium.

It is a unique independent institution for the whole spectrum of professional interests involved in television, and has over 3,500 members drawn from engineering, studio services, programme making, design, journalism and administration. It provides a forum for discussion through lectures, symposia, conventions and social functions, both in London and at regional centres throughout the United Kingdom. Professional training is provided through courses and seminars. The RTS gives awards, for television journalism and programme making, and honours, including a Fellowship.

Publications: *Yearbook & membership list*; *Television* (bi-monthly); *RTS bulletin*; monographs and society papers.

SOCIETY OF CABLE TELEVISION ENGINEERS (SCTE)
10 Avenue Road, Dorridge, Solihull, West Midlands B93 8LD; 05645 4058
Professional association, formed in 1945, for engineers involved in development and manufacture in the cable and satellite television industry. It organizes meetings and provides information.

Publication: *Cable Television Engineering* (quarterly).

2.9 Pressure groups and monitoring organizations

Many organizations have sprung up to bring pressure on the broadcasters, or Parliament and Government, concerning broadcasting policy issues. They represent a range of consumer or vested interests in the broadcasting services, and cover such areas as broadcasting freedom and standards, social action broadcasting and community service, the employment of women in the media, and committed and active sections of the listening and viewing audience.

The activities of these pressure groups include: monitoring programme output; liaison with the broadcasting authorities; lobbying Parliament and Government; organizing conferences and public meetings; campaigns through pamphlets, articles and letters in the press; and even litigation on behalf of members. These organizations are a rich source of reports, campaigning literature and information.

CAMPAIGN FOR PRESS AND BROADCASTING FREEDOM
9 Poland Street, London W1V 3DG; 01-437 2795
A broad-based, trade-union supported organization launched in 1979. It campaigns for a more accessible, more accountable and more diverse media in the United Kingdom, particularly for the freedom of the press and the airwaves, and for the three 'rights' — of reply, to know, and to fair representation.

Affiliated groups include trade unions, political party branches, civil liberties groups, academic institutions, community arts and media projects, and other community organizations. Conferences, public meetings and a range of services are provided for members.

Publications: *Media manifesto*; *Free press* (bi-monthly); books and pamphlets; videos; information packs.

DEAF BROADCASTING COUNCIL
592 Kenilworth Road, Balsall Common, Coventry CV7 7DQ; 0203 27600
The Council is a voluntary organization representing deaf and hard-of-hearing television viewers. It campaigns for improved access to television for the deaf, by way of more dedicated programmes, particularly news, with sign language, open sub-titles and speech.

Publications: Press releases; campaign literature.

THE MEDIA PROJECT
The Volunteer Centre UK, 29 Lower King's Road, Berkhamsted, Herts. HP4 2AB; 04427 73311
The Media Project was established at the Volunteer Centre in 1977, on a grant from the Home Office Voluntary Services Unit, following the recommendation of a conference on 'Voluntary action through television' in London the previous year. It is now funded by the Home Office Voluntary Services Unit with grants from the BBC and the IBA.

The aims of the Project are to provide information and advice for broadcasters and voluntary or statutory organizations involved in social action broadcasting. Such broadcasting covers almost the whole spectrum of programming — from news and current affairs through to drama and soap operas, from documentaries to continuing education — and includes programmes designed for minorities and specialist groups. The common thread is that these programmes in some way reflect social issues, and often identify ways in which the viewer or listener can do something about them.

The Project organizes conferences, seminars and meetings to debate the issues, stimulate new ideas, and improve the quality of social action broadcasting and its support services. It also runs training courses for staff from social agencies who wish to use broadcasting in their work. Other activities include monitoring of programmes for both broadcasters and agencies, undertaking research projects, and offering advice and information.

Publications: *Action stations: the directory of social action programmes* (bi-annual); *On air/off air* (bi-monthly); case studies.

NATIONAL VIEWERS' AND LISTENERS' ASSOCIATION (NVALA)
Ardleigh, Colchester, Essex C07 7RH; 0206 230123
Originating from the Clean Up TV Campaign, the Association was launched in
1966, with founder, Mary Whitehouse, as President. It is a pressure group
concerned with moral standards in the media, especially the role of television in
the creation (or destruction) of social and cultural values.

NVALA organizes conferences and meetings; lobbies Parliament and broadcasters; and monitors programmes for content to see if they contravene the
BBC Royal Charter or the broadcasting legislation.

Publications: *The viewer and listener* (newsletter); monitoring reports and
guidance notes; books and leaflets; videos.

VOICE OF THE LISTENER
101 King's Drive, Gravesend, Kent DA12 5BQ; 0474 64676
The Voice of the Listener is an independent non-profit-making society formed
to support the quality of sound and spoken word in radio broadcasting. It was
formed in 1983, orginally as a protest against the BBC report, *Broadcasting in
the nineties*, and now campaigns actively for increased awareness and appreciation of radio.

It organizes conferences, meetings, visits, and the lobbying of Parliament,
Government and the broadcasting authorities.

Publication: *Voice of the listener* (quarterly).

WIDER TELEVISION ACCESS (WTVA)
c/o Illuminations, 16 Newman Passage, London W1P 3PE; 01-580 7877
A pressure group which encourages interest in old British and American television programmes, and the greater use of archive material.

Publication: *Primetime* (irregular journal).

2.10 Audience research organizations

Research into the audiences for broadcasting services in the United Kingdom
has been conducted on a regular basis for over fifty years. It is currently
undertaken by the joint boards and committees for television, radio and cable
television research, several market research companies, as well as the research
departments of the two major broadcasting organizations. A history of audience research and discussion of the techniques and methodology used is in
Chapter 3.

BROADCASTERS' AUDIENCE RESEARCH BOARD (BARB)
Knighton House, 56 Mortimer Street, London W1N 8AN; 01-636 6866
Established in August 1980, the Board replaced the two different, and often

conflicting, systems of television audience measurement previously produced by the BBC and the ITV companies, with a single unified system for the United Kingdom.

BARB is a jointly-owned company in which the BBC and the ITV Association are the sole, and equal, shareholders; it controls and administers television audience research on behalf of its shareholders and other customers. BARB provides two basic services: the Audience Measurement Service, with data supplied under contract by AGB Research; and the Audience Reaction Service, supplied by the BBC Broadcasting Research Department. The Board operates through a committee system: one committee for audience measurement, with representation from the Institute of Practitioners in Advertising (IPA) and the Incorporated Society of British Advertisers (ISBA); another for audience appreciation, with representation of the IBA.

Publications: Available to subscribers only: *Weekly TV audience report*; *Audience appreciation reports* (weekly); *Trends in television* (monthly, annual); *Establishment survey of TV homes* (annual). BARB data available online from Interactive Market Systems.

JOINT INDUSTRY COMMITTEE FOR CABLE AUDIENCE RESEARCH
(JICCAR)
44 Hertford Street, London W1Y 8AE; 01-499 7502
JICCAR was originally conceived at a meeting at the Institute of Practitioners in Advertising (IPA) in 1983, as a means to producing authentic and reliable data on the cable audience. It was set up as a limited company in 1984 to represent the IPA and ISBA, as well as the Cable Television Association (representing the operators) and the Cable Programme Providers Group. A Technical Sub-Committee was formed to write a specification for the research, and Survey Research Associates were appointed to undertake the research. A pilot study was conducted in November 1984, with the first full survey of the cable audience undertaken in March–April 1985.

Publication: *JICCAR national survey of the cable audience*.

JOINT INDUSTRY COMMITTEE FOR RADIO AUDIENCE RESEARCH
(JICRAR)
44 Belgrave Square, London SW1X 8QS; 01-235 7020
JICRAR is the joint industry body which supervises the audience research conducted on behalf of the Independent Radio companies and the advertising industry. Surveys of audiences for individual Independent Radio stations have been conducted according to JICRAR specifications since 1974, and for the network as a whole since 1977. The network survey is commissioned by the Radio Marketing Bureau and conducted by Research Surveys of Great Britain (RSGB).

Publication: *The Independent Radio network survey*.

BBC BROADCASTING RESEARCH DEPARTMENT
The Woodlands, 80 Wood Lane, London W12 OTT; 01-743 8000
The Department, formerly Audience Research, was set up in 1938. Its principal functions are to provide continuous measurement of audience size and reactions to BBC domestic radio and television services, and to undertake a range of special projects on specific programmes or broader issues for management or individual programme departments.

The Continuous Services section is responsible for the audience measurement and reaction services. It provides data to the Broadcasters' Audience Research Board for the television reaction service, for the weekly measure of the audience appreciation of BBC TV, ITV and Channel 4 programmes. Measurement of audience reactions to specific BBC Radio network programmes, the Daily Survey of Listening, is undertaken through the department's Radio Listening Panel.

Special Projects, established in 1979 as a separate section within the Department, undertakes ad hoc research assignments on new broadcasting developments, and programme development and evaluation. The research findings of the section are primarily for management and internal use only.

Publications: *Annual review of BBC broadcasting research findings* (1974/75-. Annual); *Daily life in the 1980s* (1984); *The people's activities and use of time* (1978).

IBA RESEARCH DEPARTMENT
70 Brompton Road, London SW3 1EY; 01-584 7011
The IBA is required by the *Broadcasting Act* to ascertain the state of public opinion on Independent Television and Radio programmes. The Research Department carries out extensive research on audience reactions to radio and television services, and publishes a variety of research reports and papers. It does not, though, conduct the continuous measurement of audiences for ITV/Channel 4 and Independent Radio, which is the responsibility of the television and radio companies themselves, through their trade associations. However, the Department does have access to the continuous measurement data from AGB Research and the BBC Broadcasting Research Department, from which it produces detailed analysis and interpretation.

An annual national survey of attitudes to broadcasting covers a wide range of issues, including audience opinions on both radio and television programmes, viewing and listening patterns, and the use of television and other media in the home. Special surveys of the television audience are based on data from either the BARB service, the Television Opinion Panel or specially recruited quota samples, selected to represent the national audience. The IBA also produces studies of listening patterns, listeners' reactions to, and the requirements for individual Independent Radio stations.

The IBA also regularly funds substantial independent research projects at universities and other research bodies. It maintains close links with academic researchers in the United Kingdom and overseas.

Publications: *Attitudes to broadcasting* (annual); *Television Research Monographs*; various special reports and research papers; and books, articles in academic journals and the popular press.

2.11 Research institutes and centres for the study of broadcasting

Various institutes and centres, either independent or attached to academic foundations, have been established with the purpose of furthering the advancement of knowledge of the media, film, television and radio, through the provision of educational programmes and qualifications, publishing programmes, research projects and facilities, libraries and documentation centres. They generate academic research on the content of mass communications and broadcasting, and their effects on society, in contrast to the market research undertaken on behalf of the broadcasters or advertisers.

BRITISH FILM INSTITUTE (BFI)
21 Stephen Street, London W1P 1PL; 01-255 1444
The BFI was founded in 1933. Its aim is 'to encourage the development of the art of film and television'.

The BFI is incorporated by Royal Charter, with registered charity status, and is financed from a grant from the Department of Education and Science, through the Office of Arts and Libraries, membership fees, and various grants and donations. Membership, currently over 40,000, is open to all with an interest in film and television, particularly students, researchers, writers, and those working in the media and education. It incorporates the National Film Archive, the National Film Theatre and the Museum of the Moving Image. It has divisions covering film production, film distribution, funding and development, and information services (including a library (q.v.)).

Publications: *BFI film and TV yearbook* (annual); *Sight and sound* (quarterly); various monographs and reports.

BRITISH UNIVERSITIES FILM AND VIDEO COUNCIL (BUFVC)
55 Greek Street, London W1V 5LR; 01-734 3687
The BUFVC is the representative body for teachers in higher education who use video and other audio-visual media in their work.

It encourages the use, production and study of audio-visual media, materials and techniques for higher education teaching and research, through conferences, seminars and workshops. An information service, book library (q.v.), and film and video library are available to member organizations.

Publications: *BUFVC catalogue; Researchers' guide to British film and television collections; Researchers' guide to British newsreels; Newsletter* (3 p.a.); HELPIS (Higher Education Learning Programmes Information Service) available online through BLAISE-LINE.

BROADCASTING RESEARCH UNIT (BRU)
39C Highbury Place, London N5 1QP; 01-226 9903
The BRU was established in 1980 as an independent body for research into developments in broadcasting technologies and their impact on future broadcasting policy.

It is funded by the BBC, the IBA and the Markle Foundation of New York, with administrative support from the BFI. The BRU has undertaken research projects on many aspects of broadcasting, including the evolution of public service broadcasting, and the likely impact of cable television in the UK compared with the USA and Canada.

Publications: *Beyond broadcasting: into the cable age* by Timothy Hollins (London: BFI Books, 1984); *Invisible citizens: British public opinion and the future of broadcasting* by David Morrison (London: John Libbey, 1986); and other monographs and reports.

CENTRE FOR CONTEMPORARY CULTURAL STUDIES, UNIVERSITY OF BIRMINGHAM
P O Box 363, Birmingham B15 2TT; 021-472 1301
Postgraduate research centre for interdisciplinary research into contemporary culture and mass media. Provides courses, including BA (Combined Honours) in Communications and Cultural Studies and an MA in Contemporary Cultural Studies, as well as supervision of research projects for MA/MLitt and PhD degrees.

Publications: *Working papers in cultural studies*; monographs.

CENTRE FOR MASS COMMUNICATION RESEARCH, UNIVERSITY OF LEICESTER
104 Regent Road, Leicester LE1 7LT; 0533 523863
The Centre, established at the University of Leicester, on the recommendation of the Television Research Committee, was officially opened in March 1967.

It is a post-graduate research and teaching centre, whose original concern with the influence of television and other media on the young later broadened into a multi-disciplinary research programme covering aspects of media institutions and the mass communications process. The Centre has been supported nationally and internationally, by media institutions, research councils and other funding bodies. Though primarily a research centre, teaching and supervision of post-graduate students (including for an MA in Mass Communications), lectures and seminars are an important part of its programme.

Publications: *Register of current and recently completed British research on mass media and mass communication*; research reports and monographs.

CENTRE FOR TELEVISION RESEARCH, UNIVERSITY OF LEEDS
Leeds LS2 9LT; 0532 431751
Leeds was the first British university to establish an academic post in mass communication. The Television Research Unit, founded in 1959 with a grant

from Granada Television, became the Centre for Television Research in 1966.

Its main research has been into the role of television in political communication. A post-graduate research centre with academic staff from several disciplines — psychology, sociology and political science — it provides supervision for MPhil and PhD dissertations.

Publications: Reports; monographs (including *The challenge of election broadcasting* (1978)).

CENTRE FOR THE STUDY OF COMMUNICATION AND CULTURE
221 Goldhurst Terrace, London NW6 3EP; 01-328 2868
International institute, founded by the Society of Jesus in 1977, for interdisciplinary research on the moral problems of modern communication, and the Church's mission in communications and culture.

The Centre undertakes research projects, and provides seminars and meetings, a publications programme and a research library (q.v.).

Publications: *Communication research trends* (quarterly); various teaching aids and monographs.

EUROPEAN INSTITUTE FOR THE MEDIA
The University of Manchester, Manchester M13 9PL; 061-273 3333
Following an initiative of the European Cultural Foundation in 1978, the Institute was established at the University of Manchester in January 1983. Its objectives are: to provide a forum for discussion of media policies and aims; to undertake research on the role and influence of the media and development of media policies in Europe; and to help the Third World with development of its media.

Activities include: colloquia, consultations and seminars on European media and broadcasting policy; research and development projects; and a programme of tutorials and broadcasting production experience for visiting Fellowships; library and documentation centre.

Publications: *Media Bulletin* (quarterly); *The first three years, 1983-1986*; media monographs, colloquia proceedings.

INTERNATIONAL INSTITUTE OF COMMUNICATIONS (IIC)
Tavistock House South, Tavistock Square, London WC1H 9LF; 01-388 0671
The Institute, founded in 1969 as the International Broadcast Institute and changing to its present name in 1977, is an independent organization which acts as a forum for the analysis and discussion of the social, economic, political, cultural and legal issues related to communication in the broadest sense.

The IIC has institutional members from over seventy countries throughout the world, including, in the United Kingdom, the BBC, the IBA, the Independent Television Association and the Open University. It carries out a worldwide research and education programme on telecommunications, broadcasting and the new technologies. The Institute also offers consultancy services through its

Communications Research Unit, seminars and conferences, and a research library (q.v.).

Publications: *Intermedia* (five a year); newsletter, membership directory; annual conference papers; research reports and studies.

SOCIETY FOR EDUCATION IN FILM AND TELEVISION (SEFT)
29 Old Compton Street, London W1V 5PL; 01-734 5455/3211
SEFT, founded in 1949 as the Society of Film Teachers, is a grant-in-aid body of the British Film Institute. It aims to promote education in all aspects of film, television, video and the mass media, both nationally and internationally, with teachers, broadcasters, researchers and media workers. It is both an academic and research body, and a professional association for media teachers.

Among its activities are an annual education conference, seminars, day and weekend schools, short courses, research projects and consultancy, and lobbying on issues of media and education policy.

Publications: *Screen* (incorporating *Screen Education*) (quarterly); *Initiatives* (academic term newsletter); occasional papers; teaching papers; bibliographies; videos.

2.12 Educational organizations and courses

The further education system in the United Kingdom offers a wide range of courses in subjects of relevance to the broadcasting industry, either training courses for careers in radio and television, offered by specialist educational establishments, or courses on media studies, both theoretical and practical, provided by universities, colleges of further education or art schools.

Specialist training and educational establishments

Vocational courses directly related to the range of skills involved in radio and television production for those intending to take up careers in the broadcasting industry are provided by the principal broadcasting organizations (the BBC, the IBA and the ITV companies), some specialist training establishments, such as the National Film and Television School, as well as various colleges and universities.

The BBC regularly recruits for specific job categories, either at school-leaver level for engineering, film and secretarial areas, or at graduate level for the News Trainee, Television Production Trainee, General Trainee, and Trainee Studio Manager schemes. Courses are run by BBC Television Training at Elstree, the BBC Open University Production Centre, on television production in education and development, and at the BBC Engineering Training Department.

The ITV companies, particularly the larger 'network' companies, also administer their own trainee schemes. Thames Televison has a particularly well-established Technical Training Course. The Independent Television Association provides advice and guidance on training for the companies. The IBA recruits junior engineers each year for courses at the Harman Engineering Training College.

Training in the various engineering skills associated with broadcasting are provided by some of the electronics companies supplying the broadcasting industry. Examples of companies and courses provided are: Ampex (broadcast engineers); Pye (studio engineering, transmitters and telecine); Rank Cintel Ltd (telecine); Sony Broadcast (digital and analogue techniques).

NATIONAL FILM AND TELEVISION SCHOOL
Beaconsfield Film Studios, Station Road, Beaconsfield, Bucks. HP9 1LG; 04946 71234
The School was set up following the recommendations of a Government Committee, under the Chairmanship of Lord Lloyd of Hampstead, which looked at the need for a national film school. It has operated from Beaconsfield Film Studios since 1971.

The School is a registered charity and non-profit-making educational foundation, funded by grants from the Office of Arts and Libraries, the film industry, the BBC and television companies. It is the principal training establishment for the film and television industries. It offers courses of up to three years' full-time professional training, leading to the Associateship of the National Film and Television School (ANFTS), with graduation automatically entitling students to ACTT membership on gaining employment. Areas of instruction in film and television techniques include: directing; producing; writing; documentary production; editing; and art direction, with emphasis on practical work, not theory. Retraining courses are also available for those already in the industry.

BROADCAST TRAINING CENTRE, UNIVERSITY OF LEEDS
Springfield House, Hyde Terrace, Leeds; 0532 436447
Course: Television Production (intensive course on planning and execution of a television production for overseas students).

THE CHURCHES TELEVISION CENTRE (CTVC)
Hillside Studios, Merry Hill Road, Bushey, Watford, Herts. WD2 1DH; 01-950 4426
Courses: Radio Introductory Course, Radio Advanced Course, Radio Production; Writing for radio.

CENTRAL OFFICE OF INFORMATION
Hercules Road, London SE1 7DU; 01-928 2345
Course: News and feature writing (including radio and television).

HARMAN ENGINEERING TRAINING COLLEGE
Fore Street, Seaton, Devon EX12 2NS; 0297 22051
College established by the IBA to train its own engineering recruits, but places for non-IBA staff available.
   Courses: Trainee Broadcast Engineer.

LOCAL RADIO WORKSHOP
12 Praed Mews, London W2; 01-240 0168
Course: Introduction to radio programme making.

LONDON INDEPENDENT FILM SCHOOL
24 Shelton Street, Covent Garden, London WC2H 9HP; 01-240 0168
Course: Postgraduate Diploma: Art and Technique of Film Production.

MARCONI COLLEGE
Arbour Lane, Chelmsford, Essex; 0245 350011
Course: Analogue and digital design and techniques, broadcast transmitter techniques, colour studio cameras, and CCTV applications for broadcast engineers and technicians.

THE MEDIA PROJECT AT THE VOLUNTEER CENTRE
29 Lower Kings Road, Berkhamsted, Herts. HP4 2AB; 04427 73311
Course: Using Local Radio.

NATIONAL CATHOLIC RADIO AND TELEVISION CENTRE
Oakleigh Road, Hatch End, Middlesex HA5 4HB; 01-428 1198
Courses: Full Production Course (radio, television and video); Radio Course: Diploma in Christian Communication.

TELEVISION TRAINING CENTRE
18 Grosvenor Street, London W1; 01-629 5069
Courses: Diploma/Certificate: Television Studies, Television Direction and Production, Journalism for Television News and Current Affairs, Television Photography.

THE THOMSON FOUNDATION
Regent's College, Regent's Park, London NW1 4NS; 01-486 9648
Educational foundation set up in 1962 by Roy Thomson, later Lord Thomson of Fleet, with the purpose of making available training facilities and the assistance of experts to establish and develop radio and television stations for developing countries. The Thomson Foundation Television College near Glasgow provided training for engineers and producers from most Third World countries from 1964 to 1983, and currently from its London headquarters the

Foundation provides specialist courses in journalism, and advice, or practical in-station courses for broadcasters throughout the world.

VISNEWS INTERNATIONAL
Cumberland Avenue, London NW10 7EH; 01-965 7733
Courses: Television Programme Maker Course; Television Studio Production; Advanced Documentary Production; Cable Operation.

WOMEN'S AIRWAVES
90 De Beauvoir Road, London N1; 01-241 3729
Course: Radio Skills for beginners.

Universities

The following universities offer degree-level courses in subjects relevant to broadcasting — communications and media studies, telecommunications, electrical and electronic engineering — either as a main topic or as a subsidiary or optional element.

As well as providing the opportunities for the study of broadcasting, they are also sources of information and research into the subject. University libraries usually provide good collections of books on the subject for students following courses on communications and broadcasting. Also, they may have valuable special collections or archives relating to broadcasting and film, such as the John Grierson Archive at the University of Stirling or the Mary Adams Collection (papers on BBC Television 1936–58) at the University of Sussex. The universities are also often centres of academic research into broadcasting, with resident academic staff who are experts on various aspects of the media and broadcasting.

UNIVERSITY OF BATH
Claverton Down, Bath BA2 7AY; 0225 61244
Courses: BEng: Electronic and Communication Engineering; BSc/MEng: Electrical and Electronic Engineering (including Communication Engineering).

QUEEN'S UNIVERSITY OF BELFAST
University Road, Belfast BT7 1NN; 0232 245133
Courses: BA (Integrated Honours): Language and Communication; BEng/ MEng: Electrical and Electronic Engineering; (including Communications Theory)

UNIVERSITY OF BIRMINGHAM
Centre for Contemporary Cultural Studies, Faculty of Arts, Birmingham B15 2TT; 021-472 1301
Courses: BA (Combined Honours): Communications and Cultural Studies; MA: Contemporary Cultural Studies; MA/MLitt/PhD (research degrees).

UNIVERSITY OF BRADFORD
Bradford, West Yorkshire BD7 1DP; 0274 733466
Courses: BEng (Hons): Electronic Communication and Computer Engineering; MEng/MSc: Communications Engineering; Diploma: Electronics and Communications Engineering; MPhil/PhD: Telecommunications.

UNIVERSITY OF BRISTOL
Department of Drama, 29 Park Row, Bristol BS1 5LT; 0272 24161
Courses: BA: Drama (including Radio, Film and Television options); Certificate (Postgraduate): Radio, Film and Television.

BRUNEL UNIVERSITY
Department of Human Sciences, Uxbridge, Middlesex UB8 3PH; 0895 56461
Course: BSc: Communication and Information Studies.

CITY UNIVERSITY
Northampton Square, London EC1V 0HB; 01-253 4399
Courses: MA: Communications Policy Studies; MA/Diploma: Radio Journalism; MA/Diploma: International Journalism; MSc: Human Communication.

UNIVERSITY OF EAST ANGLIA
School of English and American Studies, Norwich NR4 7TJ; 0603 56161
Courses: BA (Hons): English Studies (including History of Television); BA (Hons): Film and English Studies (including British Television, and History of Television); MA: Film Studies; MPhil/PhD (research degrees).

UNIVERSITY OF ESSEX
Wivenhoe Park, Colchester CO4 3SQ; 0206 862286
Courses: BEng: Electronic Engineering (Telecommunications); BEng: Electronic Engineering (Computers and Communications); MSc: Telecommunications Systems.

UNIVERSITY OF GLASGOW
53 Hillhead Street, Glasgow G12 8QF; 041-339 8855
Course: MA (Joint Honours): Film and Television Studies.

UNIVERSITY OF HULL
Department of Drama, Cottingham Road, Hull HU6 7RX; 0482 46311
Course: BA (Joint Honours): Drama (Film, Television & Radio Studies).

UNIVERSITY OF KENT AT CANTERBURY
Canterbury, Kent CT2 7NZ; 0227 66822
Courses: BA: Film Studies; MA/PhD (research and thesis): Film Studies; BSc: Communications Engineering.

UNIVERSITY OF LANCASTER
Bailrigg, Lancaster LA1 4YW; 0524 65201
Course: BA (Hons): Human Communication (including Media Sociology).

UNIVERSITY OF LEEDS
Leeds LS2 9JT; 0532 431571
Course: MPhil/PhD: Research dissertations on television.

UNIVERSITY OF LEICESTER
Centre for Mass Communication Research, 104 Regent Road, Leicester LE1
7LT; 0533 523863
Courses: MA: Mass Communications; MPhil/PhD (research and thesis).

UNIVERSITY OF LIVERPOOL
Department of Communication Studies, Chatham Street, Liverpool L69 3BX;
051-709 6022
Courses: BA (Combined Honours): Communication Studies; BA (Joint Honours): English Literature and Communication Studies.

UNIVERSITY OF LONDON: DEPARTMENT OF EXTRA MURAL STUDIES
26 Russell Square, London WC1B 5DQ; 01-636 8000
Courses: Certificate: Television Study; Certificate: Community Radio: Theory and Practice.

UNIVERSITY OF LONDON: GOLDSMITHS COLLEGE
New Cross, London SE14 6NW; 01-692 7171
Courses: BA (Combined Honours): Communications Studies and Sociology;
Diploma (Postgraduate): Communications.

UNIVERSITY OF LONDON: INSTITUTE OF EDUCATION
Department of English and Media Studies, 20 Bedford Way, London WC1H
0AL; 01-636 1500
Course: MA: Film and Television Studies for Education.

LOUGHBOROUGH UNIVERSITY OF TECHNOLOGY
Loughborough, Leics. LE11 3TU; 0509 263171
Courses: BA/BSc/MA/MSc: Library Studies (including Communications and
Mass Media).

UNIVERSITY OF NEWCASTLE UPON TYNE
Department of English, Newcastle upon Tyne NE1 7RU; 091-232 8511
Courses: MA/MPhil: English and American Literature of the 20th Century
(including Television Studies).

UNIVERSITY OF NOTTINGHAM
University Park, Nottingham NG7 2RD; 0602 506101
Courses: BEd/BPhil (including Mass Media Communication option); Diploma: Mass Media Education.

UNIVERSITY OF READING
Whiteknights, Reading, Berks. RG6 2AH; 0734 875123
Course: BA (Hons): English (including Media Semiotics).

UNIVERSITY OF SOUTHAMPTON
Highfield, Southampton, Hants SO9 5NH; 0703 559122
Course: MA (Ed): Languages, Literacy and Media Studies (including Teaching Media).

UNIVERSITY OF STIRLING
Stirling FK9 4LA; 0786 73171
Course: BA: Film and Media Studies; MLitt/PhD (Research Degrees): Film and Media Studies.

UNIVERSITY OF STRATHCLYDE
16 Richmond Road, Glasgow G1 1XQ; 041-552 4400–9
Course: BA (Joint Honours): Film and Television Studies.

UNIVERSITY OF SUSSEX
Falmer, Brighton, East Sussex BN1 9RG; 0273 606755
Courses: BA (Hons): English with Media Studies; MA: Language, the Arts and Education (including Film and Television).

UNIVERSITY OF ULSTER
Coleraine, Co Londonderry BT52 1SA; 0265 4141
Course: BA (Hons): Communication Studies.

UNIVERSITY OF WALES: UNIVERSITY COLLEGE, CARDIFF
Centre for Journalism Studies, Cardiff CF1 1XL; 0222 874000
Courses: MSc (Econ): Media Studies; MEd: Journalism Studies; Diploma (Postgraduate): Radio Journalism Studies.

UNIVERSITY OF WARWICK
Joint School of Film and Literature, Coventry CV4 7A1; 0203 523523
Course: BA (Hons): Film and Literature (including Television).

Polytechnics and colleges of higher/further education

The polytechnics and colleges of higher/further education offer a variety of courses on the practical aspects of broadcasting and the media. Many provide courses at degree level, the Council for National Academic Awards (CNAA) degrees, as well as for the vocational qualifications of the Business and Technician Education Council (BTEC). Studio facilities and equipment, for the making of films and television programmes, and practical experience are provided. Courses for broadcast engineers and technicians in communications and electronics engineering are offered at the polytechnics and colleges.

ABERDEEN: ROBERT GORDON INSTITUTE OF TECHNOLOGY
Schoolhill, Aberdeen AB9 1FR; 0224 633611
Course: BEng: Electronic and Electrical Engineering (including Communications).

BEDFORD COLLEGE OF HIGHER EDUCATION
Polhill Avenue, Bedford MK41 9EA; 0234 51671
Course: BA (Hons): Combined Studies (Drama in Film and Television).

CITY OF BIRMINGHAM POLYTECHNIC
Perry Barr, Birmingham B42 2SU; 021-356 9193/6911
Courses: BA (Hons): Communication Studies; BEng (Hons)/BEng: Electronic Engineering (Control, Computers and Communications); BTEC HND: Engineering (including Communications Systems).

BOLTON INSTITUTE OF HIGHER EDUCATION
Deane Road, Bolton BL3 5YZ; 0204 28851
Course: BEng/BEng (Hons): Electronic Engineering (including Communications Engineering).

BRIGHTON POLYTECHNIC
Moulsecoomb, Brighton, East Sussex BN2 4AT; 0273 693655
Courses: BA (Hons): Combined Studies (Humanities) (including Understanding the Media); BEng/BEng (Hons): Electronic Engineering (including Communications Engineering); BTEC HND: Information Technology (including Communications); Radio/TV News Course.

BRISTOL POLYTECHNIC
Coldharbour Lane, Frenchay, Bristol BS16 1QY; 0272 656261
Course: BA/BA (Hons): Humanities (Communication & Cultural Studies).

BRUNEL TECHNICAL COLLEGE
Ashley Down, Bristol BS7 9BU; 0272 41241
Course: BTEC HNC: Communications Engineering.

CAMBRIDGESHIRE COLLEGE OF ARTS AND TECHNOLOGY
East Road, Cambridge CB1 1PT; 0223 63271
Course: BEng: Electronic Engineering (Telecommunication Engineering).

CHRIST CHURCH COLLEGE, CANTERBURY
North Holmes Road, Canterbury, Kent CT1 1QU; 0227 65548
Course: BA (Hons)/BSc (Hons): Combined Studies (including Radio, Film and Television Studies).

COVENTRY (LANCHESTER) POLYTECHNIC
Priory Street, Coventry CV1 5FB; 0203 24166
Courses: BA (Hons): Communication Studies; BA (Hons): Fine Arts (including Media Studies); BEng/BEng (Hons)/HND: Electrical and Electronic Engineering (including Telecommunication Engineering).

DARLINGTON COLLEGE OF TECHNOLOGY
Cleveland Avenue, Darlington, County Durham DL3 7BB; 0325 67651
Course: Diploma: Journalism (including Radio Journalism).

DERBYSHIRE COLLEGE OF HIGHER EDUCATION
Kedleston Road, Derby DE3 1GB; 0332 47181
Course: HND: Electrical and Electronic Engineering (Communication Systems).

DORSET INSTITUTE OF HIGHER EDUCATION
Wallisdown Road, Poole, Dorset BH12, 5BB; 0202 52411
Course: BA (Hons): Communication and Media Production.

EDINBURGH: NAPIER COLLEGE
219 Colinton Road, Edinburgh EH14 1DJ; 031-447 7070
Courses: BEng: Communication and Electronic Engineering; HND: Communication Studies.

FARNBOROUGH COLLEGE OF TECHNOLOGY
Boundary Road, Farnborough, Hants GU14 6SB; 0252 515511
Course: BTEC HND: Electronic and Communications Engineering.

GLASGOW COLLEGE OF TECHNOLOGY
Cowcaddens Road, Glasgow G4 0BA; 041-332 7090
Course: BA: Communication Studies.

HATFIELD POLYTECHNIC
College Lane, Hatfield, Herts. AL10 9AB; 07072 79000
Course: BEng/BEng (Hons): Electrical and Electronic Engineering (including Telecommunications).

HUDDERSFIELD POLYTECHNIC
Queensgate, Huddersfield HD1 3DH; 0484 22288
Course: BEng/BEng (Hons): Electrical and Electronic Engineering (including Communications Engineering).

LANCASHIRE POLYTECHNIC
Preston, Lancs. PR1 2TQ; 0772 22141
Courses: BEng/BEng (Hons): Electronic Engineering (including Communication Engineering); Diploma (Postgraduate): Radio and Television Journalism.

LEEDS POLYTECHNIC
Calverly Street, Leeds LS1 3HE; 0532 462903/4
Courses: BEng/BEng (Hons): Communication Engineering; BTEC HND: Electrical and Electronic Engineering (including Communication Studies).

LEEDS: TRINITY AND ALL SAINTS' COLLEGE
Brownberrie Lane, Horsforth, Leeds LS18 5HD; 0532 584341
Courses: BA/BEd: Communication and Cultural Studies; BA: Public Media.

LEICESTER POLYTECHNIC
P O Box 143, Leicester LE1 9BH; 0533 551551
Courses: BEng/BEng (Hons)/BTEC HND: Electronic Engineering (including Communication Engineering); MA: Graphic Design (including Television Design).

LIVERPOOL POLYTECHNIC
Rodney House, 70 Mount Pleasant, Liverpool L3 5UX; 051-207 3581
Courses: BEng/BEng (Hons): Electrical and Electronic Engineering (including Communication Engineering); HND/HNC: Electronics and Communications Engineering.

LONDON: LONDON COLLEGE OF PRINTING
Department of Photography, Film and Television, Elephant and Castle, London SE1 6SB; 01-735 9100
Courses: BA (Hons): Film and Video (ACTT accredited course); BA (Hons): Media and Production Design; BA (Hons): Visual Communication; Diploma (Postgraduate): Radio Journalism.

LONDON: MORLEY COLLEGE
61 Westminster Bridge Road, London SE1 7HT; 01-928 8501
Course: Radio Production.

LONDON: NORTH EAST LONDON POLYTECHNIC
Romford Road, London E15 4LZ; 01-590 7722
Courses: BEng/BEng (Hons): Electrical and Electronic Engineering (including Telecommunication); BTEC HND/HNC: Engineering (including Telecommunications Engineering).

LONDON: POLYTECHNIC OF CENTRAL LONDON
School of Communication, 18–22 Riding House Street, London W1P 7PD; 01-486 5811
Courses: BA (Hons): Media Studies; MA/Diploma (Postgraduate): Film and Television Studies; MPhil/PhD (Research Degrees): Film and Television/Mass Media History, Theory and Criticism; Certificate (Postgraduate): Radio Journalism.

LONDON: POLYTECHNIC OF NORTH LONDON
Holloway Road, London N7 8DB; 01-607 2789
Courses: BSc/BSc (Hons): Electronic and Communications Engineering; BTEC HND: Engineering (Electronics and Communications).

LONDON: SOUTH BANK POLYTECHNIC
Borough Road, London SE1 0AA: 01-928 8989
Courses: BEng/MEng: Electrical and Electronic Engineering (including Communications).

LONDON: THAMES POLYTECHNIC
Wellington Street, Woolwich, London SE18 6PF; 01-854 2030
Course: BSc/BSc (Hons): Computer and Communication Systems.

MANCHESTER POLYTECHNIC
School Lane, Didsbury, Manchester M20 0HT; 061-434 3331
Course: BA (Hons): Design for Communication Media.

MIDDLESBROUGH: LONGLANDS COLLEGE OF FURTHER EDUCATION
Douglas Street, Middlesbrough, Cleveland TS4 2JW; 0642 248351
Course: BTEC National Diploma: Audio Visual Studies.

MIDDLESEX POLYTECHNIC
114 Chase Side, Southgate, London N14 5PN; 01-886 6599
Courses: BA (Hons): Contemporary Cultural Studies (including Communications Studies); Diploma Higher Education: Communication Studies; BEng (Hons): Electronic Engineering (including Communications); MA/Diploma: Film and Television Studies.

NEWCASTLE UPON TYNE POLYTECHNIC
Sandyford Road, Newcastle upon Tyne NE1 8ST; 091-232 6002
Courses: BA (Hons): Media Production; BA: History of Modern Art, Design
and Film (including Television Documentary); BEng/BEng (Hons): Electrical
and Electronic Engineering (including Satellite Engineering).

NOTTINGHAM: TRENT POLYTECHNIC
Burton Street, Nottingham NG1 4BU; 0602 418248
Courses: BA (Hons): Communication Studies; BEng/BEng (Hons): Electrical
and Electronic Engineering (including Communication Engineering).

PLYMOUTH POLYTECHNIC
Drake Circus, Plymouth, Devon PL4 8AA; 0752 221312
Courses: BEng/BEng (Hons): Communication Engineering; BEng/BEng
(Hons): Electrical and Electronic Engineering (including Communications
Studies); MEng: Communication, Information and Electrical Engineering;
BTEC HND: Electrical and Electronic Engineering (including Communi-
cations Engineering).

PORTSMOUTH: HIGHBURY COLLEGE OF TECHNOLOGY
Department of Journalism Studies, Cosham, Portsmouth, Hants PO6 2SA;
0705 383131
Course: Diploma (Postgraduate): Radio Journalism.

PORTSMOUTH POLYTECHNIC
Museum Road, Portsmouth, Hants PO1 2QQ; 0705 827681
Courses: BA (Hons): Cultural Studies (including Mass Media); BEng/BEng
(Hons): Electrical and Electronic Engineerng (including Telecommunication
Systems).

READING: BULMERSHE COLLEGE OF HIGHER EDUCATION
Woodlands Avenue, Earley, Reading, Berks. RG6 1HY; 0734 663387
Course: BA/BA (Hons): Combined Studies (including Film and Drama
Studies, with Television).

SALFORD COLLEGE OF TECHNOLOGY
Department of Performing Arts and Media Studies, Adelphi Building, Peru
Street, Salford, Manchester; 061-834 6633
Course: Diploma: Media and Communication Techniques.

SHEFFIELD CITY POLYTECHNIC
Totley Hall Lane, Sheffield S17 4AB; 0742 369941
Courses: BA (Hons): Communication Studies; MA: Communication Studies;
BTEC HNC: Engineering (Industrial Electronics) (including Communications

and Society); BTEC HND: Engineering (Electrical and Electronic) (including Communication Studies).

STOKE-ON-TRENT: NORTH STAFFORDSHIRE POLYTECHNIC
College Road, Stoke-on-Trent, Staffs. ST4 2DE; 0782 45531
Courses: BA (Hons): History of Design and the Visual Arts (including Sociology of the Mass Media); BEng (Hons): Electronic Engineering (including Communications); BTEC HNC: Communications Engineering.

SUFFOLK COLLEGE OF HIGHER AND FURTHER EDUCATION
Rope Walk, Ipswich, Suffolk IP4 1LT; 0473 55885
Course: BTEC HND: Visual Communication (Television Graphics and Production)

SUNDERLAND POLYTECHNIC
Langham Tower, Ryhope Road, Sunderland SR2 7EE; 0783 76231
Courses: BA/BA (Hons)/MA: Communication Studies; BEng/BEng (Hons): Electrical and Electronic Engineering (including Communications); Diploma: Film and Television Studies.

SWANSEA: WEST GLAMORGAN INSTITUTE OF HIGHER EDUCATION
Townhill Road, Swansea SA2 0UT; 0792 203482
Course: BTEC HNC/HND: Electronics and Communications Engineering.

ULSTER POLYTECHNIC
Shore Road, Newtownabbey, Co Antrim BT37 0QB; 0231 65131
Courses: BA (Hons): Graphic Design (including Film and Television); BTEC HND: Electronics and Communications Engineering.

POLYTECHNIC OF WALES
Treforest, Pontypridd, Mid Glamorgan CF37 1DL; 0443 405133
Courses: BA (Hons): Communication Studies; BTEC HND: Electrical and Electronic Engineering.

WARRINGTON: NORTH CHESHIRE COLLEGE
Fearnhead, Warrington, Ches. WA2 0DB; 0925 814343
Course: BA: Combined Studies (including Media and Communication).

WIGAN COLLEGE OF TECHNOLOGY
Parson's Walk, Wigan WN1 1RR; 0942 494911
Courses: BTEC National Certificate: Audio and Television Equipment; BTEC Technicians Course: Telecommunications; BTEC National Diploma: Electronics and Communications.

WINCHESTER: KING ALFRED'S COLLEGE
Sparkford Road, Winchester, Hants SO22 4NR; 0962 62281
Course: BA (Hons): Drama, Theatre and Television Studies.

THE POLYTECHNIC WOLVERHAMPTON
Molineux Street, Wolverhampton WV1 1SB; 0902 710654
Courses: Diploma: Cultural Studies (including Film and Television); BTEC
HND: Design (Communication).

YORK COLLEGE OF ARTS AND TECHNOLOGY
Tadcaster Road, Dringhouses, York YO2 1UA; 0904 704141
Course: BTEC National Diploma: Electronics and Communications
Engineering.

YORK: COLLEGE OF RIPON AND YORK ST JOHN
Lord Mayor's Walk, York YO3 7EX; 0904 56771
Course: BA (Combined Honours): Drama, Film and Television.

Arts schools

Courses in film, television and video production and techniques have developed
from the curricula of art schools and the arts faculties of the polytechnics and
colleges. Such topics as graphic and production design, animation, documentaries and photography are covered, with an emphasis on aesthetic and practical
aspects of film and television.

BERKSHIRE COLLEGE OF ART AND DESIGN
Kings Road, Reading RG1 4HJ; 0734 583501
Course: BTEC HND: Graphic Design (Film and TV Graphics).

BOURNEMOUTH AND POOLE COLLEGE OF ART AND TECHNOLOGY
Department of Photography, Film and Television, Wallisdown Road, Poole,
Dorset BH1 5HH; 0202 533011
Courses: BTEC HND: Design (Film and Television); BTEC HND: Photogra-
phy, Film and Television.

BROMLEY: RAVENSBOURNE COLLEGE OF ART AND DESIGN
School of Television and Broadcasting, Wharton Road, Bromley, Kent BR1
3LE; 01-464 3090
Course: BA (Hons): Visual Communications Design; BTEC HND: Communications Engineering (Broadcasting).

CROYDON COLLEGE OF DESIGN AND TECHNOLOGY
Barclay Road, Croydon, Surrey; 01-688 9271
Course: Diploma (Postgraduate): Film and Television Animation.

EPSOM SCHOOL OF ART AND DESIGN
Askley Road, Epsom, Surrey KT18 5BE; 037 27 28811
Course: BTEC National Diploma: Audio Visual Studies.

GLOUCESTERSHIRE COLLEGE OF ART AND TECHNOLOGY
Brunswick Road, Gloucester GL1 1HU; 0452 426609
Course: National Diploma: Design (Communications).

GWENT COLLEGE OF HIGHER EDUCATION
Faculty of Art, Clarence Place, Newport, Gwent NP7 0UW; 0633 59984
Courses: BTEC HND: Film and Television Practice; Diploma: Film and Television Design.

HARROGATE COLLEGE OF ARTS AND TECHNOLOGY
Hornbeam Park, Hookstone Road, Harrogate, North Yorkshire; 0423 879466
Courses: BTEC National Diploma: Communications Design; BTEC National Diploma: Audio Visual Studies.

HARROW COLLEGE OF HIGHER EDUCATION
Faculty of Art and Photography, Northwick Park, Harrow, Middlesex HA1 3TP; 01-864 5422
Course: BA (Hons): Applied Photography, Film and Television.

LONDON: ROYAL COLLEGE OF ART
School of Film and Television, Kensington Gore, London SW7 2EU; 01-584 5020
Courses: MA/PhD: Film and Television Production; MA: Graphics in Film and Television.

LONDON: ST MARTIN'S SCHOOL OF ART
107–109 Charing Cross Road, London WC2H 0DU; 01-437 0611
Courses: BA (Hons): Fine Art (including Film and Video); BA (Hons): Graphic Design (including Film and Video); Diploma (Postgraduate): Film and Video.

WIMBLEDON SCHOOL OF ART
Merton Hill Road, London SW19 3QA; 01-540 0231
Course: BA (Hons): Fine Art (including Film and Video).

Further reading

Allen, Julia. *Careers in television and radio*. London: Kogan Page, 2nd edn, 1988.
British Council. *Media courses in Britain*. Annual. London: The Council.
British Film Institute: Education Department. *Film and television training: a guide to film and video courses*. London: BFI Education, 1987.
British Film Institute: Education Department. *Studying film and television: a list of courses in higher education*. London: BFI Education, 1987.

British Kinematograph, Sound and Television Society. *Education and training for film and television*. London: BKSTS, 3rd edn, 1982.
British qualifications. Annual. London: Kogan Page.
Careers and Occupational Information Centre. *Broadcasting*. (Job Outlines, No. 89) London: Manpower Services Commission, 1984.
Careers and Occupational Information Centre. *Occupations*. Annual. London: Manpower Services Commission.
Careers and Occupational Information Centre. *Working in the media and entertainment*. (Working in series, No. 48) London: Manpower Services Commission, 1982.
Careers and Occupational Information Centre. *Working in tv and video*. (Working in series, No. 79) London: Manpower Services Commission, 1986.
Careers in Independent Television. London: Independent Television Association, 2nd edn, 1986.
Media Project. *Where you can learn about radio: a directory of training courses*. Annual. Berkhamsted: The Media Project/The Volunteer Centre.

2.13 Awards, festivals and conventions

Award ceremonies, festivals and conventions are a regular and important feature in the broadcasting industry calendar. They provide a valuable opportunity for broadcasters to gather together, discuss current issues, 'talk shop' and receive (and hand out) the accolades of the broadcasting industry and profession. They also produce useful documentation — festival brochures, papers and award citations.

Many of the festivals are competitive, with programmes submitted by broadcasting organizations for prizes. Other festivals, such as the Edinburgh International Television Festival or the Radio Festival, are primarily forums for serious discussion of broadcasting issues. At the most highly regarded of them, the Royal Television Society Convention or the Radio Festival for example, major policy issues are debated with addresses from the Home Secretary or other key figures.

BRITISH ACADEMY AWARDS
British Academy of Film & Television Arts, 195 Piccadilly, London W1
BAFTA (q.v.) presents two sets of awards to the film and television industry — craft awards, and production and performance awards; the latter ceremony, a major event in the broadcasting year, is televised.

BROADCASTING PRESS GUILD
60 Sandford Road, Bromley, Kent BR2 9AN
Annual awards for radio and television programmes from the radio and television critics and journalists of the national, regional and trade press.

EDINBURGH INTERNATIONAL TELEVISION FESTIVAL
5 Betterton Street, London WC2H 9BU
Prestigious annual event for broadcasters held in August/September; a series of

discussion sessions on current issues in television, with screenings of associated programmes, and the MacTaggart Memorial Lecture.

GOLDEN ROSE OF MONTREUX FESTIVAL
Case Postale 97, 1820 Montreux, Switzerland
International competition for television light entertainment, music and variety programmes instituted in 1960. It is held annually in May under the patronage of the EBU, in collaboration with the Swiss Broadcasting Corporation. Prizes include: Golden, Silver and Bronze Roses; City of Montreux Prize (for the funniest entry); and the Press Prize. United Kingdom prize-winning entries have included: 1977: *The Muppet Show* (ATV); 1982: *Dizzy Feet* (Central Independent Television); 1983: *Three of a Kind* (BBC); 1985: *The Paul Daniels Magic Easter Show* (BBC) and *Spitting Image* (Central Independent Television); 1987: *Fire and Ice* (LWT).

MONTE CARLO INTERNATIONAL TELEVISION FESTIVAL
Palais des Congrès, Avenue d'Ostende, Monte Carlo, Monaco
Competitive festival for member organizations of the International Telecommunications Union, established in 1960 and held annually in February. Prizes are awarded for best programmes, performers, writers and directors, documentaries, news reporting, children's and environmental programmes. British winning programmes have included: 1985: *Death in Belfast* (ITN/Channel 4) and *Threads* (BBC).

NEW YORK INTERNATIONAL FILM AND TELEVISION FESTIVAL
246 West 38th Street, New York, NY 10018, USA
Annual competitive festival for industrial and educational films and television programmes. British winners include: 1984: *Squaring the Circle* (Channel 4/TVS); 1986: *Weekend World* (LWT), *City Safari* (LWT).

PRIX ITALIA
RAI Radiotelevisione Italiana, Viale Mazzini, 14, 00195 Rome, Italy
Europe's oldest and most respected broadcasting festival was founded in 1948. It is organized by RAI, under the auspices of the EBU, with aims to promote the quality of radio and television programmes and encourage member organizations to broadcast the programmes in the competition. The competition for national broadcasting organizations is held annually in September in different Italian cities. Awards include: six Prix Italias for best radio and television music, drama and documentary programmes; six RAI Prizes for the same categories; and two ecology prizes. British winners have included: 1980 (TV Music): *A Time There Was . . .* (LWT); 1981 (TV Music): *At The Haunted End Of The Day* (LWT); 1982 (TV Drama): *Cream In My Coffee* (LWT) and (TV Music) *Cruel Garden* (BBC); 1984 (TV Drama): *Made in Britain* (Central Independent Television); 1987 (TV Drama): *After Pilkington* (BBC).

RADIO AND TELEVISION INDUSTRIES CLUB
Corbetts House, Norwood End, Fyfield, Ongar, Essex CM5 0RW
Major annual awards for television and radio programmes.

RADIO FESTIVAL
Radio Academy, 30 Whiteladies Road, Bristol BS8 2LG
Annual conference for Radio Academy (q.v.) members, providing working sessions, plenary discussions and an address by the Home Secretary.

ROYAL TELEVISION SOCIETY
Tavistock House East, Tavistock Square, London WC1H 9HR
Organizes several important events during the year: the Journalism Awards in February; Programme Awards in May; and in September the Convention in Cambridge.

SONY RADIO AWARDS
Department SRA, Alan Zafer and Associates, 47–48 Chagford Street, London NW1 6EB
Major event in the radio broadcasting calendar with awards for all categories of radio programmes and performers.

3

Primary sources of information and documentation

The primary source material on broadcasting is the wealth of documentation and papers generated by the broadcasters and their organizations in the process of broadcasting, as well as the finished product — the radio and television programmes broadcast.

The written, oral and visual archives of broadcasting are of enormous future value, both to the broadcasters themselves for use in further programmes, and to historians and researchers looking into the social, political, cultural and broadcasting history of the twentieth century.

The primary source material on broadcasting falls into four broad categories: administrative and operational papers; programme documentation; broadcasting research; and television and radio programmes.

Collections of this source material can be found in the archives and libraries described in Chapter 6.

3.1 Administrative and operational papers

Most organizations generate an enormous amount of operational paperwork, of which only a small proportion is of long-term significance or likely to be retained long enough to become part of an archive. Guidelines would be drawn up identifying different categories of papers to be assessed for: retention permanently as documents of lasting importance and significance to the organization; or scheduled to be retained until a later review after a certain lapse of time; or as documents of no long-term value which can be destroyed after a short time.

The principal administrative papers in the broadcasting organizations are generated by the policy-making bodies within them — the boards of governors or directors, the executive or management, the advisory councils and committees.

Internal memoranda between heads of departments and other senior staff either consulting about, agreeing to, or notifying policy decisions will form a significant proportion of the retained papers, and will give considerable insight into the evolution and implementation of policy within the organization.

External correspondence between the broadcasters and the Government or other broadcasting bodies will also form an important part of an archival collection, giving a picture of the relationships with Government and within the broadcasting industry.

Another invaluable primary source of information about an organization is the annual report and accounts which may, of course, be published, but not always; this depends on the status of the organization or company.

Minutes and papers of boards, councils and committees

Most significant of the policy papers of the broadcasting organizations will be the minutes of meetings of the boards, councils, committees and advisory bodies, which record the discussions and decisions taken, together with any of the information or background papers presented at the meetings. As happens in many organizations, final policy is the result of a gradual filtering of ideas, information and proposals from the professional staff, through the executive to the policy makers.

The ultimate policy-making body in the BBC is the Board of Governors, nominated by the Home Secretary, with input of advice and information from the Board of Management, departmental meetings and the various advisory councils and committees.

In the IBA the Authority, consisting of members appointed by the Home Secretary, approves policy based on advice from the Director-General's Management Meeting and such advisory bodies as the General Advisory Council.

The Boards of Directors, consisting of honorary directors and senior members of staff on the board, decide policy for Channel 4, and the television and radio programme companies.

Various cross-industry groups in broadcasting are also important in the determination of policy. In ITV, for example, programme scheduling policy is worked out at meetings of the Network Programme Committee, under the auspices of the Independent Television Association, before approval by the IBA. Other bodies within the industry may have different internal structures, but the evolution and formulation of policy would be similar.

Internal correspondence, memoranda and files

Records of the internal structure and working of an organization, and of the advice and briefings channelled up from the professional staff to the governing body can be found in the memoranda and correspondence between senior staff or departments. Of particular interest to historians and academics would be the personal files of distinguished former members of staff, which may contain valuable information, though possibly of a confidential nature and restricted access. Files of correspondence with notable programme contributors, either on the staff or freelance, are also of enormous value.

External correspondence

Insight into the relationships of the organizations in the broadcasting industry, particularly the broadcasting authorities, with the Government of the day, and individual Government Ministers and departments, is essential to an understanding of their structure and working environment, as well as the development of British broadcasting.

Correspondence between such bodies as the BBC, the IBA and the Cable Authority, and the responsible Government Ministers, is to be found in the Public Record Office, when released, or in the archives of the individual broadcasting authorities and companies.

Annual reports and accounts

The principal source of information about the activities and finances of an organization is its annual report and accounts.

Each of the public bodies in broadcasting — the BBC, the IBA, the Welsh Fourth Channel Authority and the Cable Authority — is required under its constitution to prepare a general report of its proceedings during the year and submit it, together with audited accounts, for approval by the Home Secretary. The report will then be presented to Parliament, after which it can be published by HMSO, the Government publishers, or the body itself.

The companies providing the television and radio programme services, like other registered companies in the UK, are required by the *Companies Act 1985* to prepare a directors' report for each financial year. The report must contain a fair review of development of the business of the company, together with names and shareholdings of directors, asset values, policies for employment, training and safety, and staff share participation schemes. The Act also requires an auditors' report, giving the balance sheet with profit and loss account, and an annual return, containing information about the amount and distribution of share capital, financial situation, and names and addresses of directors and secretary of the company. Copies of the auditors' report and accounts, and the annual return must be forwarded to the Registrar of Companies; they will then be available for public examination at the Companies Registration Office in Cardiff, or its Search Room in London.

However, many companies publish their annual reports and accounts, often as glossy, prestige publications to promote themselves to the consumer and potential investors. These may provide illustrations of the organization's activities, with the basic statistical and accounting information presented graphically as bar or pie charts, flow charts and graphs.

Further reading

British Broadcasting Corporation. *Report of the Advisory Committee on Archives.* London: BBC, 1979.

Cook, Michael. *The management of information from archives.* Aldershot, Hants: Gower Publishing, 1986.

Foster, Janet and Sheppard, Julia. *British archives: a guide to archive resources in the United Kingdom.* London: Macmillan, 1982.

International Council on Archives: Committee on Business Archives. *Business archives: studies on international practices.* Munich: K.G. Saur, 1983.

3.2 Programme documentation

The making of a programme inevitably generates a large amount of documentation at every stage in the production process, from the original concept to the eventual transmission. Directors and producers, particularly those working within the large broadcasting organizations, frequently complain of the huge amount of paperwork involved. However, the need for careful and detailed planning and production, together with such operational necessities as negotiating contracts for performers and other outside contributors, arranging permission for the use of locations and facilities, determining copyright and performing right payments, and supplying information for publicity and billings for programme journals, results in a substantial body of documentation.

Some selection from this mountain of material is inevitable when the decision is made on its eventual retention and storage in a programme archive, and policy may vary from archive to archive as to how much of this material would be retained. However, programme documentation retained should represent all the key stages in the production cycle from the original concept and proposal, through the planning, recording, post-production and scheduling, to the final transmission of the programme. This documentation can provide the broadcasters with useful material for re-use in future productions, as well as valuable source material to enable later generations of researchers to recreate the evolution of the programme as part of the study of the television or radio production process.

The exact stages in the production process may vary from one type of programme to another; they would not be quite the same in a documentary as in drama production, or in news and current affairs compared with light entertainment. Television production methods are often different from radio. However, the following section, based on television production, should give some idea of the type of documentation generated at each stage in the production process, the purpose it served and the information it would contain.

Concept and proposal

The concept or idea for a programme may originate in different ways, either from the head of a particular programme department, or from the producer, or perhaps as the result of a suggestion from an outside contributor.

The original idea for a programme can appear in different forms. A *script*, or programme proposal submitted by an author or outside contributor may be the original documentation. Or a *format* may be drawn up by a drama producer, for example, giving a rough outline of the plot, characters and location, as part of a proposal for a new drama programme or series. Another form may be a *treatment* proposed by a documentary producer, for example, giving details of programme title, length and transmission slot, intended audience, résumé of the content, requirements for studio and outside broadcast facilities, production timescale and a budget estimate.

At this early stage in a proposal, special *audience research* may occasionally be commissioned to assess the likely audience for the proposed programme or series, particularly if it is an entirely new concept, perhaps representing considerable expense and commitment of resources. An important part of the early planning of the BBC *EastEnders* serial was market research; firstly questioning the various viewing panels about their attitudes to a possible new television soap opera; and then later testing reactions to the initial concept, setting and characters of the serial.

Formal programme proposals or offers are necessary in most broadcasting organizations before programme controllers/directors will approve the production and schedule it as part of a forthcoming programme plan.

Planning

Once the go-ahead is given, the executive producer or producer can draw up a detailed budget for the resources required, and assemble a production team consisting of a producer, a director (to direct the programme in the studio), production assistant, script editor (for drama) and other key personnel.

At the planning stage of a programme there are many different operational papers generated and circulating among the production team, including many versions of the basic source of programme information — the *script*.

Programme research is an early and important element in most types of programmes, providing valuable information for content, contacts and experts, interviewees (in the case of current affairs or documentaries), or historical background or accuracy (for drama). There may be research into archive film and television footage or sound recordings to be used.

A *recce* for the locations and outside facilities required is also early on in the planning process.

Correspondence with programme contributors, possibly freelance script writers, consultants and advisers, organizations, interviewees, or owners of locations may be of enormous interest to future generations of researchers.

There may also be negotiations about production crew levels with the relevant trade unions.

A *running order*, a scene breakdown of the shots for scripted productions, or a 'build-up' for unscripted news and current affairs programmes, lists sequence number and name, actors or others involved, vision sources and camera positions, sound sources, and duration.

The *floor plan*, the blueprint of a programme, giving a diagram of the studio floor and all camera positions for each shot, is vital for all on the production from the director to the designer and the lighting director.

A designer will be researching and producing *designs* for the sets and costumes of the production, and arranging for suitable properties from store to use as set furnishings.

The *lighting plot*, a matching plan to the floor plan, worked out by the lighting director, plots all the lights needed and their positions as an instruction for the electricians.

A *rehearsal script*, in the case of drama, will have been necessary for the days of outside rehearsal before the production moves into the studio. Here the floor plan is vital for marking out the rehearsal room floor to enable the actors to go through their dialogue and moves.

A *camera script* is drawn up by the director. It is a complete description of all sound and vision in a production, and serves to co-ordinate the work of the whole production team. It gives details of programme title, key dates of rehearsal, recording, editing, dubbing and transmission, the names of the cast and production team and crew, technical requirements, and all the shots to be taken in sequence, followed by the actual script of dialogue, actors' and camera movements, and instructions for lighting cues, vision mixing and special effects. In documentary production a *shooting script* fulfils a similar function; written after the recces for location and programme research are completed, it lists scenes in the sequence in which they are to be shot, giving date, sequence, shot number, description of action and any dialogue.

Camera cards are prepared from the camera script, for each camera operator, giving the shots for each camera during the production, showing the number of the shot, camera position according to the floor plan, and description.

Recording

At this point the production is fully planned and prepared, and ready to go into the studio for recording. In the studio all production staff involved in the recording — from those in the Gallery, the producer, director, production assistant, and vision mixer, the Sound and Lighting Control Rooms, and the floor managers, assistants and cameramen down on the studio floor — have copies of the camera script, the camera cards or the other instructions needed.

During the recording a *shot list* is kept, usually by the production assistant, listing each shot as taken, giving the programme title, episode, producer, production dates, camera roll numbers, slate number, take number, description and sound, tape and duration. It can also cover the archive or library film footage and still photographs used in production. The shot list, sometimes referred to as an *assembly script*, will later be a valuable aid to the producer or director in assembling the material in the post-production stage.

Publicity stills are often taken during the production by a stills photographer, both of the scenes as seen finally on the television screen or 'production shots' showing production team on location or in the studio, for later use with publicity and promotion.

Post-production

Once the recording in the studio is finished, the programme goes into post-production, where it is assembled, edited, dubbed and generally finished off.

The *assembly order*, or *cutting order*, will contain the director's instructions to the editor for assembling and editing the material shot when it reaches the film cutting room or videotape editing suite. The director will view the rough cut assembled by the film or tape editor before a final cut is made.

Transcripts are often made of unscripted interviews or discussions. The transcript is used in the discussions between the director and the film editor, and later is a valuable printed record of the programme's content.

A *commentary*, when necessary, is written for a voice-over narration and is added at the dubbing stage.

A *dubbing script* is often used for the adding of sound mixes and commentary.

A final document, the *Programme-as-Completed* (*P-as-C*), also known as the *Programme-as-Televised* in some organizations, is compiled after the production is completed, and is the definitive statement of the contents, contributors and final cost of a programme. It is used by the organization for the payment of performance fees and reproduction fees to all the artists, speakers and copyright owners involved in the production. Copies are sent internally to the relevant departments dealing with artists' contracts, locations and facilities, copyright, programme correspondence and publicity, programme sales, and the Film and VT Library and Registry. Interested external bodies, such as the Performing Rights Society, would also receive copies. In ITV it is used when a regional company sells a programme to the network. Until recently in the BBC another document, the *Programme-as-Broadcast* (*P-as-B*), was compiled from the *P-as-C*, to include details of presentation, fill-up and trade test information; it was the most accurate record of the actual transmission of a television programme.

Scheduling

Once completed, the programme is ready for transmission. The programme planners will decide about which transmission slot in the forthcoming schedules will be most suitable to attract the maximum audience, given the constraints of competition from rival channels and the requirements of programme quotas and rules. These considerations do not necessarily apply to the specialist areas of programming, such as schools and educational programmes.

Programme schedules, or *transmission plans*, are the advance notice of future programme transmission details. The exact form of the advance programme schedules varies from system to system. For the BBC the transmission form or repeat transmission forms perform the function of forward schedules. In the ITV system, the programme companies draw up quarterly schedules, which list the dates, times and titles of programmes for the next three-month period. Under the *Broadcasting Act 1981* the ITV programme contractors are required to submit their schedules to the IBA for approval. These schedules, amended through subsequent editions right up to the transmission date, are an accurate record of programmes actually shown, as opposed to billed in advance in the *TV Times*. Past copies of the ITV schedules would show, for example, how the schedulers coped with sudden and last-minute changes of programmes caused by the assassination of President Kennedy or the death of Sir Winston Churchill. Computerized schedules for Independent Television are now held by the IBA Television Statistics Office.

Programme publicity, information and support

Prior to transmission of the programme, decisions will be made about publicity material, information to programme journals and the press, and programme support services.

Programme billings will be sent in advance by the production department to the appropriate programme journal, the *Radio Times* or the *TV Times*, giving details of the programme's transmission date, time, title, cast, production credits and synopsis. This forms the basis of the information in the programme listings section of the magazine. It also gives the editorial staff ideas for articles or interviews to accompany the showing of the programme.

A *Programme Index*, containing information about all programmes transmitted, is maintained for both BBC and ITV/Channel 4 programmes. The BBC Programme Index is a detailed index to the domestic radio and television output since 1945, with the exceptions of Open University broadcasts, local radio and news bulletins. Programmes are indexed by title, sub-title, contributors and subjects. Information given in each entry includes programme title and information, producer, transmission date, time and channel. A microfiche version, starting in 1979, is now available commercially from Chadwick-Healey Ltd (q.v.). A Programme Index for Independent Television programmes is maintained by the IBA; it covers London area ITV programmes since 1955 and the Channel 4 programmes since 1982. Information corresponds to the *TV Times* programme listings for the recent programmes, though the earlier years' entries are not so detailed. Extensive indexes to television programmes are also maintained by one non-broadcasting organization, the British Film Institute Library (q.v.). Its prime source is a title index to all UK networked television programmes (excepting Open University, schools and sports broadcasts) giving title, production company, transmission date and time, cast and credits, plot/ subject summary, periodical references and awards.

Press releases, giving information about their programmes and other activities, are issued by the broadcasting organizations primarily to the newspapers and periodicals for their TV programme and listings pages. The Channel 4 weekly press information pack, for example, is a considerable compilation of over seventy pages of detailed information about their programmes. Similar press releases giving programme schedules and background are issued by the BBC and the ITV programme companies. They are a valuable source of information.

Publicity material is also often produced in connection with the promotion of programmes, in addition to press releases. It can vary enormously from single-sheet handouts or marketing promotions, intended to accompany previews or for the advertisers, to glossy booklets and even novelty items, advertised on-air for the viewers or listeners.

Programme support material is the final category of programme documentation. Nowadays a wide range of semi-published material is available to support radio and television programmes after transmission. Most listeners and viewers will now be familiar with the message that often follows educational or general interest programmes offering further information or publications. Sometimes it is the BBC or the ITV companies themselves offering leaflets or information to accompany their programmes, or perhaps advertising spin-offs of tie-in books, records or videos. However, much of the support literature, information or advice connected with educational and social action programmes on BBC, ITV, Channel 4 and Independent Radio is provided through Broadcast Support Services (BSS).

In an ideal world, a programme documentation archive would collect together all the material from each of these stages in the production-to-transmission cycle, making it possible in years to come to recreate the production process for specific programmes. However, as it is, not all of this material may be retained, and not always in the same area. Considerable sleuthing may be necessary to assemble the material to form a picture of the total process.

Further reading

Croton, Gordon. *From script to screen: documentaries.* Borehamwood, Herts.: BBC Television Training, 1986 (BBC Television Training Manuals).

Highton, David. *When the programme's over. From adult literacy to Live Aid: the story of Broadcasting Support Services.* London: Comedia Publishing, 1986.

Jarvis, Peter. *Shooting on location.* Borehamwood, Herts.: BBC Television Training, 1986 (BBC Television Training Manuals).

McLeish, Robert. *The technique of radio production.* London: Focal Press, 2nd edn, 1988.

Millerson, Gerald. *The technique of television production*. London: Focal Press, 11th edn, 1985.

Phillips, Brian. *Stand by studio!* Borehamwood, Herts.: BBC Television Training, 1987 (BBC Television Training Manuals).

Pilsworth, Michael. 'An imperfect art': TV scheduling in Britain. *Sight and Sound* 1980: 49 (4). pp. 237–41.

3.3 Broadcasting research

An important category of primary source material is the wealth of information and data produced through the research conducted on various aspects of broadcasting and its audiences.

Research into broadcasting can be grouped into two main categories: market-orientated research into the audiences for television and radio services; and academic research on media and society, programme content, production processes, and media institutions and policies. Broadcasting industry research tends to be applied research, whereas in the academic sector it tends to be pure research and often by nature highly theoretical.

Audience research, largely *quantitative research* into audience size and composition, has primarily been conducted either by (or for) the broadcasters, as part of their own evaluation and development of programmes and services, or for the advertising industry. *Qualitative research* into programme content, production processes and media institutions, as well as sociological studies of the effects of broadcasting, has largely been undertaken by the academic world, through universities, polytechnics and research institutes.

Both these areas of research can provide valuable data and information on all aspects of broadcasting in the United Kingdom. However, the broadcasting industry research findings are usually based on proprietary data, available in full only to subscribers, though simplified or summarized ratings may be more widely available in published form. Academic research, on the contrary, normally uses public-domain data, and it is widely disseminated and available.

Information about the research organizations can be found in Chapter 2.

Audience research

Broadcasting research in the United Kingdom was first conducted at the BBC in 1936, and by 1938 a separate Audience Research Department had been established. In 1939 the BBC started the first continuous measurement of audiences, the Daily Survey of Listening, which was later extended to cover television, as the Daily Survey of Viewing and Listening, in 1952. This survey used an aided-recall system of interviews with a different representative sample of people each day.

The introduction of Independent Television in 1955 brought new research methods and organizations. Advertisers became interested in the selling potential of commercial television, but they required detailed and accurate measurement of audience size and composition for both the programmes and the commercials on the new service. Audience reach, the cumulative audience who watched the service over a certain period, became an important consideration. Lifestyle information, and data on viewing patterns and their effect on buying behaviour, was also required by the advertisers.

Initially several organizations, with different systems of audience measurement, tried to provide this service. The A. C. Nielsen Company, at this time the largest audience research organization in the world, started the *Nielsen Television Index*, using their 'audimeter' system of measuring the viewing of given programmes for more than five-minute periods. Nielsen were retained by Granada Television only, to provide weekly television ratings, until 1959, when they merged with the rival Television Audience Measurement (TAM). Gallup Poll produced irregular reports based on aided-recall interviews with over 700 people about their viewing the previous day. Another company, the Pulse organization, produced the weekly *Telepulse Reports*, also using an aided-recall method of personal interviews with between 3,500 and 4,000 families in their home, to provide ratings for programmes in the London and Midlands areas. However, the company, and the system, that would emerge as the single, surviving audience measurement system for ITV was Television Audience Measurement, a company founded by Bedford Attwood in 1954. It used 'TAMmeters', in some 2,300 homes in the UK, to produce the *National TAMratings Reports*. After the Gallup and Pulse organizations dropped out in 1956, TAM became the official television ratings contractor to ITV. The BBC continued to produce its own daily survey of television viewing, which it had extended to cover ITV programmes as well as BBC.

In 1967, Audits of Great Britain (AGB), formed by four former TAM executives, won the contract to provide the official television ratings from July 1968. AGB provided their service under contract to the Joint Industry Committee for Television Advertising Research (JICTAR), which had been set up in 1961 by the Independent Television Companies Association (ITCA), the Incorporated Society of British Advertisers (ISBA) and the Institute of Practitioners in Advertising (IPA), to manage a commonly acceptable system of audience measurement for ITV. The *TVRatings*, or JICTARs, as they became known, were produced through a mixed system of meters attached to television set in a representative sample of homes, as TAM had done, and diaries. While the quantitative research on size and composition of audience for ITV was conducted by AGB for JICTAR, the qualitative research on audience appreciation was undertaken by the Independent Broadcasting Authority. During this period the two audience measurement systems, from the BBC and JICTAR, were measuring rather different things and for different requirements, and not unnaturally produced differing, and sometimes apparently conflicting viewing figures, causing some press criticism of the television ratings business. In 1977 the Committee on the Future of Broadcasting, under Lord Annan, recommended the establishment of a joint BBC/ITV audience measurement system.

Independent Local Radio started in 1973, and a Joint Industry Committee for Radio Audience Research (JICRAR) was established by the Association of Independent Radio Contractors, the IBA, ISBA and the IPA to produce audience measurement for the new advertising-supported radio system. The JICRAR surveys, conducted under contract by Research Surveys of Great Britain (RSGB), were produced by a diary method from a sample of individuals in each local radio station area.

Progress towards a common television audience measurement system was made in 1978 when the BBC and the ITCA agreed to establish a jointly conducted and financed ratings system. The BBC and ITV had different priorities for audience research; the BBC were more concerned with data on individual programmes and the national audience, whereas ITV, conditioned by its regional structure and the commercial break, and mindful of the advertisers, were more concerned with regional viewing measurement and patterns, and ratings for commercials as well as programmes. Following lengthy discussions between the two parties on the complicated technical issues involved, the Broadcasters' Audience Research Board (BARB) was established in July 1980 to supervise the new joint system. BARB now serves all of their separate interests for continuous measurement of television audiences. AGB Research Ltd were again appointed to provide the quantitative research, the Audience Measurement Service, which began in August 1981. The BARB Audience Reaction Service, provided by the BBC Broadcasting Research Department, began in April 1982.

The new cable television services also had an audience measurement system, supervised by the Joint Industry Committee for Cable Audience Research (JICCAR), providing statistics of households connected to cable systems supplying special cable programme services.

Audience research is also undertaken by the broadcasting organizations to keep themselves informed on the state of public opinion about the services they provide. Broadcasters need to know who is watching or listening to their programmes. The research findings can assist them in the planning and development of programmes, and the evaluation of the impact the programmes have on the audiences.

Techniques used in audience research are similar to those of market or social research. Audiences cannot be counted directly, so samples of the population are selected, representing the size the composition (by age, sex and socio-economic status) of the national population, to produce estimates of audience size, composition and viewing — the 'ratings'.

The methods used for the collection of this data on audiences have changed since audience research began. The *aided-recall method* was used by the BBC for their television audience measurement system until 1981, and is still used for radio audience research. It involves trained interviewers going out to ask a representative sample of people questions about their viewing or listening the previous day. The *diary method*, currently used by the BBC for the Audience Reaction Service, involves giving a selected sample of the population a booklet or questionnaire giving details of programmes broadcast over a certain period; respondents are asked to watch only the programmes they would normally, and to fill in the booklet by answering a number of questions about the programmes. Aided-recall and diary methods frequently make use of regularly changed population samples. An alternative to this is to use a regular *panel*, giving the opportunity for long-term data and studies. The *meter method* of audience measurement, introduced into this country from the United States when ITV began, uses a meter attached to the television set in panel members' homes. It records, minute by minute, when the set is switched on, and to which channel. Originally the data recorded by the meter was automatically transferred to paper tape, which had to be returned by post to the research organization for analysis. Nowadays, the meter is connected via a telephone line directly to the computer at the organizations' headquarters, and the data is transmitted automatically. A push-button handset for each member of the household (and guests), with which they press an 'on' button when starting to view and 'off' when stopping, identifies and records, again minute by minute, exactly who in the household is watching. This method, currently used for the BARB Audience Measurement Service, provides full data on the viewing audience very quickly.

Currently audience research findings for television are produced under the auspices of the Broadcasters' Audience Research Board by the BBC and AGB Research, for Independent Radio under the Joint Industry Committee for Radio Audience Research by Research Surveys of Great Britain, for cable by the Joint Industry Committee for Cable Audience Research, and by the BBC Broadcasting Research Department. A variety of other market research organizations undertake special audience surveys, often under commission from the broadcasters, the advertisers or the agencies.

Broadcasters' Audience Research Board (BARB)

Continuous measurement of television viewing in the United Kingdom is undertaken through the Broadcasters' Audience Research Board (q.v.). The services, printed reports and an online service are available on subscription for clients in the broadcasting, advertising and marketing industries. BARB produce two services: audience measurement; and audience appreciation or reaction.

The Audience Measurement Service is provided from data collected by Audits of Great Britain (AGB Research), under contract to BARB. Information is collected from a sample panel of homes throughout the country designed to be representative of all private households with television in the United Kingdom. The measurement of viewing in each household is achieved through electronic meters attached to television sets, with press-button handsets, linked directly to the AGB Research central computer. The system provides valuable continuous data on viewing levels and patterns, but it is criticized by the advertising agencies for not producing detailed enough classification data or reporting quickly enough.

Weekly TV audience report
Weekly. London BARB/AGB Research.
Known as the 'Green Book', this report gives population estimates and panel composition, followed by detailed listings of all programmes on ITV, Channel 4, BBC1 and BBC2, arranged by (ITV) region, giving the transmission time, programme title and the ratings. The audience figures are expressed as a 'TVR' ratings figure, and as the number (in thousands) and percentage of homes and individuals watching. Also included is a chronological listing of all commercials shown, with the audience ratings they obtained. In addition to the region-by-region report, a separate 'Network' report is issued, giving overall national ratings for all four channels, and analysis of the social composition of the audience.

Weekly TV audience report: Part II: and weekly schedule of commercials
Weekly. London: BARB/AGB Research.
Known as the 'Blue Book', this weekly classified schedule of commercials arranged by product or service categories gives the product brand name, with transmission dates, times, duration, company rate card cost and TVR ratings.

The week's viewing in summary
Weekly. London: BARB/AGB Research.
A single-sheet summary of hours of viewing, audience share and reach, followed by lists of the top ten highest rated programmes for ITV, Channel 4, BBC1 and BBC2, and then region by region.

Trends in television: a monthly audience research report for directors
Monthly. London: BARB/AGB Research.
Digest of developments in television, with trend data on TV ownership, viewing hours, audience share, hours of transmission, advertising revenue, top programmes and breakfast television.

Children TVRatings report
Weekly. London: BARB/AGB Research.
Viewing by children aged 4–15 of ITV, Channel 4, BBC1 and BBC2 programmes shown before 21.00 hours, expressed as a TVR figure, percentage share and thousands viewing, organized by age groupings and region.

Establishment survey of TV homes
Annual. London: BARB.
Report giving demographics for each ITV area, including analysis of TV and ITV households and individuals.

The BARB Audience Reaction Service was launched in April 1982. It monitors the audience responses to, and appreciation of, television programmes. This qualitative research, using a quantitative method of data collection and measurement, into audience appreciation is as valuable to broadcasters as the 'ratings'. The Reaction Service is carried by the BBC Broadcasting Research Department under contract to BARB. During the first four years it was conducted through self-completion booklets left with respondents for the BBC Daily Survey. However, the sample size and distribution did not provide sufficient data for minority programmes or adequate regional coverage. It was replaced in 1986 by the Television Opinion Panel (TOP), which comprised a national panel of 3,000 members and regional boost panels for each of the ITV regions. Panel members, aged 12 and over, are asked only to watch programmes they would normally and record their appreciation according to a six-point scale, ranging from 6 ('extremely interesting and/or enjoyable') down to 1 ('not at all interesting and/or enjoyable'). The scale positions 6, 5, 4, 3, 2 and 1 are treated as scores of 100, 80, 60, 40, 20 and 0, and the total value for each programme divided by the number of respondents to give an Appreciation Index (AI) figure between 0 to 100. A high AI figure indicates a high level of interest or enjoyment. The Children's Television Opinion Panel works in a similar way. The measurements are not absolute, their value is in the comparisons between them.

Audience appreciation report: national report
Weekly. London: BARB/BBC Broadcasting Research Department.
National audience appreciation report arranged by programme groups and sub-groups (e.g. UK drama: single plays; UK drama: series and serials; etc.). Within each category, programmes are arranged in descending AI figure order, giving title and transmission details, total AI figure, scale positions, and analysed by sex, age and socio-economic class.

Audience appreciation summary: national summary
Weekly. London: BARB/BBC Broadcasting Research Department.
National survey in chronological arrangement of programmes on all four television channels with their total AI figures and scale positions.

Audience appreciation report: regional report
Monthly. London: BARB/BBC Broadcasting Research Department.
The Television Opinion Panel regional panels in each of the ITV regions record their reactions to programmes for one week in four throughout the year. As with the national report, the data is arranged by programme categories and sub-categories, with programmes listed in descending AI order.

Audience appreciation summary: regional summary
Monthly. London: BARB/BBC Broadcasting Research Department.
A chronological (day-by-day) listing of programmes, AIs and scale positions for BBC, ITV and Channel 4 programmes for one week in a four-week period.

Children's appreciation report: national report
London: BARB/BBC Broadcasting Research Department.
Classified listing of children's viewing and appreciation of programmes transmitted before 9.00pm in the evening.

Children's appreciation summary: national summary
London: BARB/BBC Broadcasting Research Department.
Chronological listing of children's viewing and appreciation of programmes transmitted before 9.00pm.

Joint Industry Committee for Cable Audience Research (JICCAR)

JICCAR represents both the advertisers, through the Institute of Practitioners in Advertising and the Incorporated Society of British Advertisers, and the cable television industry, in the form of the Cable Television Association and the Cable Programme Providers Group. It has provided a regular survey of the cable audience, compiled according to a specification drawn up by a Technical Sub-Committee, since 1985.

National survey of the cable audience
London: JICCAR.
The survey provides establishment data on cable penetration, the number of homes 'passed' by (i.e. capable of receiving) cable systems, and the number of homes subscribing, as well as periodic research on usage and viewing habits. The research methodology for the cable television market is not the meter system, but the more traditional method of a personal diary kept in a representative sample of the total number of homes with cable television. The published report is a summary; data tapes are available.

Joint Industry Committee for Radio Audience Research (JICRAR)

This joint industry body, representing the radio companies and the advertising industry, has provided regular surveys of the audience for Independent Radio since 1974. The network survey is commissioned by the Radio Marketing Bureau and conducted by Research Surveys of Great Britain.

The Independent Radio network: a survey of the radio audience in accordance with the JICRAR specifications
London: Radio Marketing Bureau. Annual.
The survey provides data about the audiences for the Independent Radio network and for individual radio stations. The diary method is used to compile the data; a questionnaire, for basic demographic information about the household, and a diary are placed in a randomly selected sample of homes within each radio station's total survey area. Informants record in the diary, on a quarter-hour basis, all their radio listening, either to the Independent Radio stations, the BBC local or national radio services or Radio Luxembourg, for a seven-day period.

British Broadcasting Corporation

The Broadcasting Research Department of the BBC has provided continuous measurement of the size and reactions of audiences to radio and, later, television output since 1939. It undertakes also a wide range of special projects and ad hoc investigations associated with individual programmes or programme departments, or on more general broadcasting issues. The Department maintains its own data collection and analysis facilities, and fieldforce of part-time interviewers.

Measurement of audiences for BBC and non-BBC national and local radio services, the Daily Survey of Listening, is conducted from aided-recall interviews with a representative sample of people each day. Research on audience reactions to radio programmes was originally conducted through questionnaires completed by a Listening Panel. However, it only monitored the four national radio channels, and the largely 'self-selected' Listening Panel, recruited through broadcast appeals, was eventually felt to be biased and unrepresentative. In 1984 a more directed recruitment method for the Listening Panel was established, using respondents selected from those interviewed for the Daily Survey.

The provision of continuous measurement of television audiences for the BBC (and Independent Television) is now under the auspices of BARB. The BARB online meter method of collecting the audience data has been described previously. The BBC's own Daily Survey of Viewing, which it replaced, using the aided-recall interview method, had been a cost-effective and straightforward research method. However, the regularly changing daily sample had meant that long-term studies of audience viewing patterns could not be undertaken, and it had often produced results contradicting those of the JICTAR system of the ITV companies. The Department is responsible for the BARB Audience Reaction Service, providing the data for the *Audience appreciation reports* from the Television Opinion Panel, as previously described.

The majority of the Department's own research findings are provided for internal use only, and often of a confidential nature. They are used by management and programme staff as an aid to decision-making on programme planning and evaluation, or on broader policy issues. Audience research is part of the BBC's commitment to take note of public opinion of its output and services. However, little of the considerable research output is available in published form, or to those outside the Corporation, except for an annual review of its findings, an occasional survey of daily life in the United Kingdom and a few special reports.

Annual review of BBC broadcasting research findings
1973/74–. Annual. London: BBC.
This review contains regular summaries of viewing and listening trends and developments in audience research during the year, followed by a series of articles on the results of findings from the special projects and studies on

individual programmes or other broadcasting topics, and a list of special reports available from the department.

Daily life in the 1980s: Volume 1: *Broadcast media and associated media*; Volume 2: *General activities*. London: BBC Data Publications, 1984.
The eleventh in a series of studies for broadcasters and the general public on people's leisure pursuits, in particular their viewing and listening. Previous studies were carried out in 1939, 1947, 1948, 1950, 1952, 1953, 1961 and 1974/75. The earlier studies used self-completion diaries with members of selected households, whereas this study used face-to-face interviews conducted by professional interviewers.

Independent Broadcasting Authority

The *Broadcasting Act* requires the IBA to ascertain the state of public opinion concerning the programmes broadcast.

The IBA Research Department does not provide the continuous measurement of the size and composition of the audiences for ITV, Channel 4 or the Independent Radio system; that is undertaken by the companies themselves, through their trade associations, and is now provided by the BARB Audience Measurement Service and JICRAR.

However, the measurement of audience appreciation was undertaken by the IBA for approximately ten years until the BARB Audience Reaction Service began in 1985, and of children's appreciation of programmes until 1986.

The IBA Research Department now produces an annual survey of audience attitudes to broadcasting, a range of special research papers and reports on audiences for specific programmes or programme categories, or other broadcasting topics, and a series of published monographs resulting from research projects.

Audience appreciation report
1974–85. Weekly. London: IBA.
The reports provided data on viewers' appreciation and opinions on television programmes, compiled through Television Diaries completed by a representative sample of households in London on alternate weeks, and in each of the other ITV areas in rotation.

Children's view
1978–86. Bi-monthly. London: IBA.
The IBA maintained a panel of children aged 4 to 12 years who were representative in terms of age, sex and social class to produce this survey of their appreciation and opinions of programmes. The survey is a classified order of programme categories, with tables arranged in descending AI order, giving programme title, time, AI figure, scale positions, analysis by sex, age and class. A similar survey for adolescents, *Teenager's view*, existed until 1984.

Attitudes to broadcasting
1970–. Annual. London: IBA.
National survey of public attitudes to broadcasting, using personal interviews
with a quota sample of approximately 1,000 adults (aged 16 and over) in geogra-
phically representative areas of the United Kingdom. Questions cover such topics
as location and number of TV sets in the home, teletext and video ownership,
channel preference and viewing levels, perceived bias and offensiveness, breakfast-time viewing, family viewing, radio listening and views on commercials.

IBA Television Research Monographs
1986–. London: John Libbey.
Titles in this series of research monographs written by staff of the IBA Research
Department, and resulting from IBA research surveys, include: *Television and
sex role stereotyping* by Barrie Gunter (1986); *Behind and in front of the screen*
by Barrie Gunter and Michael Svennevig (1987); *Television and the fear of
crime* by Barrie Gunter (1987); *Violence on television: what the viewers think* by
Barrie Gunter and Mallory Wober (1988); *Attitudes to broadcasting over the
years* by Barrie Gunter and Michael Svennevig (1988).

Academic research

Research into the media, and particularly broadcasting, has gained academic
respectability and acceptance in the United Kingdom only comparatively
recently.

Communications or mass media research in the United States had followed
fairly quickly on the heels of the market-orientated 'ratings' research into radio
audiences in the 1930s, and later developed into a separate and identifiable area
of academic studies. However, in Britain, academic consideration of broadcasting and its effects did not develop until the 1950s when Professor Hilde
Himmelweit and others conducted pioneering studies on television and the
child. Even by 1963, the Television Research Committee, appointed by the
Home Secretary to initiate and co-ordinate research into television as a medium
of communication, found there was still a lack of interest in media research.
Since then, though, and partly through the Committee's influence, research
into the mass media has become a part of the programme of several academic
establishments, notably the Centre for Mass Communications Research at the
University of Leicester, the Centre for Television Research at the University of
Leeds, the Centre for Contemporary Cultural Studies at Birmingham University, and the European Institute of the Media at Manchester University.
Research centres on broadcasting are described in Chapter 2.

However, because of the initial slow acceptance of media studies and
research in the UK and Europe, the overwhelming body of research material is
American, based on US network television operating in American society,
models which are not valid for Europe.

Broadcasters and academic media researchers have broadly similar concerns — they need to know about society, the receiver or audience of the broadcast services. However, their concerns differ in detail: broadcasters are mostly interested in audience size, composition and reactions to specific programmes and services; academics are more concerned with the nature of audiences in general, and the impact of broadcasting on society.

Academic studies of the media, often highly theoretical, frequently fall within the broader disciplines and approaches of psychology, sociology, semiology and political economy.

The main categories of academic study and research into broadcasting are concerned with *media and society*; *content studies*; *production processes*; and *media institutions and policy*.

Research into *media and society* covers two broad areas: the impact or effects of the media on society; and the ways in which people use the media and the gratification they derive.

The *effects* studies have often been based on an assumption of the powerful influence of the media. However, this theory — particularly of direct influence — has been challenged as being less significant than is popularly supposed, and as being part of a far more complex process of interaction between the media and its audience. The advertising analogy, that if the media can be used to sell products then they must as surely influence other forms of social behaviour or attitudes, has also been discredited. Short-term effects might be defined as either a change of opinion or attitude, or a change of behaviour. Longer-term effects would be a more widespread and fundamental change in the culture, values and structure of a society through the influence of the media.

Most concern in this area of research has been with the negative effects of the media, of possibly causing social or psychological problems, such as violence, crime, delinquency, civil unrest, deviance or permissiveness. Prominent among these is the research undertaken on the effects of television violence on society, particularly on the more vulnerable members of society — children and young people. Notable research on the possible relationship between television violence and aggressive behaviour includes: in Britain, the enquiry by William Belson on television violence and the adolescent boy, conducted through the London School of Economics and sponsored by the Columbia Broadcasting System; and in America, the studies of television and aggression led by J. Ronald Milavsky for the National Broadcasting Company, and by George Gerbner and Larry Gross from the University of Pennsylvania's Annenberg School of Communications. However, research by Barrie Gunter argues that it is a far from simple matter because most audiences are discriminatory, they perceive so-called 'violent' incidents in different ways, particularly according to whether it is fact or fiction, and make subtle and complicated judgements about what they have seen according to the context and circumstances. There is concern that violence on television, whether news coverage or fictional, might have a desensitizing effect on audiences, and that some evidence would seem to point to a small minority of viewers admitting to feeling more violent (though not necessarily acting violently) after watching a violent programme. The fact that aggressive people may tend to watch more violent programmes on television and that some people are more easily influenced than others further confuses the issue. However, despite the considerable body of research, there is still little convincing evidence to support the hypothesis of a direct causal link between violence on television and violence in society. Many of these issues continue to be fiercely debated but remain largely unresolved.

The *uses and gratifications* approach to research into media and society examines how the people use the media and the gratification they derive according to their psychological and social needs. Different people satisfy different needs from the media. The amount of time spent watching television, for example, would seem evidence that audiences derive gratification, however illusory, from the medium. Another aspect would be examination of how audiences perceive and categorize programme types, and how that might differ from the broadcasters' own programme classification. Do they, for example, make the same distinctions between news and current affairs, or current affairs and programmes of opinion, as do the broadcasters?

Another broad category of academic research into the media and broadcasting is *content analysis*, the systematic and quantitative description of the contents of broadcasts. It can form part of a quantitative analysis of a programme or, increasingly, form a semiotics approach through the analysis of the meaning, symbolism and message content of a television programme or series. It aims to be a non-selective and objective method of analysis; the programme or commercial is analysed by pre-determined categories perhaps representing the frequency or number of appearances of characters by race, sex or age, or specified images, messages or geographical locations, for example. The results can be constituted statistically to substantiate or disprove claims of media coverage bias or impartiality. Content analysis is frequently used for studies of the representation on television of race, women, trade union or industrial affairs, minority interests and concerns, and the portrayal of controversial issues such as alcoholism, crime and homosexuality. It can challenge the assumptions broadcasters make about their programmes, and be offered as evidence of the likely impact the programmes may have on the audience, though it does not actually measure impact. It is often used to draw conclusions about the motives and intentions of programme makers. However, the claim made for content analysis of total objectivity is suspect at the point where the categories are pre-determined, and with definitions used. Certainly, it cannot serve as the sole basis for claims about media effects. This method of media research has often brought the social scientists into conflict with the broadcasters, most notably the studies of television news reporting and coverage of industrial affairs by the Glasgow University Media Group.

A related category to content studies, and one overlapping with it, is the study of *production processes* — looking, not at the audience or exclusively at content, but at the process of making programmes. It relies on broadcasters allowing researchers full access to a production. This area of research examines the decisions made by programme makers during production, particularly with news and current affairs. Decisions, for example, about 'news values' and what attributes make an event 'newsworthy'. The disorder of the real world is organized and given shape by news editors and those on the production team who make these decisions, often termed 'gatekeepers' because they open the gate on some items of news and close it on others. Raw news from reporters is filtered through to the news editors, who select and process it into a version of reality ready for the programme. News department staff need guidelines for the selection, construction and presentation of news; these naturally establish the attributes of newsworthiness and their exploitation for programmes. Operational decisions have to be made on the deployment of resources, particularly staff, in order to cover news stories; these have to be based on predictions of the location and importance of the events. Advance notice of important events, essential for planning, often relies on official sources, such as Parliament and Government departments, giving them the ability to control the timing and release of information. News gathering is the result of specialisms — specialist reporters and correspondents covering self-contained subjects, for example: foreign affairs, crime or sport. Finally, there is the assessment of likely audience appeal, and shaping the news to 'entertain' as well as to inform. All these elements in the production of news can have an influence on the eventual programme. Broadcasters would all defend their professional standards and independence, and their responsibility to the audience as they see it, but few of their decisions made during production can be said to be entirely objective or impartial. The results of this process — the finished programmes — have been criticized on the grounds of: bias or lack of impartiality; agenda-setting the terms of reference and topics for debate according to the dominant culture or political system; or establishing false priorities for the importance of news. Examples of research into the production process are by Stanley Cohen and Jock Young into the response of the mass media to deviant behaviour and social problems, the investigation into the social context and production of broadcast news by Peter Golding and Philip Elliott, the analysis of the ITV soap opera *Crossroads* by Dorothy Hobson, and the study of BBC news by Philip Schlesinger.

A final category of research on *media institutions and policy* includes investigation of the internal structure and dynamics of media organizations, and the various external influences on them — the state and legal system, commercial environment, public service or private enterprise, ownership and control, competition, the state of the technology, and the audience. Such research can only be undertaken with full permission by the institutions concerned, and access to confidential material and interviews. Notable studies of the BBC by Asa Briggs and Tom Burns use this approach.

None of these categories of media research are mutually exclusive, and many research projects combine elements from more than one. The methodology of academic research into the media ranges from surveys using data collection (through random sample or regular panel interviews) and analysis, longitudinal research, construction of experiments, content monitoring and analysis, field observation, control groups, case studies, archive research and many other methods. For studies in all these areas of the media, *communication models* can be used as simplified descriptions in graphic form of structures and processes involved, and the relationships between them. These models can clearly show the transmission of ideas or information through symbols in diagram form. Models are used to illustrate television effects on behaviour, uses and gratifications of the media, media organizations communications, agenda setting, news flow, the 'gatekeeper' approach, and many other concepts.

Most academic research into broadcasting and the media is in the public domain and published, even if only as a summary or report of a substantial body of research findings. Published and unpublished research findings should be available in the libraries of the research centres sponsoring media research, and other broadcasting archives and libraries.

Further reading

Belson, William. *Television violence and the adolescent boy*. London: Saxon House, 1978.

Blumler, Jay and Katz, Elihu. *The uses of mass communications: current perspective on gratifications research*. Beverly Hills, Calif.: Sage Publications, 1974.

Briggs, Asa. *Governing the BBC*. London: BBC, 1979.

Burns, Tom. *The BBC: public institution and private world*. London: Macmillan, 1977.

Cohen, Stanley and Young, Jock. *The manufacture of news: social problems, deviance and the mass media*. London: Constable, 1973.

Gerbner, George and Gross, Larry. Living with television: the violence profile. *Journal of Communication* 1976: 26, 2. pp. 173–99.

Glasgow University Media Group. *Bad news* (1976); *More bad news* (1980). London: Routledge & Kegan Paul; *Really bad news*. London: Writers and Readers, 1982.

Golding, Peter and Elliott, Philip. *Making the news*. London: Longman, 1979.

Goodhardt, G. J., Ehrenburg, A. S. C. and Collins, M. A. *The television audience: patterns of viewing*. Aldershot, Hants: Gower, 2nd edn, 1987.

Gunter, Barrie. *Dimensions of television violence*. Aldershot, Hants: Gower, 1985.

Gunter, Barrie and Wober, Mallory. *Violence on television: what the viewers think*. London: John Libbey, 1988.

Halloran, James. *The effects of television*. London: Panther Books, 1970.

Hobson, Dorothy. *Crossroads: the drama of a soap opera*. London: Methuen, 1982.

James, Gabrielle. The birth of BARB. *Broadcast* 1981: 20 July. pp. 24–5.

Jenkins, Peter. The design, testing and launch of the Television Opinion Panel. *Annual review of BBC broadcasting research*, No. 12, 1986. London: BBC Data Publications, 1987.

Katz, Elihu. *Social research on broadcasting: proposals for further development*. London: BBC, 1977.

McCron, Robin. Social research on broadcasting in Britain. *Combroad* 1986: October/December. pp. 27–8.

McQuail, Denis. *Communication*. London: Longman, 2nd edn, 1984.

McQuail, Denis and Windahl, Sven. *Communication models for the study of mass communications*. London: Longman, 1981.

Meneer, Peter. Television audience measurement in the United Kingdom. *Annual review of BBC broadcasting research findings*, No. 11, 1985. London: BBC Data Publications, 1985. pp. 27–36.

Milavsky, J. Ronald *et al. Television and aggression: the results of a panel study*. New York: Academic Press, 1982.

Phillips, William. Persistence of vision: 1: Thirty years of ratings. *Admap* 1986: February. pp. 56–67.

Reiss, Pamela. Continuous research for television: the eighties approach. *Television* 1983: 20 (5). pp. 202–6.

Schlesinger, Philip. *Putting 'reality' together: BBC news*. London: Methuen, 1987.

Shannon, C. E. and Weaver, W. *The mathematical theory of communication*. University of Illinois Press, 1949.

Silvey, Robert. *Who's listening?: the story of BBC audience research*. London: Allen & Unwin, 1974.

Tuck, Mary. Television and violence: a note on recent research. *Home Office Research and Planning Unit Research Bulletin* 1986: (22). pp. 28–32.

3.4 Television and radio programmes

Most essential of the primary sources of information about television and radio programme output are the actual programmes. They are the final and visible result of the broadcasting process. They are also the raw material for the study of television and radio production, as well as of the impact and effects of broadcasting on society.

Until comparatively recently, television and radio were considered ephemeral media. Originally broadcasting was essentially a 'live' medium, and it was neither technically easy nor financially feasible to record programmes for posterity, nor was it even considered necessary. Indeed, much of the early programme output of the BBC and ITV has not been preserved, for reasons of technical or organizational difficulties, costs or just lack of concern. Most broadcasting organizations are primarily concerned with making new programmes, and are less concerned about maintaining large and expensive archives unless they are convinced of the value of the material for programme re-use. What preservation there is of television and radio programme output by the broadcasting organizations is according to criteria concerned more with programme re-use than with an eye to the interests of posterity. The emphasis has been on 'selection', with only a small proportion of the final programme output being preserved.

The question of archiving of the output of British broadcasting, and its associated documentation, has been extensively discussed over the last few years. Academics are as much concerned over the broadcast output that has not been preserved, and is lost to posterity, as with the material that is, which they consider to have been rather arbitrarily and randomly selected. An argument against 'selection' is that it is difficult to predict now with any certainty what will prove to be of historical significance in the future. Certainly selection diminishes the value to historians and social scientists of these records of the most pervasive (and persuasive) media of communications; they need a comprehensive record of exactly what the public saw and heard. However, now there is a greater understanding of the value of television and radio programmes for study and research, as well as programme re-use, and the need to preserve and make them available for future generations. Increasing dependence on overseas sales of programmes, repeat transmissions and video sales of old programmes will ensure that the broadcasters will now keep more of their programme output. Even so, the bulk of television and radio output is 'wiped' within weeks or months of transmission, unless particular requests are made for retention. Acts of cultural vandalism or an inevitable policy born of necessity? However one sees it, that is the reality of television and radio archiving.

There is, as yet, no statutory legal deposit of television and radio programmes in the United Kingdom, as there is for published books with the British Library or for official records at the Public Record Office. Pressure from the academic community in Britain for a legally backed and adequately financed system of statutory deposit of films, and recordings of television and radio programmes has not yet been successful. Their objective of a 'National Archive of Mass Communications or Audiovisual Records', to preserve and administer the programme archives of the national broadcasting organizations, and offer access and viewing/listening facilities for accredited researchers, as the Institut National de l'Audiovisuel does in France, has not been realized. Until such time, researchers requiring access to recordings of television and radio programmes will need to approach either the National Film Archive and the National Sound Archive for selected television and radio programmes or the broadcasting organizations. See Chapter 6 for details of the national archives, and the broadcasting organizations' film and videotape libraries.

Television programmes

Originally television programmes were transmitted 'live' — what viewers saw on their television sets at home was being performed live in the television studio or at an outside broadcast. Recordings of these early programmes are only available if they were also simultaneously filmed in the studio; a few such filmed records of the pre-war BBC Television programme output from Alexandra Palace do exist. Eventually the technique of 'telerecording' — filming programmes direct from the television monitor — made it possible to make recordings on film. Increased use of filmed programmes also resulted in more programmes being stored and re-used. However, in both cases stringent selection was necessary because of the high cost of film and the large amount of space taken up with storage. The introduction of videotape recording in the late 1950s made possible large-scale preservation of television programmes though storage problems remained until the later development of smaller tape formats.

The viewing of old television programmes for study purposes can often be a lonely and less than rewarding experience for the academic researcher.

Originally such programmes were made as home entertainment for family viewing, not for scholarly consideration years later by academics or researchers. Television, more than almost any other medium, reflects exactly the social style and attitudes of its time, and therefore dates quickly. For historians and social scientists, of course, this is part of its value as a record of the times and what viewers were watching. Earlier black and white programmes on the previous line standard — 405-lines — seem indistinct compared to the present-day colour and higher definition 625-line image.

The researcher needs to make allowance for all these points when viewing earlier television output, and must be able to develop a sense of perspective by seeing it in its exact historical time and place, taking into account the state of the technology and the social context of its production.

Retention and storage of television output by the originating broadcasting organizations is either as: selected complete programmes or series kept for later repeat transmission, sale to foreign broadcasting organizations for showing abroad, or sale or hire as videocassettes for home consumption through video sales outlets; or as 'stock shots', selected portions of programmes suitable for re-use as establishing shots, inserts or backgrounds.

Apart from the broadcasting organizations, there are other sources of television material. There are two national bodies — the National Film Archive, which has selectively preserved BBC and ITV television output for over twenty years, and the Imperial War Museum, which has valuable collections of film and television material on the two World Wars and other conflicts. Many regional archives and record offices, such as the North West Film Archive or the Scottish Archive, have collections of television programmes, particularly from local news and interest programmes, and often donated by the local ITV company or BBC service. Specialized archives like the Church House Record Centre or the House of Lords Record Office can have television material connected with their work or interests. Such commercial film and newsreel libraries as British Movietone Film Library or Visnews may also contain television material in their collections.

Access to the television material held by the broadcasting organizations may not be easily available; their film and videotape libraries' main responsibility is to serve their own production requirements. Beyond that they will co-operate with other broadcasting organizations, but probably would not be able or willing to cater for outside researchers.

Selection, however unpopular with the broadcasters themselves or the academic community, may still be a necessary part of the preservation and storage policy of television archives and libraries. An example of the selection policy used by the broadcasters (or the National Film Archive) is that of the BBC Film and Videotape Library — selection according to: importance to the history and development of television; people or events of historic interest; showing items of sociological interest, objects of art or geographical places; as well as individual complete programmes or series for repeat transmission.

Copies of television programmes, whether at the national archives or the various film and vt libraries, may be on film (16mm or 35mm) or videotape (VHS viewing copies, or 1in/2in broadcast-standard videotape). Viewing would be in viewing booths, at Steenbeck editing or viewing tables, or on television monitors. Retrieval from the collections is usually through catalogues and card indexes.

Radio programmes

Early radio, like television, was essentially 'live', though early developments in sound recording enabled the use of commercially-issued cylinder and disc recordings in programmes, and the ability to record the programmes broadcast. However, few recordings were made until the 1930s, when the BBC began recording programmes on discs for immediate re-use on the Empire Service.

The principal source of recordings of radio programmes in the United Kingdom is, of course, the BBC. The BBC Sound Archives department contains BBC radio programmes and extracts from programmes dating back to the 1920s. It also contains a wealth of unbroadcast material, specialized collections of natural history and folk music recordings, and sound effects. The oral history of the BBC is a recently developed project by the Archives involving recorded interviews with former BBC staff recalling earlier days in the Corporation and broadcasting generally. However, there are a few other sources of radio programmes and sound archive material. The National Sound Archive has received copies of most recordings added to the BBC Sound Archives, and is also permitted to record BBC programmes off-air; it also contains selected programmes from Independent Radio stations. The Imperial War Museum has a collection of the BBC's Second World War recordings. The Parliamentary Sound Archive has recordings of broadcast debates and proceedings in the Houses of Parliament. Other specialized or regional archives or societies have often acquired, or recorded off-air by arrangement, radio programmes within their area of interest. Many of the BBC Local Radio or Independent Radio stations have made recording arrangements with their local public libraries, record offices and societies.

Selection of sound recordings is as necessary as it is with television, and for largely the same reasons, and only a small proportion of radio output is retained for preservation. An archive of sound recordings in a broadcasting organization would aim to develop a collection of material suitable for use in both radio and television programmes, as well as selected complete programmes representing the total broadcast output and suitable for use as repeat broadcasts. Criteria for selection would be similar to those of television material: events and voices of people of historic importance; social history and general interest; language, dialect and regional accents; drama and entertainment; music of all kinds; natural history; and sound effects. Decisions would have to be made also on the future value of the material, whether the archive already had similar items, whether it was technically suitable for preservation, what copyright restrictions there might be on the future re-use of the material, and whether to preserve the whole programme or only a part.

Further reading

Bredin, James. *A television archive for Britain. A paper for discussion by James Bredin, a BP Press Fellow at Wolfson College, Cambridge*. London: British Petroleum, 1987.

Briggs, Asa. National treasure. *Times Educational Supplement* 1986: 25 April. p. 55.

British Broadcasting Corporation. *Report of the Advisory Committee on Archives*. London: BBC, 1979.

Harrison, Helen. *Film library techniques*. London: Focal Press, 1973.

Hearst, Stephen. A second chance to see . . . *The Listener* 1985: 113 (2911). p. 21.

Hewlett, Richard. The BBC's written archives. *ASLIB proceedings* 1975: 27 (10). pp. 414–21.

Jeavons, Clyde. Opening the box to everyone. *Guardian* 1986: 30 June. p. 13.

Lance, David. (ed) *Sound archives: a guide to their establishment and development*. London: International Association of Sound Archives, 1983.

Madden, Paul. What's in store for TV archives? *Broadcast* 1980: 21 (1046). p. 14.

Markosky, Cheryl. Programmes vanish while archive plans stay in cold storage. *Television Weekly* 1984: 13 January. pp. 18–19.

Oliver, Elizabeth. *Researchers' guide to British film and television collections*. London: British Universities Film and Video Council, 2nd edn, 1985.

Panorama of audiovisual archives. A contribution to the development of international film and video archive practice. Editor of English language edition: Anne Hanford. London: BBC Data Publications, 1986.

Pronay, Nicholas. Archive film/television preservation: the historian's perspective. *The Audiovisual Librarian* 1979: 5 (1). pp. 24–5.

Smith, Anthony. The right to record. *BFI film and television yearbook, 1988*. London: British Film Institute, 1987. pp. 16–20.

Wyver, John. Why we need a national TV archive. *The Listener* 1982: 108 (2790). pp. 6–7.

4

Printed and electronic reference sources

This selection of basic published sources of information on broadcasting in the United Kingdom covers both books, periodicals and electronic publishing. It is intended to be a reference work, as well as both a guide to information resources for researchers and an indication of a basic stock list for a small specialist library or collection on broadcasting.

Many of the titles included are traditional reference sources such as directories, yearbooks, dictionaries and glossaries; others are histories, surveys, textbooks and non-book materials. All, however, are relevant to the subject, whether in total or in part. In some cases, general reference works, such as the basic official statistical series for the United Kingdom, have been described in some detail because, even though broadcasting is only a small part of their contents, they are important sources.

For each category, the most important or useful items are included. Each entry contains full bibliographical details and a short descriptive annotation summarizing the subject coverage and contents, and highlighting any useful features.

The works described should be available in the libraries specializing in the subject of communications and broadcasting, and a selection of them will be represented on the shelves of the larger public reference libraries.

Increasingly, however, print sources are available as online databases either directly from the producer or through various host systems; a selection of those relevant to the media, broadcasting and advertising are also outlined. In many cases, the print or hard-copy version is described as well as the online version.

4.1 Histories

General

Briggs, Asa. *The BBC: the first fifty years*. Oxford: Oxford University Press, 1985. xvi, 439 pp.
Invaluable single-volume history of the BBC, chronicling developments from 1922 to 1972, and relating them to the social, cultural and political changes in Britain. Useful chronology and detailed bibliography.

Briggs, Asa. *History of broadcasting in the United Kingdom*. London: Oxford University Press.
Volume I: The birth of broadcasting (-1927). 1961. xiii, 415 pp.
Volume II: The golden age of broadcasting (1927-39). 1965. xvi, 688 pp.
Volume III: The war of the words (1939-45). 1970. xviii, 766 pp.
Volume IV: Sound and vision (1945-55). 1979. xiv, 1,082 pp.
Comprehensive and detailed chronological account of broadcasting in the United Kingdom, from the early Marconi experiments in wireless telegraphy, through the formation and development of the BBC, to the beginning of Independent Television. Written by the leading social historian of broadcasting with full access to the BBC Archives. Extensive references and bibliography.

Paulu, Burton. *Television and radio in the United Kingdom*. London: Macmillan, 1981. xiv, 476 pp.
This highly regarded American media academic considers broadcasting in the United Kingdom to be the best in the world, and ascribes this pre-eminence to our system of controlled competition. He examines the legal structure, financial basis, personnel policies and technical facilities of British broadcasting, with reference also to programming and audience research. Extensive bibliogrpahy.

Pawley, E. *BBC engineering 1922-72*. London: BBC, 1972. xiv, 569 pp.
History of the development of radio and television engineering in the BBC, by a former Chief Engineer. Bibliography.

Sendall, Bernard. *Independent Television in Britain*. London: Macmillan.
Volume 1: Origin and foundation, 1946-62. 1982. xviii, 418 pp.
Volume 2: Expansion and change, 1958-68. 1983. xvii, 429 pp.
Volume 3: Politics and control, 1968-80 by Jeremy Potter. Forthcoming, 1989. ix, 360 pp.
Volume 4: Companies and programmes, 1968-80 by Jeremy Potter. (In preparation).
Authorized history of Independent Television begun by the former Deputy Director General of the ITA (later IBA), and continued by the former Director of Corporate Affairs at London Weekend Television. Written with full access to IBA archives. Extensive references and bibliography.

Smith, Anthony. *British broadcasting*. Newton Abbot, Devon: David & Charles, 1974. 271 pp. (David & Charles Sources for Contemporary Issues Series).
A history of broadcasting in the United Kingdom explained through extracts from key constitutional documents, official sources and texts.

Radio

Baron, Mike. *Independent radio: the story of commercial radio in the United Kingdom*. Lavenham, Suffolk: Terence Dalton, 1975. 192 pp.
The development of commercial radio in Britain, beginning with the challenge to the BBC from Radio Paris and the International Broadcasting Company's Radio Normandy service in the 1920s, and from Radio Luxembourg in the 1930s, to the offshore pirate radio stations of the 1960s and the start of Independent Local Radio in 1973.

Henry, Stuart and Joel, Mike von. *Pirate radio: then and now*. Poole, Dorset: Blandford Press, 1984. 129 pp.
Well-illustrated and researched chronology of twenty years of pirate or illegal broadcasting, from the official launch of Radio Caroline in 1964 to Radio Laser 558 and Radio Nova in 1984.

Hill, Jonathan. *Radio! Radio!* Bampton, Devon: Sunrise Press, 1986. 244 pp.
A comprehensive radio enthusiasts' history of the technical developments in wireless telegraphy and radio, and the evolution of the design of the wireless set. It contains information about wireless manufacturers and full details for all radios sold in the UK up to the 1960s. Profusely illustrated.

Parker, Derek. *Radio: the great years*. London: David & Charles, 1977. 160 pp.
Affectionately written, well-illustrated history of radio from 2LO and Savoy Hill to the era of local radio and disc jockeys.

Pegg, Mark. *Broadcasting and society, 1918-39*. London: Croom Helm, 1983. 272 pp.
Extensively researched, academic study of the social, cultural and political influence of radio before the Second World War, looking at audience research and listening patterns, the wireless organizations, broadcasting and leisure. Detailed list of references and selected bibliography.

Reid, Colin. *Action stations. A history of Broadcasting House*. London: Robson Books, 1987. 160 pp.
Recollections, by a former BBC Duty Officer, of the BBC headquarters, known as 'BH' to its inhabitants, and as the flagship and symbol of the BBC to millions throughout the world.

Television

Black, Peter. *The mirror in the corner: people's television*. London: Hutchinson, 1972. 232 pp.
An authoritative account, by a respected columnist and critic, of the development of British television since 1946, covering the birth of Independent Television and the effect of subsequent competition on the BBC and British television generally.

Burns, Russell. *British television, the formative years*. London: Peter Peregrinus, 1986. xv, 488 pp. (IEE History of Technology Series, 7).
History of British television, from Baird's first experiments in 1923 to the closedown of the BBC Television service in 1939, which considers the technical and financial factors which led to the establishment of the world's first high-definition television service.

Davis, Anthony. *Television: the first forty years*. London: Severn House, 1976. 159 pp.
Short, illustrated historical survey of television in Britain, arranged by category of programme.

Geddes, Keith and Bussey, Gordon. *Television: the first fifty years*. Bradford: National Museum of Photography, Film and Television, 1986. 36 pp.
Well-illustrated museum guide, which concentrates on the pre-war developments and the BBC Television service, and the technical improvements for both the broadcaster and the viewer since the war.

Henry, Brian (ed.) *British television advertising: the first thirty years*. London: Century Benham, 1986. 528 pp.
This essential history of television advertising in the United Kingdom was sponsored by the History of Advertising Trust. A detailed chronology of developments from the beginning of advertising-supported television (ITV) in 1955, by the editor, is followed by essays from twelve distinguished practitioners, including Lord Aylestone, Asa Briggs and David Bernstein, giving their personal viewpoints on such topics as the television commercial, advertising regulation, television advertising and the social revolution, and the advertising agencies. Useful features include colour illustrations of key commercials, a glossary of abbreviations, appendices of various codes and constitutional documents. Detailed index.

Highton, David. *When the programme's over. From adult literacy to live aid: the story of Broadcasting Support Services*. London: Comedia Publishing Group, 1986. 114 pp.
History of Broadcasting Support Services (BSS), which began modestly in 1976

as a national referral service to support the *On the move* adult literacy series, and has become an essential element in public service broadcasting by providing audiences with support and off-air services for radio and television programmes.

ITV Books and *TV Times. 25 years on ITV: 1955–1980*. London: ITV Books and Michael Joseph, 1980. 279 pp.
Profusely illustrated chronology of programmes and the major news events for each year form 1955 to 1980.

Institution of Electrical Engineers. *International conference on the history of television from early days to the present*. London: IEE, 1986. 185 pp. (IEE Conference Publication, 271).
Conference papers by representatives from the BBC, the IBA and the electronics industry on technical aspects of television history, including television systems, colour television, technical standards, telecine, video recording, transmitters and receivers.

Marschall, Rick. *History of television*. London: Bison Books, 1986. 255 pp.
A glossy and profusely illustrated popular history of television in the United States and the United Kingdom, from the early experimental period, through the decades of public television service and programmes since the 1940s.

Moss, Nicholas. *BBC TV presents: a fiftieth anniversary*. London: BBC Data Publications, 1986. 120 pp.
History of BBC Television, with an opening chapter on the development of the medium, followed by sections for each decade from the 1930s to the 1980s on the programmes. Unique illustrations.

Norman, Bruce. *Here's looking at you: the story of British television, 1908–39*. London: BBC and the Royal Television Society, 1984. 224 pp.
Well-researched history of British television from the early experiments to the closedown of BBC Television at the outset of war in 1939. Details and photographs of the experimental television service from 1932–5, as well as of the regular public service from 1936–9, with a 'Who's who in early television' and a bibliography.

4.2 Directories and yearbooks

Blue book of British broadcasting. 1974–. Annual. London: Tellex Monitors.
Listing of the programmes and key administrative and production personnel in the BBC, ITV companies, IBA, Channel 4 and local radio. Alphabetical indexes to personnel and classified index of programmes.

British Film Institute. *BFI film and television yearbook*. Annual. 1984–. London: BFI.
Yearbook and directory containing the annual report and accounts of the BFI, and extensive listings of film and television awards, courses and training in film and television, production companies, publications, television companies and trade organizations.

Broadcast yearbook and diary. Annual. London: *Broadcast*.
Diary for the broadcasting industry in the United Kingdom, with directory section of information about broadcasting organizations, television and radio stations, cable television operators and programme services, production companies, training courses, professional and trade associations, festivals and conferences.

Cable and satellite Europe yearbook. 1985–. Annual. London: 21st Century Publishing.
Yearbook containing articles and directory entries on cable and satellite television in each European country, including the United Kingdom. Coverage includes communications satellites, DBS, satellite and cable programme channels, and TVRO. For each country, a general article on the current cable and satellite situation is followed by listings of government and regulatory bodies, trade associations, telecoms, cable networks, relay systems, up-grade systems, programme channels, space segment, programme producers and consultancy.

Directory of international broadcasting. Annual. London: BSO Publications.
Directory of broadcasting organizations, systems, manufacturers and suppliers in the United Kingdom and throughout the world.

Independent production handbook. Annual. London: Association of Independent Producers.
Guide to independent film and television production in the United Kingdom, with directory listings of production companies, broadcast and cable television companies, trade organizations and festivals, together with a list of AIP members.

International television and video almanac. 1955–. Annual. New York/London: Quigley Publications.
This directory, though primarily American in coverage, has a substantial section on the industry in the United Kingdom with listings of production companies, television stations, cable television operators, as well as an extensive 'Who's who'.

International TV and video guide. Annual. London: Tantivy Press.
Guide with articles on broadcasting and television developments, followed by

directory section for countries of the world, giving statistics, broad surveys of the television and video industry, and lists of organizations. Illustrations of television programmes.

Kemps international film and television yearbook. Annual. London: Kemps Group.
Long-established trade directory for the film and television production industries, with lists of agents, studios, production companies, film libraries and technical services in the United Kingdom and abroad.

Professional tv and radio media directory. Bi-annual. Abingdon, Oxon.: Professional Books.
Directory of the UK television and radio industry, listing key personnel in the BBC, IBA, ITV companies, Channel 4, cable and satellite television, hospital and student broadcasting services, and local and community radio. Also listed are suppliers to the broadcasting industry of production facilities, specialist services and equipment.

Screen International film and TV yearbook. 1945–. Annual. London: King Publications.
General trade directory listing film and television production companies, studios, cinemas and facilities houses, together with an extensive 'Who's who' section on actors, directors, producers and writers.

4.3 Company information and industry sector surveys

Sources of information about the structure and finances of the television and radio companies can be found from their annual reports and accounts, as published and/or deposited with the Companies Registration Office, or in general company information sources, such as the *Stock Exchange Official Yearbook* or the McCarthy or Extel services. However, a few specialist services publish industry sector surveys of the television and radio industries.

Financial Times Business Information. *Key issue briefs*. 1982–. London: Financial Times Business Information Consultancy.
Series monitoring developments in the communications industry in the UK, Europe and the USA, as reported in the media, giving an overview of trends and changes in the sector. Separate briefs cover cable television, radio, satellite communications, teletext and videotex.

Inter Company Comparisons. *ICC financial surveys*. 1979–. Annual. London: ICC Financial Surveys.
Financial and market profiles on quoted and unquoted companies within particular industry sectors, including cinema, TV and radio producers. Each entry

contains three-year figures for turnover, pre-tax profits, assets, liabilities, ratio on capital employed and profit margins.

Key Note Publications. *Key Note reports*. London: Key Note Publications.
Series of over 200 reports on a wide range of industrial and commercial market sectors, including commercial radio, commercial TV and videotex, each covering the industry structure, market size, recent developments, future prospects and major company profiles.

4.4 Statistical sources

Statistics on most aspects of broadcasting in the United Kingdom, including radio and television manufacturing, production and distribution, television ownership and audiences, are collected and published by various official and non-official organizations.

Official statistics

Official statistics in the UK from the Government Statistical Service are collected by the statistics divisions of individual Government departments and agencies and, in many cases, are co-ordinated and published by the Central Statistical Office through Her Majesty's Stationery Office (HMSO).

For statistics of production and distribution, it is useful first to consult the Standard Industrial Classification Scheme for the appropriate activity codes used by most of the official statistical series.

Central Statistical Office. *Standard Industrial Classification. Revised 1980.* London: HMSO, 1979. iii, 69 pp.
The official system of industrial classification, whereby all economic activities of production, or services, in the United Kingdom are classified into broad classes and then sub-divided into progressively narrower groups and activities so that the classification can be used with varying amounts of detail, and for differing purposes. These Standard Industrial Classification (SIC) codes follow the same broad principles as the relevant international standards. Many official statistical publications organize their statistics according to SIC codes, so it is necessary to ascertain the code for the required activity first, before consulting the source.

Central Statistical Office. *Indexes to the Standard Industrial Classification. Revised 1980.* London: HMSO, 1981.
Numerical and alphabetical indexes to the SIC, enabling the researcher to trace activity codes for specific industries, as well as related areas of industrial activity.

The most relevant groups of SIC codes to the broadcasting industry and services in the United Kingdom are given in Table 9:

Table 9.   Standard Industrial Classification codes relevant to broadcasting

Class	Group	Activity	Description
34	344	3441	Telegraph and telephone apparatus and equipment
		3443	Radio and electronic capital goods
		3444	Components other than active components, mainly for electronic equipment
	345	3452	Gramophone records and other pre-recorded tapes
		3454	Electronic consumer goods and miscellaneous equipment (including the manufacture of domestic radio receivers and video cassette recorders)
61	615	6150	Wholesale distribution of household goods (including radio and television receivers, video cassette recorders)
64	648	6480	Retail distribution of household goods (including retailers of radio and television receivers and video cassette recorders)
79	790	7902	Postal services and telecommunications (including British Telecom, cable company and associated relay stations' telecommunications services)
84	846	8460	Hiring out of consumer goods: 1. Television and radio receivers
97	974	9741	Radio and television services. Broadcasting and local relay stations for radio and television on air, or over cable

Business Statistics Office

The Business Statistics Office was set up in 1969 to co-ordinate an integrated system of collecting industrial statistics, whereby over 400,000 firms in the United Kingdom are required to supply (either quarterly or monthly) figures of their production, orders and sales. Results of these statistical submissions appear in the *Business monitors* series, which are the primary and, in many cases, only source for this information. They are arranged by the SIC (80) activity codes. Most industries have their own *Business monitor*.

Business monitors are organized as follows: Series P (Production Monitors) — PA (annual series), PQ (quarterly series), PM (monthly series); Series SD (Services and Distributive Monitors); Series M (Miscellaneous Monitors).

Business monitors: annual series

The PA series of Annual Census of Production Monitors contains statistics on the structure of manufacturing industry — total sales, stocks, work in progress, capital expenditure, operating ratios, employment, wages, and analysis of cost and output.

Business Statistics Office. *Business monitor: Report on the census of production.* Annual. London: HMSO.

PA 344   *Telecommunications equipment, electrical measuring equipment, electronic capital goods and passive electronic components.*
Covers SIC (80) activity codes 3441–4, and includes the output and costs, capital expenditure, employment and labour costs within the telecommunications manufacturing industry.

PA 345   *Miscellaneous electronics equipment.*
Covers SIC (80) activity codes 3452–4, and includes statistics for the manufacturers of gramophone records and other pre-recorded tapes, domestic aerials and other television equipment and components, radio and television receivers, and video cassette recorders.

Business monitors: quarterly series

The PQ quarterly series gives comprehensive, up-to-date sales figures for over 4,000 products, including the number of products, total sales value, imports and exports (collected by HM Customs and Excise), prices and employment. They appear approximately three months after the quarter to which they refer.

Business Statistics Office. *Business monitors: Production series.* Quarterly. London: HMSO.

PQ 3441   *Telegraph and telephone equipment.*
Covers telephone exchange equipment; PMBX; transmission equipment for telephone, telegraph, radio-relay and microwave systems; telecommunications equipment.

PQ 3443   *Radio and electronic capital goods.*
Includes radio and television transmitters; closed-circuit television equipment; radar equipment

PQ 3452   *Gramophone records and pre-recorded tapes.*
Includes video recordings.

PQ 3453   *Active components and electronic sub-assemblies.*
Includes domestic aerials; television and radio tuners; television line output and EHT transformers; cathode-ray tubes; and integrated circuits.

PQ 3454   *Electronic consumer goods and miscellaneous equipment.*
Includes television and teletext receivers; radio receivers; video cassette recorders.

Business monitors: monthly series

The PM monthly series is available only for a limited number of industries. They contain volume indices of sales and orders, with five-year comparisons.

Business Statistics Office. *Business monitors: Production series*. Monthly. London: HMSO.
PM 1000   *Engineering*.

> Includes volume index numbers for all combined engineering industries together, as well as divided into broad categories (e.g. electrical engineering industry) and then specific industries, according to the SIC (80) activity codes (e.g. 3443 radio and electronics capital goods). Statistics give five-year comparisons for total sales, and then divided into home and export sales.

Business monitors: Service and Distributive series

The SD series deals with aspects of the service industries and distributive trades, and covers the areas of finance houses, consumer credit, computer services and retailing.

Business Statistics Office. *Business monitors: Service and Distributive series*. London: HMSO.
SDM 28   *Retail sales*.

> Includes the value of retail sales per week, with weekly figures for the current year, and annual figures for the past five years for comparisons; retail sales analysed by form of organization and by detailed type of business (e.g. electrical and music goods retailers, TV and other hire and repair businesses, etc.).

Business monitors: Miscellaneous series

The M series, which covers subjects outside the scope of the other series, can be issued monthly, annually or quarterly.

Business Statistics Office. *Business monitors: Miscellaneous series*. London: HMSO.
MA4   *Overseas transactions*. Annual.

> Includes tables for the value of overseas transactions in films and television material, and the expenditure and receipts of the BBC and the IBA programme contractors analysed by area of the world and type of transaction.

Central Statistical Office

The Central Statistical Office occupies a central position in the Government Statistical Service. It co-ordinates the statistics collected by other Government departments, and produces the digests needed for central economic and social policies, such as the national accounts and balance of payments. The CSO is also responsible for a number of key statistical publications, including the *Annual abstract of statistics*, the *Monthly digest of statistics*, *Regional trends* and *Social trends*.

Central Statistical Office. *Annual abstract of statistics*. 1946–. Annual. London: HMSO.
Compiled by the CSO in collaboration with the statistics divisions of other Government departments, this abstract covers ten-year comparisons of annual statistics for population, social conditions, law enforcement, education, employment, production, agriculture, transport, distribution and trade, national income and expenditure, prices, etc. The SIC (80) activity headings and codes are used for the production statistics. In the broadcasting field, it covers the current broadcast receiving licences in force for television sets, and annual production figures for radio, television and electronics goods.

Central Statistical Office. *Monthly digest of statistics*. 1946–. Monthly. London: HMSO.
Statistical tables covering national income and expenditure, population, employment, social services, law enforcement, agriculture, production, energy, transport, retailing, trade, finance, prices and wages, and entertainment. Figures given are monthly or quarterly, with comparisons for current and past two years, and annual figures for the past five years. Each issue has a subject index. Tables relevant to broadcasting cover: output of production industries (including electronic engineering); total UK sales of manufactured goods (including SIC (80) codes 3441, 3443, 3452, 3453, 3454 for the electronics industries); the value of imports and exports of telecommunications equipment; export and import volume index numbers analysed by SIC (80) classes (including class 34 for telecommunications and electronics industries); a general index of retail prices analysed by area of expenditure (including entertainment, with and without television); index numbers of producer prices analysed by SIC (80) classes; and current broadcast receiving licences for the United Kingdom.

Central Statistical Office. *Regional trends*. Annual. London: HMSO.
Gathers together detailed information on regional variation in the United Kingdom on a wide range of social, demographic and economic topics. Text, maps and statistical tables cover regional profiles, population, housing, health, law enforcement, education, employment, environment. Figures for the percentages of households owning television sets are analysed by region.

Central Statistical Office. *Social trends*. 1970–. Annual. London: HMSO.
Statistical tables, charts and text, with original sources indicated, cover population, education, employment, income and expenditure, social services, communications and leisure. Relevant statistics are: the ownership of television sets,

with other European country comparisons; radio listening and television viewing figures; and readership of selected magazines, including *Radio Times* and *TV Times*.

Central Statistical Office. *Statistical news*. Quarterly. London: HMSO.
A survey of developments in British official statistics aimed at both the statistician and the general user, with articles and analysis on the latest results from Government statistical publications, and a cumulative subject index. Topics relevant to broadcasting include an annual table and article on the overseas transactions by television companies, giving the earnings from sales of television programmes abroad, and other occasional items on statistics of production.

Department of Employment. *Family expenditure survey*. 1957–. Annual. London: HMSO.
Continuous survey of a representative sample of private households, giving data on expenditure, incomes and other aspects of household finances. Figures are given for average weekly expenditure on purchase of television, video and audio equipment, television and video rentals, and television licences.

Department of Trade and Industry. *British business*. Weekly. London: HMSO.
Weekly magazine, formerly entitled *Trade and Industry*, giving news, articles and statistics about all aspects of UK commerce and industry. Each issue has a 'Business trends' index to the year's issues arranged by subject headings. An article and statistics on the net overseas earnings by television companies from sales of television programmes abroad appear annually.

Office of Population Censuses and Surveys: Social Survey Division. *General household survey*. 1971–. Annual. London: HMSO.
Continuous survey, based on a sample of the UK population living in private households, covering areas of population, housing, employment, education and health. Tables on housing include percentage of households with television sets, videos, etc.

Welsh Office/Y Swyddfa Gymreig. *Digest of Welsh statistics/Crynhoad o ystafegau Cyrmu*. Annual. Cardiff: Welsh Office.
Annual statistics covering population, social conditions, Welsh language, education, production, communications, finance and the environment. A chapter on communications includes summaries of BBC Wales (finances, hours of output, and percentage of population served by UHF and VHF transmissions), the IBA television and radio services in Wales, and Sianel 4 Cymru. The number of broadcast receiving licences current in Wales is also given. Similar statistics of television licences in Northern Ireland and Scotland are given in *Northern Ireland abstract of statistics* (Annual. Belfast: HMSO); *Scottish abstract of statistics* (Annual. Edinburgh: Scottish Office).

Central Statistical Office. *Guide to official statistics.* 1976–. London: HMSO.
An official and comprehensive guide to official and some non-official UK
statistics. Organized into sections for general statistics, environment, population, social conditions, labour, agriculture, production industries, transport,
distribution, public services, prices, the economy, finances, business and overseas transactions. Appendices include a bibliography of sources, a list of Government departmental contacts and an alphabetical keyword index (with many
references to broadcasting, radio and television). Another useful guide to
major current statistical publications is *Government statistics: a brief guide to
sources* (Annual. London: HMSO).

Non-official statistics

Statistics are also collected, and sometimes published, by a variety of non-
govenmental bodies, such as trade associations, societies and research
organizations.

Advertising Association. *Advertising statistics yearbook.* 1983–. Annual.
London: Advertising Association.
Statistical information on broad trends in UK advertising expenditure, compiled from annual and quarterly surveys of the media, the advertisers and the
advertising agencies, and also data from other trade associations — the Independent Television Association and the Association of Independent Radio
Contractors. Statistical tables of annual figures, in many cases dating back to
1970, for cinema, direct mail, poster, press radio and television advertising
revenue.

British Broadcasting Corporation: International Broadcasting & Audience
Research Library. *World radio & television receivers.* Annual. London: BBC.
Statistics of population, and the number of radio and television sets for individ-
ual countries, continents and the world.

British Radio and Electronic Equipment Manufacturers' Association
(BREMA). *The UK market for domestic audio equipment.* Annual. London:
BREMA.
Statistical tables of market development, availability, imports and exports of
radio receivers, tape recorders, music centres, compact disc players and car
radios. Appendices cover tax-rate changes since 1940, radio hire purchase and
rental regulations.

British Radio and Electronic Equipment Manufacturers' Association. *The UK
market for domestic television receivers and video.* Annual. London: BREMA.
Statistics of television sets, including sets in use and market penetration since
1946, market development, imports and exports, trade and manufacturers'

stocks, availability of television and teletext sets, and video recorders. Appendices cover prices of television sets compared with other consumer goods since 1960, a history of television hire purchase and rental regulations, and tax-rate changes since 1946.

European Broadcasting Union (EBU). *International comparison of broadcasting statistics*. 1979–. Annual. Geneva: EBU.
Annual synthesis of data supplied by twenty-eight broadcasting organizations in Europe (including the BBC and IBA for the United Kingdom) on broadcasting institutions, finance, personnel, radio and television programmes, audiences, transmitters and transmission coverage, cable distribution and external broadcasting. Confidential to member organizations.

Independent Television Association. *An introduction to Independent Television*. 1987–. London: ITV Association.
Introductory survey to Independent Television (replacing *ITV facts and figures* (1978–85) with statistical tables on homes with television/teletext sets, television advertising expenditure, ITV net revenue, programme transmissions on ITV, and other information.

Media Expenditure Analysis. *MEAL digest*. Monthly/quarterly. London: Media Expenditure Analysis Ltd.
MEAL is a subscribers' service offering detailed advertising expenditure figures on individual products and brands in television and print media. Figures for television advertising are taken directly from each ITV company's daily post-transmission log; the drawback to their total accuracy is that the figures are based on published rate card costs, though much advertising time is bought at negotiated (and undisclosed) discounts, and not the full rate card rates. MEAL data is available online through various databases, including MAGIC, MAID Systems, Comshare and Interactive Market Systems.

The Performing Right Society. *The Performing Right yearbook*. Annual. London: PRS.
Yearbook covering all aspects of the work of the PRS, and includes statistics of the royalties paid by British and Irish radio and television to the Society.

Other non-official statistics relevant to broadcasting may be traced through *Sources of unofficial UK statistics*, compiled by David Mort and Leona Siddall (Aldershot, Hants: Gower, 1986), which contains details of published statistics from trade associations, research organizations, societies, trade magazines, publishers, national industries and public bodies.

4.5 Legal guides

Broadcasters are affected by a far wider body of statutory and case law than the broadcasting legislation alone. Certainly the various Acts of Parliament, from the *Television Act 1954* onwards, which govern the IBA, and the BBC's Royal Charters and Licences and Agreements establish certain responsibilities and obligations for the broadcasting authorities. However, the broadcasters, as any other institutions, are subject to the law of the land, laws governing competition, defamation, contempt of court, representation of the people, copyright and performing rights, and many other areas. Several legal guides have attempted to draw together this plethora of statute and case law for broadcasters.

Bate, Stephen de B. *Television by satellite — legal aspects.* Oxford: ESC Publishing Ltd, 1987. vi, 146 pp.
Collection of conference papers on the legal and practical questions involving satellite television, including legal issues relating to transmission and telecommunications aspects, as well as to the contents of programmes (copyright, advertising and sponsorship).

Mosteshar, Said and Bate, Stephen de B. *Satellite and cable television: international protection.* London: Oyez Longman Publishing, 1984. xv, 130 pp.
Report bringing together the existing body of law, both domestic legislation and international conventions, on cable and satellite television in the United Kingdom and Europe. Areas covered include legal protection for broadcasters, competition, copyright and performers' rights.

Ploman, Edward W. *International law governing communication and information: a collection of basic documents.* London: Frances Pinter, 1982. xvi, 367 pp.
Collection of all major international legal instruments applicable to telecommunications and information from the United Nations, Unesco, the International Telecommunications Union and other agencies.

Robertson, Geoffrey and Nicol, Andrew G. L. *Media law: the rights of journalists and broadcasters.* London: Oyez Longman Publishing, 1984. 450 pp.
Guide to the legal rights of broadcasters, producers, film makers, programme editors, journalists and anyone who publishes news or views through the communications media. It covers freedom to communicate, defamation, obscenity, copyright, contempt of court, court reporting, relationships with Parliament and Government, public complaints (including the Broadcasting Complaints Commission), and regulation of the media (particularly the statutory obligations of the IBA, the work of the BBC).

Townley, Stephen and Grayson, Edward. *Sponsorship of sport, arts and leisure: tax and business relationships*. London: Sweet and Maxwell, 1984. xliii, 333 pp.
Detailed, practical guide to the legal background to sports and leisure sponsorship in the United Kingdom, particularly in relation to broadcasting. Regulation by the BBC, the IBA and the EBU is discussed, with citing of both statute and case law.

4.6 Dictionaries and glossaries

Special terminology and jargon abounds in broadcasting, particularly in television engineering and production, and the related areas of advertising, media studies, telecommunications and the 'new technologies'. In an industry with a decidedly transatlantic flavour, many terms used in the United Kingdom are of American origin, therefore some dictionaries from the United States have been included. However, this is not always so and in some cases the use of terms is quite different to that across the Atlantic. These are dynamic, rapidly-changing industries where the terminology changes constantly and terms become quickly dated or obsolete, so only recently published works have been included.

Aries, S. J. *Dictionary of telecommunications*. London: Butterworths, 1981. 329 pp.
Comprehensive guide to the terminology of telecommunications in the UK and the USA, containing definitions of varying lengths, occasionally with explanations and diagrams.

Armstrong, Brian. *The glossary of tv terms*. London: Barrie and Jenkins, 1976. 94 pp.
This light-hearted guide to the television production industry 'shop-talk' contains 1,200 regularly used phrases, expressions and jargon, from 'A and B rolls' to 'Zip-up tower'.

BKSTS dictionary of audio-visual terms, edited by Bernard Happe. London: Focal Press, 1983. 138 pp.
Collection of 2,400 entries for technical terms, abbreviations and acronyms used in the film and television industries. The short definitions occasionally have diagrams or illustrations. Appendices: image areas and picture aspect ratios (for television and motion pictures); television single waveforms and colour bars; and the electro-magnetic spectrum.

Connors, Tracy Daniel. *Longman dictionary of the mass media and communication*. New York: Longman, 1982. 256 pp.
Over 7,000 entries on a wide range of subjects within the mass media world, including broadcasting, television, advertising, marketing and film.

Delson, Donn and Michalove, Edwin. *Delson's dictionary of cable, video and satellite terms*. Thousand Oaks, Calif.: Bradson Press, 1983. 63 pp.
Compact dictionary of commonly used terms in the cable and satellite television industry; UK, US and international in coverage.

Graham, John. *The Penguin dictionary of telecommunications.* Harmondsworth, Middlesex: Penguin Books, 1983. 199 pp.
Collection of over 1,500 terms relating to telephony, data transmission, radio and television. Terms have been spelt, and defined, in accordance with international practice and the convention within the television industry, in which the North American influence is evident. Published in the United States as *The Facts on File dictionary of telecommunications* (New York: Facts on File, 1984).

International Telecommunications Union. *Provisional glossary of telecommunications*. Geneva: ITU, 1979. 948 pp.
Tri-lingual glossary (English/French/Spanish) of 15,000 telecommunications terms in each language, based on analysis of the CCIR and CCITT texts.

Longley, Dennis and Shain, Michael. *Dictionary of information technology*. London: Macmillan, 1982. 381 pp.
Encyclopaedic dictionary of over 6,000 terms and phrases used in information technology, including telecommunications, broadcasting, data transmission, videotex and consumer electronics.

Meadows, A. J., Gordon, M. and Singleton, A. *A dictionary of new information technology*. London: Century Publishing, 1982. 206 pp.
Dictionary aimed at bringing together and codifying the specialized terms currently in use in the various constituent parts of this diverse field, including cable and satellite television, videotex and computers. Key terms and techniques are described at length, and act as reference points to more specialized entries.

O'Sullivan, Tim, Hartley, John, Saunders, Danny and Fiske, John. *Key concepts in communication*. London: Methuen, 1983. xiv, 270 pp. (Studies in Communication).
Multi-disciplinary glossary of commonly-used terms in communication, cultural and media studies. Over 280 entries, varying in length from a few lines to several pages, offer a brief definition followed by a discussion of the origins and usage, cross-references and further reading.

Roberts, R. S. *Dictionary of audio, radio and video*. London: Butterworths, 1981. 248 pp.
Dictionary of British and American terms used in audio, radio and video engineering, giving definitions and explanations of their meaning and applications.

Appendices cover classification of radio frequencies and emissions, lists of commonly-used acronyms and abbreviations, and European television system standards.

van Minden, Jack J. R. *Dictionary of marketing research*. London: St James Press, 1987. 200 pp.
Glossary of some 2,000 terms relevant to the marketing research practitioner, covering the media and media research among other topics. Arranged in two parts: an alphabetically arranged list of all terms included in the book with page references; a subject or 'concept' arrangement of full definitions of all terms.

Watson, James and Hill, Anne. *A dictionary of communication and media studies*. London: Edward Arnold, 1984. 185 pp.
Dictionary for students of mass communications and media containing 1,000 entries for terms in broadcasting, radio, television, cinema and the press. Entries include definitions, technical meanings, relevant quotations and references to further reading.

4.7 Production manuals

Manuals on radio and television production or engineering are as necessary for those already working in the field — practitioners or trainees — as for students or those who may want to pursue a career in broadcasting. A wide range of manuals is produced by the broadcasting organizations, professional associations and specialist publishers. Only a selection can be listed as a guide to the types of manuals, the range of production areas covered and sources for other manuals.

Alkin, Glyn. *Sound recording and reproduction*. London: Focal Press, 1981. 224 pp.
Manual for the professional recording engineer and the amateur.

Alkin, Glyn. *TV sound operations*. London: Focal Press, 1975. 176 pp.
Guide to the art and practice of sound recording covering all areas of studio acoustics, equipment, types of recording and editing. Diagrams, glossary of terms and further reading list.

British Broadcasting Corporation. *Writing for the BBC*. London: BBC, 8th edn, 1988. 103 pp.
Guidance for potential contributors who wish to write for radio and television. Information on the organization of the BBC, writing for radio and television, how to submit material, with specimen pages of various types of scripts, and useful addresses.

British Broadcasting Corporation: Television Training. *BBC Television training manuals*. Borehamwood, Herts.: BBC Television Training, 1986–.
Series of illustrated manuals on production methods and techniques used in television documentary and drama programmes. Titles include: *After tea we'll do the fight* . . . by Mike Crisp (1987); *Editing film and videotape* by Ed Boyce (1986); *From script to screen: documentaries* by Gordon Croton (1986); *Shooting on location* by Peter Jarvis (1986); *Stand by studio!* by Brian Phillips (1987); *Directing situation comedy* by Harold Snoad (1988).

Bermingham, Alan *et al. The small television studio: equipment and facilities.* London: Focal Press, 1976. 163 pp.
Manual on planning the facilities, functions and equipment of a typical small television studio. Diagrams, glossary and reading list.

Bland, Michael and Mondesir, Simone. *Promoting yourself on radio and television*. London: Kogan Page, 2nd edn, 1987. 128 pp.
Manual for those appearing before the camera or microphone, giving techniques for interviewees, with sample interviews, and guidance on making the best use of the opportunity for promotion and advertising.

British Kinematograph, Sound and Television Society. *BKSTS training manuals*. London: BKSTS, 1972–.
Series of technical training manuals made up from papers given at various lectures and courses by distinguished television engineers. Titles include: *Image quality and control of motion picture and television film* (2nd edn, 1973); *Photographic sound recording and reproduction* (1975); *16mm production for television* (1974); *Sound for film and television* (3rd edn, 1973); *Television technology* (1972); *Video recording systems present and future* (1972).

Davis, Desmond. *The grammar of television production*. London: Barrie and Jenkins, 3rd edn, 1974. 80 pp.
Standard textbook on television production by noted film and television director, with simple, illustrated guidelines arranged in sections on editing, composition, camera, recording and filming.

Englander, A. Arthur and Petzold, Paul. *Filming for television*. London: Focal Press, 1976. 266 pp.
Illustrated manual on the contribution of film (and the camera operator) to television, covering planning, reconnoitring, location and studio shooting, equipment, lighting and types of programmes.

Evans, Elwyn. *Radio: a guide to broadcasting techniques*. London: Barrie and Jenkins, 1977. 175 pp.
Manual on the techniques of radio production, including scriptwriting,

interviewing, discussion programmes, disc jockeys, phone-ins, drama, documentaries and outside broadcasts.

Hulke, Malcolm. *Writing for television*. London: Adam and Charles Black, 1980. 263 pp.
Handbook for aspiring writers for television, which covers step-by-step the techniques of scriptwriting and production, concentrating on drama, but also covering commercials, documentaries, news bulletins, educational programmes and presentation.

McLeish, Robert. *The technique of radio production: a manual for broadcasters*. London: Focal Press, 2nd edn, 1988. 288 pp.
Manual of radio production techniques based on BBC radio practice.

Millerson, Gerald. *The technique of television production*. London: Focal Press, 11th edn, 1985. 448 pp. (Library of Communication Techniques).
Established standard textbook on television production used by broadcasting, film and television schools and in training. A practical manual which covers all aspects of production — the studio, television engineering, cameras, editing, lighting, scenery, make-up, sound, film, videotape, graphics, visual effects, location and production routines. Glossary and reading list. Other works by Gerald Millerson include: *Basic tv staging* (2nd edn, 1982); *Effective tv production* (2nd edn, 1983); *Tv lighting methods* (2nd edn, 1982); *Video camera techniques* (1983).

Nisbett, Alec. *The technique of the sound studio*. London: Focal Press, 4th edn, 1979. 560 pp. (Library of Communication Techniques).
Standard manual on sound in television and radio, covering studios, microphones, stereo, sound effects and editing. Glossary, book list.

Parker, Bruce and Farrell, Nigel. *Tv and radio: everybody's soapbox*. Poole, Dorset: Blandford Press, 1983. 192 pp.
Entertaining advice to those appearing on radio or television on production techniques, interview techniques and legal issues.

Redfern, Barrie. *Local radio*. London: Focal Press, 1978. 164 pp.
Manual for a small radio station, explaining studio layout, equipment, production techniques, and the various types of programme formats from studio interviews and discussions to phone-ins and outside broadcasts.

Rowlands, Avril. *The production assistant in tv and video*. London: Focal Press, 1987. 211 pp.
The production assistant is an essential part of the team in television who, acting as the director's personal assistant, is involved at every stage of the

production — planning, organizing, filming on location and in the studio. This guide to what is expected of a production assistant is for both the student of broadcasting and for those intending making a career in television or video production.

Sheppard, Roy. *The DJ's handbook: from scratch to stardom*. Poole, Dorset: Javelin Books, 1986. 192 pp.
Practical guide by former disc jockey giving advice on sound quality, lighting equipment, phone-ins and how to get into radio.

Tyrrell, Robert. *The work of the television journalist*. London: Focal Press, 2nd edn, 1981. 180 pp.
Primer for those new to television on the work of television journalists, covering writing, directing, editing, reporting, interviewing and presentation.

Yorke, Ivor. *The technique of television news*. London: Focal Press, 2nd edn, 1987. 214 pp. (Library of Communication Techniques).
Guide for journalists or aspiring journalists to the processes of gathering, processing and transmitting television news. Aspects covered include writing, reporting, editing, foreign assignments, production and presentation, all brought up to date to embrace the electronic newsroom, videotex, cable and satellite television.

4.8 Programme information: companions, guides and indexes

It can be difficult finding out information about radio and television programmes. Though it is possible to approach the broadcasting organizations — the BBC, the IBA, Channel 4 or the ITV companies — for information about their programmes, the results may not be entirely satisfactory, depending on whether the programme is current or not, and how much information is required. Researching through the programme journals — *Radio Times* and *TV Times* — can produce interesting material on programmes, but it can be a lengthy process. There are now many illustrated companions to popular programmes, such as *The Avengers*, *The Professionals*, *Coronation Street*, *East-Enders*, *Brookside* and *Dallas*. In many cases there may also be 'novelizations' of the story lines from such long-running series as *Emmerdale Farm* or *East-Enders*.

However, for quick information about programmes — date of transmission, production company and team, cast and plot synopsis — the programme companions and guides are the basic published sources. Whether they have been designed as aids to the memory for the armchair viewer or as serious reference works for the researcher, they are invaluable in providing information about programmes. As so many programmes shown on television in the United Kingdom are from the United States or international in origin, not to mention the popularity of British programmes in America and overseas, a few American reference works have been included.

British Broadcasting Corporation. *BBC programme index*. Cambridge: Chadwyck-Healey, 1979–. Microfiche.   •
BBC radio and television programmes since 1979 arranged in four sequences of titles, contributors, subjects and the main entries. Details given include programme title, date, channel, time, producer and brief descriptive annotation.

British Broadcasting Corporation. *BBC Television drama index, 1936–75*. Cambridge: Chadwyck-Healey, 1976. Microfiche.
Microfilmed version of the BBC card catalogue of plays, drama series and serials shown on television since 1936. Collection arranged in three sequences — authors, titles and chronological, each entry having details of director, producer, actors, transmission and repeat dates.

Brooks, Tim and Marsh, Earle. *The complete directory to prime time network tv shows, 1946–present*. New York: Ballantine Books, 3rd edn, 1985. 1,125 pp.
Compendium of over 3,000 American peak-hour television shows, with detailed programme billings including cast, synopses and history of the programmes. This contains far more detailed information on American series popular on British television (*Dallas*, *Hill Street Blues* or *Cagney and Lacey*, for example) than the programme companions published in the United Kingdom.

Brown, Les. *Les Brown's encyclopaedia of television*. New York: Zoetrope, revised edn, 1982. 496 pp.
American source-book for television organizations, personalities and programmes. It covers many US series shown on British television, and the many British programmes shown in the United States. Illustrations.

Gifford, Denis. *The golden age of radio: an illustrated companion*. London: Batsford, 1985. 319 pp.
An entertaining and nostalgic companion to the programmes and personalities of the 'golden age of radio', the services of the BBC and some commercial stations such as Radio Luxembourg from the 1930s to the 1960s. Entries for programme titles, catch-phrases, characters, dance bands, entertainers and personalities. Illustrations.

Granada Televsion. *Granada Television programme index. Year twenty-one: 3 May 1956 to 2 May 1977*. London: Granada Television, 1977. 132 pp.
A catalogue of the programmes produced and transmitted by Granada Television since it began in 1956. It is also an indication of many programmes networked nationally throughout the ITV system for that period. Arranged into two sequences: programmes listed by categories with date; an alphabetical

index by programme title with details of content, director or producer, writer, date and running time.

Halliwell, Leslie and Purser, Philip. *Halliwell's television companion*. London: Grafton Books, 3rd edn, 1986. 941 pp.
Compendium of over 10,000 entries for television programmes and personalities arranged in one alphabetical sequence. Programme entries include details of country of origin, year of transmission or production, number and length of episodes, colour or black and white, production company, synopsis, credits with cast, awards received and extracts from reviews. Useful reference work despite rather personal and often idiosyncratic comments, and occasional inaccuracies.

Passingham, Kenneth. *The Guinness book of television facts and feats*. Enfield, Middlesex: Guinness Superlatives, 1984. 298 pp.
Collection of facts about milestones in television history, with dates, statistics, anecdotes and programme information. Name, subject and programme title indexes.

Preston, Mike. *Tele-tunes; television and film music on record*. 1979–. Annual (quarterly supplements). Hastings: Tele-tunes Publications.
Alphabetical listing by title of theme music and scores of films, television programmes and commercials. Entries contain details of programme title, channel, transmission date, title of music, composer, performers, record label and number.

4.9 Biographical dictionaries

Biographical dictionaries can be broadly categorized as either current 'who's whos' or retrospective dictionaries.

At present there are few separately published 'who's whos' for those currently prominent in broadcasting, whether in front of the camera or microphone, or behind as production or administrative personnel. Some general directories for the film and television industry, already described in Chapter 4, such as the *Screen International film and tv yearbook*, have 'who's who' sections. Biographies also appear for actors or presenters in casting directories like *Spotlight* and *Network International*, or for producers, directors and writers in the membership lists or directories of professional organizations, such as the *Directors Guild of Great Britain directory of members*. There are no retrospective biographical dictionaries for broadcasters, equivalent to a 'Who was who in broadcasting' or the *Dictionary of scientific biography*. However, past current dictionaries are now useful for retrospective research: *Who's who in broadcasting* (London: Pitman, 1933); *Radio & television who's who* (London: Vox Mundi/George Young, 1st edn, 1947; 2nd edn, 1950; 3rd edn, 1954).

Directory of women working in film, tv and video. London: Women's Film, TV and Video Network, 1984. 122 pp.
Directory of women skilled and experienced in all areas of production from designers, electricians, film editors, camera operators, to producers and directors. Entries include occupation, main area of experience, union membership, qualifications and production credits.

Who's who in broadcasting. Ayr: Carrick Publishing, 2nd edn, 1985. 210 pp.
1,000 short biographies of broadcasting administrators and production personnel, though not many on-air personalities. Entries, compiled through self-completion questionnaires, contain details of current position, birth, education, career, production credits and address.

Who's who on radio. Kingswood, Surrey: World's Work, 1983. 220 pp.
Biographical entries for reporters, commentators, correspondents, newsreaders, disc jockeys and musicians on radio.

Who's who on television. London: ITV Books and Michael Joseph, 3rd edn, 1985. 272 pp.
Popular 'who's who' for viewers with over 1,000 entries for 'the best known faces on British television' — actors and personalities.

4.10 Programme journals

Programme journals can be a valuable source of information about programmes and personalities, through both the programme billings and any accompanying articles or interviews.

However, for retrospective research, the programme journals can be less than satisfactory. Neither of them has cumulative indexes, so searching for billings and information on past programmes, without first already knowing the exact transmission date of the programme, can be very laborious. *Radio Times* articles (though not billings) are indexed by the FIAF *International Index to Television Periodicals* (q.v.), but not the *TV Times*.

Another problem with researching from the *Radio Times* or *TV Times* is that because they go to press some time in advance of the programme week they cover, during which time there can be later changes to the programme schedules, the transmission times, or even the actual programmes shown, often are not as billed. These changes might be due to a programme being pulled from the schedules because of an over-running news bulletin, or possible offence caused by the subject in relation to a recent disaster or event. For whatever reason, they cannot be assumed always to be entirely accurate as to the programmes that were shown. Only the programme schedules or post-transmission logs would give reliable transmission information.

A final problem for the researcher is that the information given on programme casts and credits in the billings, particularly purchased programmes from the USA or elsewhere, is often quite inadequate.

Currently the BBC and the ITV companies (jointly through Independent Television Publications) own the copyright on information about forthcoming BBC and ITV/Channel 4 programmes, and therefore have the monopoly of advance programme listings for their own programme journals — *Radio Times* and *TV Times*. This monopoly was challenged in 1985, but upheld by the Monopolies and Mergers Commission (*The British Broadcasting Corporation and Independent Television Publications Ltd* (Cmnd 9614) London: HMSO, 1985).

Cable television services have promotional programme listings journals — *British Cable TV Programme Guide* and *National Cable and Satellite Guide*, and *Satellite TV Europe* for satellite-delivered programme services.

British Cable TV Programme Guide. 1985–. Monthly. Oxford: British Cable Services Ltd, 1985–.
Formerly entitled *Cable TV Guide*, this programme journal for subscribers to British Cable Services contains listings for Sky Channel, Lifestyle, Screensport, Children's Channel, Premiere and MTV programmes, with illustrated section of brief programme descriptions.

National Cable and Satellite Guide. 1986–. Monthly. Croydon, Surrey: Cable Guide.
Glossy programme journal for cable television services with articles, interviews and a reference guide to programmes on Arts Channel, Bravo, Cable News Network, Home Video, MTV, Premiere, Sky Channel, Super Channel, Screensport, Children's Channel, TV5, Worldnet.

Radio Times. 1923–. Weekly. London: BBC Enterprises Ltd.
Reputable programme journal for BBC television and radio services, containing illustrated articles, interviews, letters page, crosswords and generally informative programme billings. Chadwyck Healey publish a microform edition of *Radio Times*.

Satellite TV Europe. 1986–. Monthly. London: 21st Century Publishing.
Articles on European satellite television and programmes, with listings for Sky Channel, Premiere, Super Channel, Filmnet, TV5, Worldnet, Screensport, MTV, TV3, Arts Channel, 3Sat, Sat1 and others.

TV Times. 1955–. Weekly. London: Independent Television Publications.
Popular illustrated magazine covering ITV and Channel 4 programmes, with billings, interviews, articles and pull-out supplements on popular programmes. The programme listings tend to be less detailed than those in *Radio Times*. *TV Times* is published in separate editions for each of the fourteen ITV regions, including a local edition for the Channel Islands (*Channel TV Times*) and an

edition for Wales containing a Welsh language supplement (*Sbec*) for programmes on S4C.

4.11 Periodicals

Broadcasting is a rapidly changing area of public life in the United Kingdom,
with new technical innovations and Government initiatives constantly
expanding the range and type of services available. In such an area, periodical
literature is especially useful, if not essential, in providing the latest information
on new developments and services. Broadcasting is covered by a wide range of
types of periodicals — trade papers, general magazines, house journals, technical press, academic journals, trade union newsletters and professional society
bulletins.

Admap. 1964–. Weekly. London: Admap Publications Ltd.
Magazine for the advertising and marketing industry, with articles on television
and radio advertising, and audience research.

Airwaves. 1984–. Quarterly. London: Independent Broadcasting Authority.
Formerly *Independent Broadcasting* (1974–84). IBA house journal which contains illustrated articles by staff and contributors from the radio and television
industry on all aspects of broadcasting in the UK and abroad. Strong on IBA
policy, and audience research findings.

Ariel. 1936–. Weekly. London: BBC.
BBC staff newspaper with news stories, general articles on BBC policy and
developments, often by the Director-General and senior staff, obituaries, job
vacancies and retirement notices.

BETA News. 1985–. Bi-monthly. London: Broadcasting and Entertainment
Trades Alliance.
Formerly *The Association of Broadcasting Staff Bulletin* (1942–72), *Broadcast*
(1973–8) and *ABStract* (1978–85). Trade union members' journal with news,
conference reports and developments in sections of the broadcasting industry
represented — the BBC, IBA, ITVA and ILR.

British Telecommunications Engineering. 1982–. Quarterly. London: Institution of British Telecommunications Engineers.
Formerly *The Post Office Electrical Engineers Journal*. Journal for British
Telecom and Post Office engineers covering telecommunications, particularly
television engineering standards and developments.

Broadcast. 1973–. Weekly. London: International Thomson Publishing.
Formerly *Television Mail* (1959–73), and incorporating *Television Weekly*

(1983–5). *The* trade magazine for the broadcasting industry in the United Kingdom including television, radio, satellite and cable television, advertising, video and facilities houses. It contains news, analysis, articles, statistics, diary of events and audience research ratings. The *Invision* supplement, issued ten times a year, covers production technology with articles and product reviews.

Broadcast Systems Engineering. 1985–. Monthly. Croydon, Surrey: Link House Magazines.
Commercial magazine for engineers and technicians with articles on radio, audio, television and video studio engineering, and reviews of new products and equipment.

Cable & Satellite Europe. 1984–. Monthly. London: 21st Century Publishing.
Glossy magazine with news and features on UK and European cable and satellite television systems and programme channels, as well as communication satellites, transmission systems and new products.

Cable Television Engineering. 1945–. Quarterly. Solihull, West Midlands: Society of Cable Television Engineers.
Formerly *Relay Engineer.* Professional association members' journal with articles on cable and satellite television engineering, society news, reviews of new products and books.

Cablegram. 1987–. Irregular. London: The Cable Television Association.
Formerly *Cablevision News* (1973–84). Newsletter of the trade association for the cable operators and programme providers. Contains items on cable systems, legislation, sponsorship, CTA news, JICCAR cable audience research findings, and a contacts guide.

Combroad. 1966–. Quarterly. London: Commonwealth Broadcasting Association.
Members' journal containing substantial articles, written mainly by Commonwealth broadcasting executives, about the policies, structures and administration of broadcasting in their countries. Other features include news about member organizations, book and equipment reviews.

Communication Research Trends. 1980–. Quarterly. London: Centre for the Study of Communication and Culture.
International survey of communications research. Each issue contains an in-depth review of major research and recent policy developments in a topic, with an annotated bibliography.

EBU Review (Programmes, Administration, Law). 1950–. Bi-monthly. Geneva: European Broadcasting Union.
Journal for member organizations and individuals containing articles, written

by broadcasters, about broadcasting systems and policies in Europe, news about developments in member countries and EBU activities, statistical tables, book reviews and diary of events.

EBU Review (Technical). 1950–. Bi-monthly. Brussels: European Broadcasting Union.
Technical journal concerned with the practice and theory of broadcast engineering, containing original articles, reports of technical committees and meetings, abstracts and reviews, official EBU texts and a calendar.

Electrical and Electronic Trader. 1923–. Weekly. Sutton, Surrey: Consumer Industries Press.
Formerly *Wireless Trader* and *Wireless and Electrical Trader.* Trade paper for radio and television retailers, containing news items on radio, television, video and audio equipment, features, conference reports and new product reviews.

Electrical and Radio Trading (ERT). 1890–. Weekly. Sutton, Surrey: Consumer Industries Press.
Formerly *Electricity.* Trade paper for electrical dealers with trade and product news, special features, promotions, diary of meetings, conferences, trade fairs and company shows.

Electronic Technology: Journal of the Society of Electronic and Radio Technicians. 1965–. Monthly. London: Society of Electronic and Radio Technicians.
Formerly *SERT Journal.* Members' newsletter containing news items and reports, notices of meetings, book reviews and new product reviews.

Electronics and Power. 1871–. Monthly. Stevenage, Herts.: Institution of Electrical Engineers.
Formerly *The Journal of the Institution of Electrical Engineers.* Journal for professional electronics and electrical engineers, containing articles and news items.

Electronics & Wireless World. 1911–. Monthly. Sutton, Surrey: Reed Business Publishing.
Formerly *Wireless World.* Magazine for technicians in radio, electronics, television and allied industries, containing articles, product reviews, research notes, up-dates, calendar and letters.

Electronics Engineer. 1980–. Fortnightly. Harpenden, Herts.: Electronic Engineering Publications.
Newsletter for members of the Institution of Electronic & Radio Engineers and the Society of Electronic & Radio Technicians, with news on electronic and radio technology, and recruitment notices.

Electronics Letters. 1965–. Fortnightly. Stevenage, Herts.: Institution of Electrical Engineers.
Newsletter on current developments in electronic science and engineering, particularly microwave and optical communication.

Electronics Times. 1978–. Weekly. London: Morgan-Grampian Publishers.
Trade paper for the electronics industry, containing articles, news items, business and company news, and product reviews.

Electronics Weekly. 1960–. Weekly. Sutton, Surrey: Reed Business Publishing.
Trade newspaper for the electronics and communications industry, with articles, news items, business and product news.

European Journal of Communications. 1986–. Quarterly. London: Sage Publications.
Academic journal on communication research into mass communications and mass media in Europe containing scholarly articles, periodic overviews of national communications literature, and book reviews.

Film & Television Technician. 1957–. Monthly. London: Association of Cinematograph, Television and Allied Technicians.
Formerly *Journal of the Association of Cine Technicians* (1935–7) and *Cine Technician* (1937–57). Trade union members' newspaper giving news of the activities of the ACTT, and the film and television industry.

Historical Journal of Film, Radio and Television. 1981–. Bi-annual. Abingdon, Oxon.: Carfax Publishing.
'An interdisciplinary journal concerned with the evidence provided by the mass media for historians and social scientists.' It contains historical articles on British broadcasting, archival reports on public records and documents, reviews of television and radio programmes of historical importance, and book reviews.

IEE News. 1964–. Monthly. London: Institution of Electrical Engineers.
Professional association newsletter for electrical and electronic engineers, containing news, features, council reports, members' information, Parliamentary reports, diary of events and obituaries.

IEE Proceedings. 1871–. Stevenage, Herts.: Institution of Electrical Engineers.
Issued in ten parts (A–J) covering all aspects of electrical, electronics, communications and power engineering. Academic journals comprising articles, correspondence, book reviews and abstracts.

Image Technology: Journal of the BKSTS. 1931–. Monthly. London: British Kinematograph, Sound and Television Society.

Members' journal containing BKSTS news, diary of events, articles on training techniques and equipment, standards, products and services.

InterMedia. 1973–. Bi-monthly. London: International Institute of Communications.
Journal for broadcasters and academics on international communications and broadcasting, particularly such issues as satellite broadcasting, copyright, telecommunications law, international news flow and the new technologies. Features include authoritative articles written by practitioners, news briefings, book reviews and conference reports.

International Journal of Advertising. 1983–. Quarterly. London: Cassell.
Formerly *Advertising Quarterly* (1964–78), *Advertising* (1979–81) and *Journal of Advertising* (1982). Academic journal on advertising and marketing published for the CAM Foundation and the Advertising Association, containing lengthy articles, statistics and book reviews.

Journal of Advertising History. 1977–. Bi-annual. Bradford, West Yorkshire: MCB University Press.
History of Advertising Trust journal containing academic articles on the history of advertising, including commercial radio and television, research findings, the preservation of archives and book reviews.

Journal of Broadcasting and Electronic Media. 1955–. Quarterly. Washington, D. C.: Broadcast Education Association.
American academic journal on the media and broadcasting, frequently containing articles by British media practitioners and academics, and about broadcasting in the United Kingdom.

Journal of Media Law and Practice. 1980–. Quarterly. London: Frank Cass.
Legal journal covering media law in the UK and abroad, in particular articles, news briefings and case reports on such issues as broadcasting law and regulation, copyright and performing rights, video recording, control of advertising, the relationship between Government and the media, and the freedom of information.

Journal of the Institution of Electronic and Radio Engineers. 1926–. Monthly. London: Institution of Electronic and Radio Engineers.
Formerly *Journal of the British Institution of Radio Engineers* (1926–62) and *The Radio and Electronic Engineer* (1962–). Members' journal offering original papers, articles, book reviews and information about conferences, courses and exhibitions.

Line Up. 1988–. London: BSO Publications.
Members' journal of the Institute of Broadcast Sound for radio and television sound engineers, containing news, articles, new product reviews and reports on IBS events.

The Listener. 1929–. Weekly. London: BBC Publications.
A weekly magazine for the serious listener and viewer, containing features on broadcasting-related topics, transcripts of programmes and broadcast talks, book and programme reviews.

Media Bulletin. 1984–. Quarterly. Manchester: European Institute for the Media.
Newsletter offering reports on the activities of the European Institute for the Media, and conferences and meetings held by other European institutions, articles on television services and media issues in Europe, up-dates on media developments in European countries, and a diary of forthcoming events. Available in English or French editions.

Media, Culture and Society. 1979–. Quarterly. London: Sage Publications.
Academic journal, from the Polytechnic of Central London School of Communications, intended as a forum for research and discussion on the media within their social, political, cultural and historical context. Topics covered include media and politics, women and the media, media images of society, and public service broadcasting.

Media Week. 1985–. Weekly. London: Media Week.
Trade magazine containing news, features, analysis and statistical data on television, radio, advertising, publishing and the press.

Now Radio. 1986–. Weekly. Kettering, Northants: Now Radio Communications.
Desk-top published newsletter for those interested in all aspects of radio — local, community, pirate and student radio.

On Air/Off Air. 1986–. Bi-monthly. Berkhamsted, Herts.: The Media Project at the Volunteer Centre.
Formerly *Media Project News* (1977–86). Newsletter of the Media Project covering social action programmes on radio and television, often written by broadcasters or welfare agency workers.

Practical Wireless. 1932–. Monthly. Poole, Dorset: Practical Wireless.
Serious hobbies magazine providing constructional projects, articles, features, book reviews and equipment reviews.

Primetime. 1981–. Irregular. London: Wider Television Access (WTVA).
Articles, interviews and episode checklists of such series as *The Saint* and
Minder — for aficionados of old television programmes.

Producer. 1987–. Quarterly. London: Association of Independent Producers.
Formerly *AIP & Co.* (1977–87). Journal for those working in the independent
production sector. Contents include news, competitions, industry analysis,
profiles and articles about the production, distribution and exhibition of independent films and television programmes.

Radio Academy News. 1984–. Quarterly. Bristol: The Radio Academy.
Newsletter for Radio Academy members containing news, articles by broadcasters, conference reports and the Academy annual report.

Radio and Electronics World. 1981–. Monthly. Brentwood, Essex: Radio and
Electronics World Magazines.
Magazine for radio enthusiasts and engineers containing features, product
news, news items on amateur radio and short wave.

Radio Communication. 1925–. Monthly. Potters Bar, Herts.: Radio Society of
Great Britain.
Official journal for amateur radio members of the Radio Society of Great
Britain. Contents include Society news and information, articles, letters, diary
of events and Club news.

Radio Today. 1986–. Bi-monthly. London: TX Publications.
A listings magazine for unlicensed, offshore and community radio stations,
which also includes background articles, news and letters.

Relay. 1981–. Quarterly. London: Relay.
A magazine for those interested in community, ethnic and hospital radio services offering articles, reviews and letters.

Screen (incorporating Screen Education). 1959–. Bi-monthly. London: Society
for Education in Film & Television.
Academic journal for teachers and media workers providing articles on media
education, film and television criticism, and book reviews.

Screen Digest. 1971–. Monthly. London: Screen Digest.
News digest service covering the film and television industry, cable, satellite and
video. Contents include news briefings, statistical tables, calendar of events and
well-researched supplements.

Screen International. 1975–. Weekly. London: King Publications.
Formerly *Daily Cinema* (1915–69), *Today's Cinema* (1969–71) and *Cinema TV Today* (1971–5). Film and television industry trade magazine, containing news, articles, in-production details and reviews.

Sight and Sound. 1932–. Quarterly. London: British Film Institute.
Film and television criticism journal comprising articles, interviews, book and film reviews.

Stage and Television Today. 1880–. Weekly. London: The Stage.
Trade paper for the entertainment industry, with insert supplement, *Television Today*, of news, articles, lectures and conference reports largely concerned with television programming and policies.

Television. 1928–. Bi-monthly. London: Royal Television Society.
The world's earliest journal for television professionals, with articles on the creative, technical, administrative and historical aspects of television.

Television. 1950–. Monthly. London: IPC Magazines.
Magazine for television engineers which contains articles on the developments in and servicing of television and video equipment, trade news, test reports, TV fault finding, news and a service bureau.

Televisual. 1982–. Monthly. London: Centaur Communications.
Formerly *Corporate Video* (1981–2). Business magazine for independent producers, facilities houses and the broadcasting industry. Contents include news, features, trade show information, exhibition details, awards, production directory and diary of events.

The Viewer. 1988–. Quarterly. London: Independent Television Association.
Glossy magazine aiming to provide an outlet for reporting and commenting about Independent Television, particularly as a major British business, employer and exporter.

World Broadcasting Information. Weekly. Caversham Park, Reading: BBC Monitoring Service.
News from broadcasters about developments in radio, television, satellite communications and cable television throughout the world.

4.12 Abstracting and indexing services

As in many other subject areas, there has been an enormous increase recently in the periodical literature for communications and broadcasting, making it increasingly necessary to have good abstracting and indexing services.

Abstracting services, usually published as serials, can either offer full, informative abstracts or indicative abstracts of brief descriptions only. In both cases, full bibliographical details of the article (e.g. author, title, name of journal, volume and part number, page references and date) would be followed by a summary of the text of varying length and an indication of the status of the author.

Indexing services are generally subject-arranged listings of periodical articles with bibliographical details and, at most, a brief annotation of the contents of the article.

General indexing services, notably the *Biography Index*, the *British Humanities Index*, the *Essay and General Literature Index*, the *Research Index* and the *Current Technology Index*, will have many references to broadcasting topics, as will some specialized abstracting services covering related areas to broadcasting, such as *Sociological Abstracts* and *Psychological Abstracts*. However, the following specifically cover communications and broadcasting.

Communication Abstracts. 1978–. Quarterly. Beverly Hills, Calif.: Sage Publications.
An international abstracting service which contains abstracts from over 200 media journals, reports, papers and monographs on mass communication, broadcasting, radio and television. Cumulated author and subject indexes.

Electrical and Electronics Abstracts. 1966–. Monthly. Hitchin, Herts.: INSPEC (Institution of Electrical Engineers).
Formerly *Electrical Engineering Abstracts* (1898–1966). The principal abstracting service in the subject area of electrotechnology, telecommunications and broadcast engineering. Each monthly issue has full abstracts in a classified arrangement, with indexes for authors, bibliographies, books, conferences and corporate authors. A subject index to articles in the abstracts journal is issued six-monthly. Service is available in printed hard-copy, on microform and online.

Electronics and Communications Abstracts. 1961–. Monthly. London: Multi-Science Publishing.
Abstracting service covering periodical articles, patents, conference proceedings and book reviews in the fields of information theory, telegraphy, radar, radio and television. Annual indexes for authors, subjects and patents.

International Index to Television Periodicals. 1979–. Regular. London: International Federation of Film Archives (FIAF).
Indexing service resulting from the collaborative work of librarians and archivists in over 20 countries, co-ordinated by FIAF in London, covering the contents from over 40 world-wide television periodicals. Subjects covered include broadcasting, advertising, television programmes and production, cable and satellite television, and sociological aspects of television. Entries,

arranged by subject, contain bibliographical details and a short summary of the article. Originally issued on cards, with printed biennial cumulations, it changed to a microfiche service in 1983.

Market research abstracts. 1963–. Bi-annual. London: Market Research Society.
Abstracting service which covers over 30 journals in advertising, market research, statistics, psychology and marketing. Entries contain full, descriptive abstracts. Subject and author indexes. .

4.13 Registers of research, theses and dissertations

Valuable research on broadcasting and the media is being undertaken continuously in the academic community, often as part of studies and theses or dissertations for higher degrees. The results of such research projects undertaken in universities and colleges, as well as Government departments and other organizations can, unless the findings are commercially published, be difficult to identify and locate. However, several published indexes do list theses or dissertations, which would then be available at the original university or college, or on loan through the British Library Document Supply Centre. Ongoing research projects on the media can also be traced in published registers of current research.

ASLIB. *Index to theses accepted for higher degrees by the universities of Great Britain and Ireland, and the Council for Academic Awards*. 1950/51–. Bi-annual. London: ASLIB.
This index covers details of the 10,000 or so theses presented for higher degrees in British and Irish universities. Published in two parts each year, it is arranged by broad subject headings, with an extensive and detailed subject index. For full abstracts of all the theses listed, the companion microfiche service, *Abstracts of theses*, should be consulted.

British Library Document Supply Centre. *British reports, translations and theses*. 1981–. Monthly. Boston Spa, West Yorkshire: British Library.
Bibliography of 'grey literature' or semi-published material — including doctoral theses accepted at British universities and polytechnics, and report literature and translations produced by Government bodies, industry and learned institutions. Arranged into subject categories, according to SIGLE (System for Information on Grey Literature in Europe), including 'Mass media', 'Performing arts' and 'Communications'. Entries include details of author, title, corporate authority, pagination, report number, date, ISBN or ISSN, thesis and degree, and Document Supply Centre reference number.

British Library Document Supply Centre. *Current research in Britain*. Volume

3: *Social sciences.* 1978–. Annual. Boston Spa, West Yorkshire: British Library.
Formerly *Research in British universities.* The national register of current research in the social sciences in academic, Governmental and other research institutions. Arrangement is firstly by the name or place of research institution, then by name of researcher, with project and dates. Broad subjects include business studies, economics, education, information science, psychology and sociology, with many research projects on broadcasting and the media. Indexes of university and polytechnic departments, names, study areas and subject keywords.

Centre for Mass Communication Research, University of Leicester. *Register of current and recently completed British research on mass media and mass communication.* 1977–. Occasional. Leicester: The Centre.
Register of research projects on the media undertaken by universities and polytechnics, the broadcasting authorities, institutes and individual researchers. Arrangement by subject headings — television, radio, broadcasting, press, multi-media, advertising, communication and society. Entries contain name of researcher, project title and summary, sponsor, duration of project, institution and degree. Indexes of subject cross-references and contributors.

Economic and Social Research Council. *Information and communication technologies: social science research and training.* London: ESCR, 1986. Volume 1: *An overview of research.* iv, 150 pp.; Volume 2: *National directory.* xxiii, 586 pp. London: ESRC, 1986.
Guide to social science research in the UK, which surveys the work of centres for mass communications research, communication policy and media research, giving details of academic staff, research programmes and published reports. Volume 2 contains entries compiled through a questionnaire for current and planned research projects, with accompanying research and training indexes.

Kittross, John M. *A bibliography of theses and dissertations in broadcasting: 1920–1973.* Washington, D. C.: Broadcast Education Association, 1978. 238 pp.
A listing of over 4,300 studies undertaken for degrees at 199 colleges and universities in the United States, on all aspects of broadcasting, including studies of broadcasting in the United Kingdom. Alphabetical author arrangement, and indexes for subject keywords and broad topics.

4.14 Bibliographies

There are only a handful of separately published bibliographies specifically covering British broadcasting. However, many of the works discussed in other sections, notably such standard histories as Asa Briggs' *History of broadcasting in the United Kingdom* and Bernard Sendall's *Independent Television in Britain*, contain substantial bibliographies or lists of references.

Blum, Eleanor. *Basic books in the mass media*. Urbana, Ill.: University of Illinois, 2nd edn, 1980. xi, 427 pp.
An annotated, selected booklist covering general communications, publishing, broadcasting, editorial journalism, film and advertising; though American, it contains many items on the United Kingdom.

Higgens, Gavin. (ed.) *British broadcasting 1922–82: a selected and annotated bibliography*. London: BBC Data Publications, 1983. 279 pp.
Contains over 1,200 annotated entries for books and periodicals on all aspects of British broadcasting — history, organization, policies, engineering, programmes and personalities. Appendices list periodicals, BBC Engineering Monographs and BBC Lunchtime Lectures.

Langham, Josephine. *Radio research: a comprehensive guide 1975–85. An annotated bibliography of radio research sources*. London: BBC Data Publications, 1986. xvii, 298 pp.
Result of a project, initiated by the Radio Academy and funded by the IBA, intended to present an overview of the state of radio research in the United Kingdom through a descriptive bibliography of accessible research material. It is organized into four parts: BBC research; IBA research; other British research on advertising, local radio, community radio and academic research; and foreign research projects. A list of bibliographies, and separate author and subject indexes complete the work.

Snow, Marcellus S. and Jussawalla, Meheroo. *Telecommunications economics and international regulatory policy: an annotated bibliography*. New York: Greenwood Press, 1986. xiv, 216 pp.
American bibliography containing references and full abstracts for books and articles with an international focus on telecommunications and regulatory economics, including the United Kingdom.

Unesco. *List of documents and publications in the field of mass communications*. 1977–. Annual. Paris: Unesco.
Comprehensive, international bibliography of documents and publications held by the Unesco Communication Documentation Centre. It is divided into three parts: a main list of full entries containing bibliographic details and keyword abstracts; a subject index; and an author index. Good coverage of United Kingdom media.

Wedell, George, Luyken, Georg-Michael and Leonard, Rosemary (eds). *Mass communications in Western Europe: an annotated bibliography*. Manchester:

European Institute for the Media, 1985. xiii, 327 pp. (Media Monograph, No. 6).
Bibliography comprising over 700 annotated entries for books, legislation and reports, published between 1975 and 1985, on mass communications from 20 European countries, including the United Kingdom. Subjects covered include the press, radio, television, film, telecommunications and informatics.

4.15 Ephemera and memorabilia

Ephemera and memorabilia are generally undervalued and largely overlooked sources of information. The ephemera of broadcasting can be leaflets, hand-bills, posters and postcards. Equally valuable would be such memorabilia and collectibles as commemorative issues of postage stamps, cigarette card series, board and card games, toys, children's annuals and comics, and a myriad of other items. Such items would often be produced for the moment, perhaps for immediate promotional use, or as part of off-air exploitation of interest in radio and television programmes. The essence of ephemera is that it is rarely kept for long, is poorly documented and only collected by a few enthusiasts. Past ephemera and memorabilia on broadcasting are now nostalgic or amusing mementoes of earlier days of radio and television and are often eagerly sought-after collectors' items. However, they can also provide valuable information on the social history, programmes and personalities of radio and television.

This category of broadcasting source material is so large and diverse that only a couple of examples of printed collectibles can be included here as an indica-tion, and to acknowledge that these are an interesting but largely overlooked and untapped information resource.

Collections of broadcasting ephemera and memorabilia can be found in the archives and museums described in Chapter 6.

Cigarette cards

From the 1890s, British tobacco companies began issuing cards with packets of cigarettes, starting originally as advertisements but gradually evolving into sets of cards on subjects or themes to be collected. Popular series covered history, monarchs, army uniforms, highwaymen, birds, butterflies, sportsmen, film stars and many other topics. Marking the increasing popularity of radio in the 1930s, *Radio celebrities* (Bristol: W. D. and H. O. Wills, 1st series, 1934; 2nd series, 1935) was issued; the two series each contained fifty portraits and short biographies of 'Stars of the Air' — announcers, actors, comedians, singers and conductors — from announcer Stuart Hibberd ('Good night, everybody, *Good* night') to bandleader Henry Hall ('Hello, everyone, this *is* Henry Hall'). Other sets issued on the subject included *Broadcasting* (Liverpool: Ogden Ltd, 1935).

Children's annuals and comics

Children's literature provides a valuable insight into the impact and influence of broadcasting on young audiences. *Children's Hour* was an immensely popular programme for young audiences, which ran from 1926 until 1961; it was originally presented by radio 'Uncles' and 'Aunts', notably Uncle Mac (Derek McCulloch), and consisted of poetry and short story readings, dramatized series (*Toytown*, *Jennings at School* and *Norman and Henry Bones* (the boy detectives)) and competitions. *The Children's Hour Annual* (London: Collins, 1935-7), edited by Derek McCulloch, provided collections of stories, features and interviews.

Children's comics featuring popular broadcasting personalities also give of a flavour of the times and the enormous popularity of radio. *Radio Fun* (1938-61. Weekly. London: Amalgamated Press) and *TV Fun* (1953-9. Weekly. London: Amalgamated Press) contained strip cartoons, stories and features built around radio, and later television, personalities and characters from Arthur Askey to Benny Hill. *The Radio Fun Annual* (London: Amalgamated Press) collected together the cartoons and stories. Other similar popular magazines included *Radio Magazine* and *Radio Pictorial*.

4.16 Online services

Increasingly, information that was previously available only in printed form is now accessible through computer technology and telecommunications links as online databases and services. Such computerized files or databases are now growing rapidly and, having originally developed in the field of scientific and technical bibliographic databases, they now cover most subject fields and many different types of data. The online market was originally dominated by the United States, and such large database hosts as the Lockheed DIALOG service and Mead Data Central. However, British and European online hosts and databases have recently developed to balance up the market, particularly in the subject areas of news, the media and business information. As the full text of major newspapers and journals becomes available online, so information from a wide range of sources on the media and broadcasting in the United Kingdom will be easily and widely accessible. Some computerized sources of information in the media — the MEAL advertising data or the AGB/BARB Audience Measurement Service — result from the internal computer systems used to analyse and generate the specialized data, which had previously been available to subscribers only in hard-copy or print versions.

Discussion of this area of information sources will be under two headings — online host services, and databases.

Online host services

Online hosts are the computer services companies who develop specialist databases and make them available commercially. The following host services are a selection of those who provide databases relevant to broadcasting, tele-communications or advertising.

COMSHARE INC.
HQ: PO Box 1588, 3001 South State Street, Ann Arbor, MI 48106, USA
UK: 32–34 Great Peter Street, London SW1P 2DP
International computer services company operating in the USA, Canada, Europe, and in the UK since 1971. It offers a range of computing services in financial and marketing management, banking and government.
  Databases: Mentor (a marketing management and research service offering MEAL and Target Group Index data).

DIALOG
HQ: DIALOG Information Services, 3460 Hillview Avenue, Palo Alto, CA 94304, USA
UK: Learned Information Ltd/DIALOG, Woodside Hinksey Hill, Oxford OX1 5AU
The DIALOG Information Retrieval Service originated from the pioneering development by the Lockheed Missiles and Space Company of computerized information storage, and has been providing a commercial service since 1972. It now offers access to nearly 300 separate databases of over 152 million records, with a SearchSave facility to search more than one database using a single command and combined search terms.
  Databases: INSPEC; PTS Marketing and Advertising Reference Service; PsychINFO; Sociological Abstracts.

ESA-IRS
HQ: Via Galileo Galilei, C.P. 64, 00044 Frascati, Italy
UK: IRS-Dialtech, Department of Trade and Industry, Ashdown House, 123 Victoria Street, London SW1E 6RB.
The European Space Agency Retrieval Service is the oldest of the European online hosts. It offers access to over fifty-five databases covering a wide range of subjects.
  Databases: INSPEC; World Reporter; Textline/Newsline/Dataline.

INTERACTIVE MARKET SYSTEMS
HQ: 55 Fifth Avenue, New York, NY 10003, USA
UK: Grosvenor Gardens House, Grosvenor Gardens, London SW1W 0BS
An international company providing time-sharing and other computer services to the media, advertising and marketing industries, who are provided with interactive access and analysis to media and market research data.

Databases: BARB (1982–); JICTAR (1981–2); MEAL; Nielsen TV Index.

MEAD DATA CENTRAL
HQ: PO Box 933, Dayton, Ohio, OH 4501, USA
UK: 1 St Katherine's Way, London E1 9UN
Began in 1970 and now the world's largest resource of full-text databases offering information on case law and regulation, news and current affairs, business and finance, science, technology and medicine.

Databases: NEXIS (Advertising and Marketing Intelligence Abstracts, and BIS Infomat); LEXIS.

PERGAMON ORBIT INFOLINE
HQ/UK: 12 Vandy Street, London EC2A 2DE
Originally Infoline, a small UK host for scientific and technical databases, before being acquired by Pergamon Press in 1980 and transformed into a major host for a wide range of databases, many of which are unique.

Databases: Dun & Bradstreet Key British Enterprises; MAID; Who Owns Whom; and interhost connection with ESA-IRS files.

PREDICASTS INC.
HQ: 11001 Cedar Avenue, Cleveland, OH 44106, USA
Online suppliers of business information since 1960. The PTS databases contain article abstracts, forecasts and statistics from world business and trade publications, investment analysts' reports and industry studies.

Databases: PTS PROMT; PTS Marketing & Advertising Reference Services (MARS); Infomat International Business; PTS Forecasts.

PROFILE INFORMATION
HQ/UK: Sunbury House, 79 Staines Road West, Sunbury-on-Thames, Middlesex TW16 7AH
Profile Information, originally as Datasolve, part of the Thorn–EMI Information Technology Division before being acquired by the Financial Times Group in 1987, offers full-text news and business databases.

Databases: MAGIC; World Exporter; World Reporter.

TELMAR GROUP
HQ: 90 Park Avenue, New York, NY 10016, USA
UK: 87 Jermyn Street, London SW1Y 6JD
Established in 1968, this international computer services company specializes in providing databases, systems and consultancy to the advertising industry throughout the world. Mostly American but some UK data.

Databases: BARB; Target Group Index; Nielsen TV Index; Arbitron.

Databases

This category covers single-source databases, and collections or clusters of databases related by subject coverage or type of data, available under a group or service name.

BARB (Broadcasters' Audience Research Board)
Television audience measurement data supplied by AGB Research to BARB since 1982; covers BBC1, BBC2, ITV and Channel 4 viewing levels and appreciation.
 Producer: BARB, Knighton House, Mortimer Street, London W1N 8AN.
 Hosts: Interactive Market Systems; Telmar Group.

INSPEC
The largest English language database of citations and abstracts in the field of electrotechnology, telecommunications, broadcast engineering and computers from 1969 to date. The online version of *Computer and Control Abstracts*, *Electrical and Electronic Abstracts*, *Physics Abstracts* and *IT Focus*.
 Producer: INSPEC — Institution of Electrical Engineers.
 Hosts: BRS; DATA-STAR; DIALOG; ESA-IRS.

MAGIC (Marketing and Advertising General Information Centre)
Cluster of databases for the advertising and marketing industry, offering full-text information on the media and broadcasting, taken from *Marketing Surveys Index*, MEAL, Mintel Market Intelligence Reports, British Rate and Data, *Campaign*, *Marketing* and *Media Week*.
 Producers: Mintel, MEAL, British Rate and Data, and others.
 Host: Profile Information.

MAID (Market Analysis and Information Database)
A full-text service for the advertising and marketing industry, from the Economist Intelligence Reports, Euromonitors, MEAL data and trade magazines.
 Producers: Economist Intelligence Unit, Euromonitor, MEAL, etc.
 Hosts: MAID Systems; Pergamon Orbit Infoline.

MEAL
Data on advertising expenditure on television and the press in the UK arranged by product categories and brand names.
 Producer: MEAL — Media Expenditure Analysis Ltd.
 Hosts: Comshare; Interactive Market Systems, MAID; Profile.

NEXIS
One of the largest databases in the world with full-text coverage of about 160 newspapers, magazines, wire services and broadcast transcripts, including

Financial Times, The Guardian and BBC Summary of World Broadcasts.
   Producer/Host: Mead Data Central.

PTS Marketing and Advertising Reference Service (MARS)
Citations and abstracts to literature on US and international advertising indus-
try, including broadcasting, from trade and national press 1984–.
   Producer: Predicasts Inc.
   Hosts: BRS; DATA-STAR; DIALOG.

Target Group Index
Demographic, media and marketing data from 1977 based on data collected
through a postal questionnaire to a randomly selected sample of 24,000 of the
adult population each year. In broadcasting areas it measures television viewing
frequency and behaviour, and radio listening.
   Producer: British Market Research Bureau Ltd (BMRB).
   Hosts: Interactive Market Systems; Telmar Group Inc.

Textline
Database providing citations and abstracts of articles from approximately 150
UK and European newspapers and magazines, including *Financial Times,
Daily Telegraph, The Guardian, The Observer*, regional and local newspapers,
and such trade papers as *Campaign* and *Marketing*. It concentrates on
industries, companies, markets, products, legislation, and economic and politi-
cal affairs.
   Producer: Finsbury Data Services Ltd.
   Hosts: Direct from Finsbury Data Services, or as a Gateway service through
ESA-IRS.

   Other database hosts and services offering media-related information can be
traced through the *Online business sourcebook* (Bi-annual. Headland,
Cleveland: Headland Press) and *Cuadra directory of online databases* (Quarterly. New York: Cuadra/Elsevier).

4.17 Videotex services

Videotex in the United Kingdom covers two types of service — viewdata and
teletext.
   Viewdata is a system using television monitors linked by telephone line to
computers to provide on-screen information from computer databanks. Public
viewdata services in the United Kingdom started in 1979 with Prestel, provided
by British Telecom. Information carried is supplied by a wide range of information providers, including publishers, travel agents, public bodies, libraries.
Interactive services, such as tele-shopping, allow the customer to interrogate the
system. Many organizations have private viewdata systems.
   Teletext services utilize the spare or unused lines in the television picture to

transmit on-screen data through a decoder to an adapted domestic television set. Originally developed as a way of providing sub-titling of television programmes for the deaf, it was later decided to provide textual and graphic information for viewers. Teletext is not interactive. Services are provided by the BBC (CEEFAX) and ITV companies (ORACLE).

Viewdata service

Prestel
Frequently changing services relevant to broadcasting, including selected radio and television programme listings, a guide to the National Museum of Photography, Film and Television, and information on television, video and amateur radio.
   Producer: British Telecom.

Teletext services

CEEFAX
Available on BBC1 and BBC2 are listings of the current day's programmes on BBC1, BBC2, BBC Radio, ITV, Channel 4 and S4C, with films on television, BBC educational programmes, TV choice and sub-titled programmes for the week. Also details of BBC shows, videos, records and books currently available.
   Producer: BBC.

ORACLE
Transmitting since 1975, ORACLE provides different services on ITV and Channel 4 in each ITV region. ITV carries a guide to the current programmes on ITV, Channel 4, BBC1 AND BBC2, as well as news, gossip, quizzes, record charts and films. Channel 4 lists details of C4 and S4C programmes, IBA Engineering Information, city news, viewers' letters and telesoftware.
Producer: ORACLE Teletext Ltd.

5

Researching into broadcasting: notes of guidance

The following notes are designed as guidance to researchers approaching the subject of broadcasting, with a few general principles and some specific lines of research indicated. These notes can only skim the surface of a rather broad and complex research area.

5.1 General principles

Formulating the research enquiry is important when embarking on a project — deciding on your objective, exactly what you need to know, the amount of detail and the purpose of the research. Clarity of purpose at the beginning, and then keeping the objective firmly in mind at each stage of the project is important.

Preparatory research is essential before approaching specialist sources. Consult local sources and basic reference works first. One should not always assume that only the specialist library or organization can help, because some of the basic reference works on broadcasting are widely available in most public libraries and can answer many questions. Certainly preparatory research, even if not actually answering the enquiry, can result in a more informed approach to the specialist organization.

Approaching specialist institutions should be done carefully. Many of them are not always totally available to the public, and do not have an obligation to help outside researchers. It is wise to check first in the various guides to archives and libraries, such as *British archives*[1] and *The shorter ASLIB directory of information sources in the United Kingdom,*[2] for the appropriate sources to approach, the conditions of access, and details of opening hours and study facilities. Then a telephone call to check the details, and make an appointment if necessary, is a good idea.

When undertaking research, always keep complete notes on referrals from one source to another, on exact quotes and source references used, and the conditions of use and reproduction of the material found. If this has not been done scrupulously at the time, it will be difficult and time-consuming to reconstruct afterwards.

5.2 Constitutional background and history of broadcasting

The history of broadcasting in the United Kingdom can be traced through its constitutional documents — the various Acts of Parliament, Government and Committee of Enquiry reports, Royal Charters and Licences. Lists of the constitutional texts appear in Chapters 1 and 2 of this book and in some other sources, including the *Researcher's guide to film and television collections*,[3] and with extracts and comments in *British broadcasting* by Anthony Smith (q.v.). The full text of the Acts of Parliament, together with interpretation, can be found in *Halsbury's statutes of England*.[4]

For narratives of the history of broadcasting, there are several authoritative 'official' histories, described in Chapter 4. They cover their subject in considerable detail, with copious footnotes, references and extensive bibliographies leading the reader to further source material.

Biographies, memoirs and diaries of important figures in broadcasting are a valuable source. The autobiographical writings of such influential figures in broadcasting as Lord Reith,[5,6] Lord Clark[7] and Lord Hill of Luton[8] provide valuable background information and insights into the subject.

Literature searches would reveal articles from the newspapers and periodicals. *The Times Index*[9] would provide references to contemporary comment on broadcasting developments this century. Periodical articles can be traced through indexing services, either such general indexes as the *British Humanities Index*[10] or special indexing services like the *International Index to Television Periodicals* (q.v.). If the required topic is current, recent newspaper and periodical articles may be traced through such news online services as *World Reporter* (q.v.), *NEXIS* (q.v.) or *Textline* (q.v.).

From this point, recourse to special libraries or archives will be necessary to trace rarer printed sources or specialist collections.

For the primary source material for the constitution and history of broadcasting — Government and official records — approach must be made to the appropriate archives: the Public Record Office or Post Office Archives for Government papers; the BBC Written Archives Centre; and other institutional archives (outlined in Chapter 6). Useful material may also be in the form of recorded interviews with prominent broadcasters of the past available from sound archives. Access to the archives of some organizations in broadcasting may be limited; approach should be made to the Librarian or Archivist, or possibly the Secretary of the company or body, outlining the research project.

5.3 Broadcasting institutions and services

For a brief overview of the current structure and services of British broadcasting, the Central Office of Information provides two useful sources — *Broadcasting in Britain*[11] and a chapter on television and radio in *Britain: an official handbook*.[12]

For more detailed information about the organizations and services in the broadcasting industry, various directories provide up-to-date information: *Broadcast yearbook and diary* (q.v.), *BFI film and television yearbook* (q.v.), *The professional radio and tv media directory* (q.v.) and *Screen International film and tv yearbook* (q.v.).

The press or publicity offices of most organizations in broadcasting are usually only too willing to supply promotional leaflets giving information about the organization or system.

For fuller information about these bodies — their constitution, current activities and finances — the annual report and accounts is the basic source. The broadcasting authorities — the BBC, the IBA and the Cable Authority — are required to provide annual reports for Parliament, and the radio and television companies, as with all registered companies, have to supply annual reports and accounts according to the Companies Acts. Most will be fully published, but if not they will be available at the Companies Registration Office.

Statistics of broadcasting are compiled by Government departments, trade associations, industry bodies and research organizations.

Coverage of the very latest developments in the industry would be found in the trade press — *Broadcast*, *Campaign* and *Marketing*. Other sources would be a company information service like Extel[13] or such reference works as *Key British Enterprises*[14] and the *Stock Exchange Official Yearbook*.[15] Many of these sources would form the basis of the online services and databases that cover the broadcasting industry — MAGIC (q.v.) and MAID (q.v.). Various company research organizations, such as ICC Company Surveys (q.v.) and Keynote (q.v.), provide regular surveys of the commercial sector of broadcasting, giving analysis of present and future performance.

Further study of the broadcasting industry or individual companies would have to be made through the relevant organizations.

5.4 Programme research

The basic sources for information about programme output are the broadcasting organizations and their programme journals — *Radio Times* for BBC television and radio programmes, *TV Times* for ITV and Channel 4, and the cable systems operators and their cable television guides.

For information about current television or radio programmes, the sources are the programme journals, the summaries of viewing in the daily and weekly newspapers and magazines, and the appropriate frames/pages on Prestel, CEEFAX and ORACLE.

For retrospective research into past programmes, the programme journals are but one of many sources, including programme guides and companions, programme indexes and publicity, newspaper reviews and cuttings, audience research findings and programme archives.

The programme journals — *Radio Times* and *TV Times* — contain billings for each programme transmitted giving, at most, details of the day and time of transmission, title, writer, brief synopsis, short cast list and production credits. Occasionally there may be an accompanying article in the feature section about the programme, or interview with leading actors, the writer or director. However, the programme billings are neither detailed enough nor always accurate. They are often brief and uninformative, particularly in the case of imported programmes. Changes to the schedules may result in the programme eventually shown not being as billed in the *Radio Times* or *TV Times*. Neither of them have indexes of any kind so, unless the exact transmission date of a programme is already known, it will be very time-consuming tracing billings and articles for past programmes. So the programme journals are imperfect tools for programme research.

Perhaps the most common and seemingly simple enquiry is 'when was a particular programme shown', and yet can prove surprisingly difficult to trace. There is no published general programme index to all television and radio programmes shown in the United Kingdom. From some basic reference books, such as *Halliwell's television companion* (q.v.), the year of transmission of major television programmes can be traced. Other published sources giving more precise transmission dates are two microfiche publications, *BBC Television drama index, 1936–76* (q.v.) and the *BBC programme index, 1979–* (q.v.), and the *Granada Television programme index* (q.v.). Otherwise an approach to the broadcasting organizations will be necessary to trace the exact transmission date and time: for BBC programmes, the BBC Programme Correspondence Section; for ITV and Channel 4 programmes, the IBA, Channel 4 or the individual ITV companies; or the BFI Library, whose television programme index covers BBC, ITV and Channel 4. The ITV Weekly Programme Schedules or BBC transmission logs are ultimately the most accurate record of programmes actually shown, their date and exact time of transmission.

For fuller information about programmes, a literature search through such periodical indexing services as the *International Index to Television Periodicals* (q.v.) may produce useful background articles on the production and performers from the trade press, critical journals or enthusiasts' magazines. Information about the programme during production can be found in such trade magazines as *Broadcast* (q.v.) or *Screen International* (q.v.). Press and public opinion of programmes is also valuable source material: programme reviews and criticism usually appear in the newspapers and magazines within a week of transmission, and audience reaction to the programme may be found in the weekly ratings and appreciation reports.

In some cases, notable programmes may have books written about them, either about the making of the programme, such as *The making of The Jewel in the Crown*[16] or *EastEnders: the inside story*,[17] or academic studies of the production process, such as Dorothy Hobson's *Crossroads: the drama of soap opera*.[18] Many popular programmes have published 'spin-offs' or 'tie-ins', particularly long-running soap operas, such as *The Archers*, *EastEnders* and *Emmerdale Farm*, which spawn 'novelizations' using their characters and story-lines.

Further research into the production process would neccessitate visits to the relevant programme archives, for access to the scripts and other production documentation, viewing or listening to the programme itself, and possibly locating and interviewing the production staff on the programme.

5.5 Biographical research

Biographical research can be for the performers on radio and television, for production personnel or broadcasting administrators.

A variety of published sources give biographies of radio and television actors and personalities, including *Halliwell's television companion* (q.v.), *Who's who on radio* (q.v.), *Who's who on television* (q.v.), and the biographical sections in such general directories as *Screen International film and tv yearbook* (q.v.). *Spotlight*,[19] the casting directory, can be useful for tracing actors and actresses, and details of their agents for further information.

Information about production personnel — directors, producers, writers and technicians — may also be in some general directories, but more likely in the membership lists and yearbooks of the various professional bodies, such as the Directors Guild of Great Britain.

Broadcasting executives and administrators, often the most difficult to trace, are listed in the *Blue book of British broadcasting* (q.v.) and, with short biographies, in the *Who's who in broadcasting* (q.v.). Current information about them can often be found in the trade press, *Broadcast* and *Screen International*, and even the newspapers and general magazines for the more prominent figures. Press releases from the relevant organizations can also be a valuable source of information on newly appointed or promoted senior staff.

Research into prominent broadcasters in the past would require access to published biographies or autobiographies, back files of biographical dictionaries such *Who's who in radio and television* (q.v.), specialist sources such as *Biography Index*[20] and *Current Biography*,[21] newspapers and press cuttings files, archive recordings, and any personal papers held in archives.

These notes have, by necessity, been brief, but I hope they will have drawn together the material discussed throughout the book, and indicated lines of approach and useful sources.

References

1. Foster, Janet and Sheppard, Julia. *British archives: a guide to archive resources in the United Kingdom*. London: Macmillan Press, 1982.
2. *The shorter ASLIB directory of information sources in the United Kingdom* edited by Ellen M. Codlin. London: ASLIB, 1986.
3. *Researcher's guide to British film and television collections*. London: British Universities Film and Video Council, 2nd edn, 1985.
4. *Halsbury's statutes of England*. London: Butterworths, 4th edn, 1985–.
5. Reith, J. C. W. *Diaries*. London: Collins, 1975.
6. Reith, J. C. W. *Into the wind*. London: Hodder and Stoughton, 1949.
7. Clark, Kenneth (*later* Lord Clark). *The other half: a self portrait*. London: John Murray, 1977.
8. Hill of Luton, Lord. *Behind the screen: the broadcasting memoirs of Lord Hill of Luton*. London: Sidgwick and Jackson, 1974.
9. *Index to The Times*. 1906–. Monthly. London: Times Newspapers.
10. *British Humanities Index*. 1962–. Quarterly. London: Library Association.
11. Central Office of Information. *Broadcasting in Britain*. London: HMSO, 1981.
12. Central Office of Information. *Britain: an official handbook*. 1950–. Annual. London: HMSO.
13. *Extel British Company Information Service*. London: Extel Statistical Service.
14. *Key British enterprises*. Annual. London: Dun and Bradstreet.
15. *The Stock Exchange official yearbook*. 1934–. Annual. London: Macmillan.
16. *The making of The Jewel in the Crown*. London: Granada Publishing, 1983.
17. Smith, Julia and Holland, Tony. *EastEnders: the inside story*. London: BBC Books, 1987.
18. Hobson, Dorothy. *Crossroads: the drama of a soap opera*. London: Methuen, 1982.
19. *Spotlight*. 1927–. Annual. London: Spotlight.
20. *Biography Index*. 1946–. Quarterly. New York: H. W. Wilson.
21. *Current Biography*. 1940–. Monthly. New York: H. W. Wilson.

6

Institutional sources of information

The principal categories of institutional sources of information on broadcasting are: *archives* — for the original documentation generated by broadcasting regulation, administration or production, or for recordings of the actual radio and television programme output; *libraries* — for published source material on broadcasting; and *museums* — for exhibitions of the artifacts, ephemera and memorabilia of broadcasting. Another valuable source of information in the broadcasting organizations, but outside the scope of this directory, are the press or information offices and programme correspondence sections, which keep a variety of specialist material — programme information, press releases and promotional literature.

The following directory can only claim to cover the principal archives, libraries and museums in the United Kingdom.

6.1 Archives

The two types of archives covered by this directory — national and institutional archives — have very different functions and rules for access for research and study purposes.

The national and public archives are largely supported by public funds, with the primary purpose of preservation of material, and making it available to researchers and members of the general public.

The papers and records from the two Government ministeries responsible for broadcasting since its inception — the Post Office and the Home Office — are held by the Post Office Archives and the Public Record Office. They have been deposited with them under the *Public Records Act 1958* (and 1967), whereby official records may be made available for public inspection after a thirty-year period, unless otherwise prescribed by the Lord Chancellor.

For films and television programmes of permanent value, the National Film Archive is also designed to be a national repository; to this end it selects and preserves the material to make it permanently available for research and study purposes. A national collection of sound recordings is also available — provided under the aegis of British Library by the National Sound Archive. Only two collections — the Imperial War Museum and the National Film Archive — are recognized by the International Federation of Film Archives (FIAF) as conforming to their required standards for film and television archives.

The institutional archives and film libraries do not have the same obligations as the national archives to make their collections available to the public. They were established by their organizations essentially for their own purposes — to select, preserve and document their own records, with a view to internal re-use; any consideration of public access would be secondary to that purpose. The BBC Written Archives Centre, in acknowledgement of the enormous value of its collection for the study of the history of the twentieth century, as well as BBC history, provides facilities for serious researchers. Access to the archives and film libraries of other broadcasting organizations and television companies would be by negotiation.

National and public archives

NATIONAL FILM ARCHIVE
21 Stephen Street, London W1P 1PL; 01-155 2444

Contact:	Cataloguing Department (in first instance).
Access:	Viewing Service: provides private viewings for bona fide students and researchers on the Archive's premises for which a small handling fee is charged.
	Production Library: supplies extracts of films and television programmes preserved in the Archive to filmmakers and TV producers for use in compilations or other productions when no other source exists.
History:	Established in 1935 by the British Film Institute as a 'national repository of films of permanent value'; the preservation of television material began in the 1950s.
Coverage:	Any British or British-related television programmes transmitted for reception within the United Kingdom, or of relevance to the objects of the BFI.
Holdings:	Independent Television, including Channel 4, and a selection of BBC TV programmes. Since 1985 a direct recording scheme is in operation, adding over 4,400 programmes as well as acquiring independently another 3,000 programmes per year.

Special collections:	Advertising. Open University.
Catalogues:	Title List (NFA holdings of films and television programmes). Indexes: Subject; Personality; Cast; Production Company; Director.
Publications:	*Non-fiction films 1895–1978* (London: NFA, 1980). *Keeping television alive: the television work of the National Film Archive* (London: BFI, 1981).

NATIONAL SOUND ARCHIVE
29 Exhibition Road, London SW7 2AS; 01-589 6603

Contact:	Information Service.
Access:	Reference Library: general public, students and researchers without appointment. Listening Service: by appointment.
History:	The British Institute of Recorded Sound began in 1955, and was renamed the National Sound Archive on becoming a department of the British Library in 1983.
Coverage:	Comprehensive collection of sound recordings, especially British, including broadcast material, and commercially issued recordings of drama, spoken word, popular music of all kinds, oral history, sound effects, wildlife sounds and documentary material.
Holdings:	750,000 discs; 45,000 hours of tape recordings; 8,000 books and periodicals.
Special collections:	BBC Sound Archive recordings (on disc) 1923–; BBC Transcription Service discs; selected off-air recordings of BBC programmes; selected recordings from Independent Local Radio stations; British Library of Wildlife Sounds; British in India Oral Archive; International Music Collection.
Catalogues:	Card catalogues of printed materials. Record company catalogues supplemented by Archive card and microfiche catalogues of sound recordings. Various departmental catalogues.
Publication:	*POMPI: Popular Music Periodicals Index* (1985–).

POST OFFICE ARCHIVES
23 Glass Hill Street, London N1; 01-432 4521

Access:	Public: material has public records status so Crown copyright and the thirty-year rule apply.
Coverage:	Archives of the Post Office, including those of British Telecommunications. Subject coverage includes postal services, telegraphy, telephony and broadcasting.
Holdings:	Post Office administrative records since 1672; books on postal history and telecommunications.

Special collections:	Papers of two telecommunications pioneers — William Preece (Post Office Engineer-in-Chief, 1892–9) and Guglielmo Marconi (and the Marconi Wireless Company). Proceedings, reports and evidence from the Broadcasting Committees, 1923–. Television Advisory Committee minutes and papers. BBC Royal Charters, Licences and correspondence with the Postmaster General.
Catalogues:	Postmaster General's Minutes (for papers on wireless telegraphy and broadcasting); English Minutes, 1794–1920; Scottish Minutes, 1842–1920; Irish Minutes, 1831–1920; General Minutes, 1921–1940; Documents (Subjects) Volumes 1–4.
Publication:	*A guide to the Post Office archives* compiled by Jean Farugia (London: Post Office, 1987).

PUBLIC RECORD OFFICE
Chancery Lane, London WC2A 1LR; 01-405 0741
Ruskin Avenue, Kew, Richmond, Surrey TW9 4DU; 01-876 3444

Access:	Public: Reader's Ticket issued free to applicants who satisfy the Keeper of Public Records of their suitability to be allowed access to the records and can produce evidence of identity.
History:	Established in 1838 to provide for the preservation of public records and allow for their public use.
Coverage:	Public records received from Government departments, Courts, Tribunals and other public bodies subject to the Public Record Acts. These records selected for permanent preservation are normally available for public inspection thirty years after their creation, though some unrestricted papers may be more recent.
Holdings:	Cabinet papers; papers of private offices of Ministers; minutes, papers and correspondence of Commissions and Committees; Conference documents.
Special collections:	Collections applicable to broadcasting from the Home Office and the Post Office: Television Advisory Committee; Broadcasting Committee 1949 (Chairman: Lord Beveridge); BBC Charters and Licences; Broadcast Receiving Licences; Government White Papers on broadcasting (1951 and 1952); Television Act 1954; Radio Luxembourg 1945–56. Home Office Radio and Broadcasting Departments. International Telecommunications Conferences, 1857–1966. Ministry of Information, Broadcasting Division, 1939–46. Board of Customs and Excise responsibility for the Television Advertising Duty.
Catalogues:	MS: *Current Guide* (providing up-to-date information about

all classes of records at the PRO): Part 1: administrative history, functions and organization of each institution or Government department; Part 2: classified list in alphanumeric order giving class, title, dates covered, numbers of pieces and description; Part 3: alphabetical indexes to the current guide.
MS: separate listing of the current year's newly opened files of public papers.
MS: *Class Lists* (Classes: HO (Home Office) 254: Broadcasting Committee 1949; HO 255: Radio Department, 1922–78; HO 257: International Telecommunications Conferences, 1957–66; HO 258: Television Advisory Committees, 1933–67; HO 262: Ministry of Information, 1939–46).

Publications: *Guide to the contents of the Public Record Office.* Volume 1: *Legal records, etc*; Volume 2: *Date papers and departmental records*; Volume 3: *Documents transferred 1960–1966.* London: HMSO, 1963–8.

Institutional archives: documentation

These 'paper' archives, maintained by the broadcasting authorities, television companies and related organizations, contain the unpublished, internal documentation associated with broadcasting: administrative papers — correspondence, internal memoranda, contracts and agreements, committee minutes and papers; and programme documentation — scripts, transcripts, contributors' correspondence, and other operational papers.

The BBC Written Archive Centre, as mentioned earlier, is the most professional and accessible documentation archive, with a unique collection of administrative and programme records dating back to the beginning of the BBC, and well-organized facilities for visiting researchers. The BBC also maintains other archival collections of radio and drama scripts, photographs and other material, with varying rules for access by outside researchers.

Access to the archives of Independent Broadcasting is more problematic. The ITV contractors are private companies with, until recently, no obligation to make their archives publicly available. Also, with relatively short-term contracts for their franchise to provide television services, they have not taken a long-term view of the value of their past programming and its documentation. Consequently, in the past, the archives of the earlier companies not reappointed to the franchise have often been dispersed, if not disappeared. In some instances the programme contractor succeeding to the franchise has inherited the archives, as in the case of ABC Television archives by Thames Television. In other cases the archives have been donated to other bodies — Rediffusion Television production archives and files to the IBA, and Southern Television archives to the British Film Institute. However, to prevent this situation happening again the agreement between the IBA and the programme contractors for the period 1982–92 contains an 'archive' clause, requiring the companies to accumulate and preserve an archive of recordings of their programmes and the related documents, and in the event of the company not being reappointed making arrangements for their preservation agreeable to the IBA. Some of the companies do now maintain archives of programme material, and provide research facilities; only those that allow some access by outside researchers have been listed in this directory.

Although outside the coverage of this directory, some colleges and universities offering courses in radio and television studies have archival collections of relevance to broadcasting. Examples are the John Grierson Archive at the University of Stirling, and the Mary Adams papers (on BBC Television, 1936–58) at the University of Sussex.

BRITISH BROADCASTING CORPORATION
Access to BBC archives and libraries is restricted to BBC users. Intending users from outside the Corporation should telephone or write in the first instance to discuss their requirements.

BBC Data Enquiry Service
Room 7, 1 Portland Place, London W1A 1AA; 01-927 5998

Contact:	Manager.
General:	The BBC Data Enquiry Service, now part of BBC Enterprises Ltd, operates a commercial, fee-based service from printed information sources, which is applicable to outside users of some, though not all, of the BBC libraries and information services. Where application must be made through BBC Data Enquiry Service, it is mentioned in the section on 'Access' in the entries for BBC archives and libraries listed in this and following sections of the directory.

BBC Photograph Library
Unit 1, Royal London Trading Estate, 29 North Acton Road, London NW10 6PE; 01-743 8000, ext. 3314

Contact:	Assistant-in-Charge.
Access:	A commercial sales operation run by BBC Enterprises Ltd Charges: a research fee on all requests, and a scale of reproduction fees. First contact must be made in writing, and visits to view material are by appointment. No requests from general public, fans and collectors.
Coverage:	BBC's main collection of still photographs on broadcasting dating from 1922.
Holdings:	*c.* 1,000,000 items (monochrome negatives and colour transparencies).
Special collections:	Picture Publicity Library; The *Radio Times* and Enterprise collections of programme stills, personality and technical photographs.

BBC Radio Drama Information Centre
Broadcasting House, Portland Place, London W1A 1AA; 01-580 4468, ext. 5495

Contact:	Information Assistant.
Access:	BBC staff; available to non-BBC users by appointment in writing or by telephone.
Coverage:	Microfilmed scripts of BBC Radio Drama Department — plays, features and poetry.
Holdings:	50,000 scripts.
Catalogues:	Author, Title and Subject Indexes.
Publication:	*Giles Cooper Awards* (Annual. London: Eyre Methuen).

BBC Radio Programme Index
Woodlands, 80 Wood Lane, London W12 0TT; 01-743 8000

Contact:	Assistant-in-Charge.
Access:	Direct access by BBC departments only. Public may write to Programme Correspondence Section; students and researchers apply to the BBC Written Archives Centre; commercial enquirers apply to BBC Data Enquiry Service.
Coverage:	Programme Index covers BBC radio broadcasts from 1945 on the national domestic networks (excluding news bulletins, local radio and Open University programmes).
Catalogues:	Programme Index: Title/Contributor/Subject (microfilm 1945–76; computer sorted microfilm 1976–).
	Script Library: card catalogue 1922–72 (thereafter via Programme Index records).

BBC Television Script Unit
252 Western Avenue, London W3; 01-576 1390/1392

Contact:	Assistant (General).
Access:	BBC staff by appointment only; non-BBC users on payment of a fee.
Coverage:	BBC Television drama scripts form 1936.
Holdings:	Copy scripts as transmitted (mostly on microfilm).
Catalogues:	Comprehensive indexes to writers, producers and directors of all BBC drama.
	Indexes for ITV drama productions, writers and production companies (title and date).
	Drama chronological lists from 1936 (showing all drama transmissions by title, writer, producer, director, original or repeat length and transmission date).
Publication:	*BBC Television market information for writers.*

BBC Written Archives Centre
Caversham Park, Reading RG4 8TZ; 0734 472742, ext. 280

Contact:	Written Archives Officer.
Access:	BBC users throughout opening hours; bona fide researchers and students by appointment only.
Coverage:	The whole sphere of the BBC's activities from 1922 to the mid-1960s. A major source of twentieth century social and political history, the Second World War, education, science, music and literature as well as material on eminent figures in all these fields.
Holdings:	200,000 files of correspondence, minutes of meetings, programme logs, scripts, news bulletins and other records relating to the development and influence of BBC radio and television at home and abroad.
	BBC Programmes-as-Broadcast (P-as-Bs), –1954.
	BBC Programme Index: Radio –1976; Television –1982.
Special collections:	Some deposited collections from people closely associated with the BBC. Complete sets of BBC publications. A unique collection of broadcasting press cuttings 1922–mid 1960s.
Catalogues:	Shelf lists and some detailed descriptive lists and indexes.

BRITISH FILM INSTITUTE
BFI Library Services
21 Stephen Street, London W1P 1PL; 01-255 1444

Contact:	Head of Library Services.
Access:	Members of the BFI, ACTT, RTS, FIAF and FIAT. Weekly and daily passes available. Access to some collections is restricted.
Coverage:	Material is collected on the structure, personnel and programmes of UK television, and covers social, economic and aesthetic aspects. World television and telecommunications covered in more general terms.
Holdings:	See 'Libraries' entry.
Special collections:	Channel 4 (1982–) and Southern Televsion (1958–81) programme archives.
	Deposited collections from Roger Graef, Trevor Griffiths, Troy Kennedy Martin, Irene Shubik and other television figures.

BFI Television Stills Collection
21 Stephen Street, London W1P 1PL; 01-255 1444

Contact:	TV Stills Officer.
Access:	Visits by appointment.
Coverage:	Television programmes transmitted in the United Kingdom, including advertising, technical areas (e.g. cameras, studios),

trade marks, personalities, representative international programmes.

Holdings: British television programmes, 1936 to the present. Programming from various international markets (e.g. USA). Selection of British television advertising; studio productions (1930s/1940s); technical equipment; TV news; British and American TV posters.

Special collections: John Logie Baird Collection.

CENTRAL INDEPENDENT TELEVISION
Reference/Stills Library: Broad Street, Birmingham B1 2JP; 021-643 9898, ext. 4535

Contact: Librarian.
Access: Central Television staff only; bona fide researchers may apply in writing only.
Coverage: Drama, documentary and light entertainment programme material from ATV Network Ltd and Central Independent.
Holdings: Scripts — ATV Network, 1955–81.
Scripts — Central Independent Television, 1982–.
Programme publicity photographs and stills — Central Independent Television, 1982–.
(Rights to ATV programme photos held by ITC Entertainment Ltd.)
Catalogue: Selective artiste index to programme photographs.

CHANNEL FOUR TELEVISION COMPANY
Channel Four Archive: 60 Charlotte Street, London W1P 2AX; 01-631 4444

General: Channel Four is to transfer its archive to the British Film Institute. A research project is underway to establish policies and procedures for the formation of the archive, categories of papers to be included, and access by researchers.

GRANADA TELEVISION
Archives Department: Quay Street, Manchester M60 9EA; 061-832 7211

Contact: Archivist/Picture Librarian.
Access: Granada Television staff only; no public access.
Coverage: Granada Television programmes, administration, engineering and buildings.
Holdings: Scripts (on microfiche), 1956–.
2,000 boxes of programme and administrative files.
c. 78,000 colour transparencies of Granada TV programmes.
c. 30,000 black and white stills of locations, subjects and personalities.

Special collections:	*Coronation Street* story lines, 1960–.
	Transmission logs, 1956–.
	Studio and Outside Broadcast Schedules.
Catalogues:	Card catalogues: Programme Transmissions (A–Z); Programme/Production Files (A–Z); Administration Files (Classified & A–Z).
	Index: Producers/Directors (A–Z).
	Card catalogue for stills of actors/actresses in Granada TV programmes, 1956–.
Publication:	Annual calendar of Granada Television transmissions.

HISTORY OF ADVERTISING TRUST
Archives: Unit 202, Butler's Wharf Business Centre, 45 Curlew Street, London SE1 2ND; 01-403 0756

Contact:	Archivist.
Access:	Accredited researchers; advertising agencies and client firms. A fee is charged where appropriate.
Coverage:	Advertising business records; institutional archives; and some visual material.
Holdings:	Selected television commercials and radio recordings; business and advertising agency archives; library of historical books and annuals on advertising; some television scripts and associated documentation.
Special collections:	Archives of the Advertising Association, Association of Independent Radio Contractors, Esso Advertising, National Dairy Council, and J. Walter Thompson.
Catalogues:	Catalogues of individual collections.
	Book catalogue.
Publications:	*Advertising in Britain: a history* by T. R. Nevett (London: Heinemann, 1982).
	British television advertising: the first thirty years by Brian Henry (London: Century Benham, 1986).
	Journal of Advertising History (q.v.).

LONDON WEEKEND TELEVISION
Archives: 'Hatfields', 59 Upper Ground, London SE1 9LT; 01-928 1728

Contact:	Company Archivist.
Access:	LWT staff; bona fide researchers only by appointment.
Coverage:	LWT programme production files and associated paperwork, 1968–.
Holdings:	Scripts, studio and OB planning sheets; running orders; Programmes-as-Televised (P-as-T); and all documentation for all

production areas, including drama, light entertainment, current affairs, arts and sports.

Special collections:	Personal archives of senior management past and present donated for historical retention.
Publication:	*A history of London Weekend Television* by David Docherty (forthcoming, 1989).

ROYAL TELEVISION SOCIETY
Archives: Tavistock House East, Tavistock Square, London WC1H 9HR; 01-387 1970

Contact:	Archivist.
Access:	RTS members; public with references by appointment.
Coverage:	Society records and publications, 1927–.
Holdings:	Books; periodicals; documents; MSS; photographs; videos; audio tapes; miscellaneous ephemera.
Catalogue:	Computerized catalogue in progress.

TELEVISION SOUTH — TVS
Library and Records Management Centre: Television Centre, Southampton SO9 5HZ; 0703 634211

Contact:	Librarian.
Access:	TVS staff; outside users for educational and research purposes only.
Coverage:	TVS (1982–) and Southern Television (1958–81) documentation and programme material.
Holdings:	TVS cuttings, Group publications, publicity material and programme records. TVS programmes, news, documentary and current affairs items (video and film). TVS slides and stills. TVS and Southern Television documentation and ephemera.
Catalogue:	Integrated Computer Database for Programme Library/ Archive and Records.

THAMES TELEVISION
Documentation Archive: 365 Euston Road, London NW1 3AR; 01-387 0911, ext. 233

Contact:	Archivist.
Access:	Thames TV staff; outside researchers by appointment only. All material for reference only.
Coverage:	Thames Television (1968–) and ABC Television (1956–68) programme documentation.
Holdings:	Thames Television/ABC Television programme files, 1956–.

	ITV/Channel 4 advertising logs (part on microfilm).
Special	*Thames News* bulletins: scripts (part on microfilm).
collections:	Press Office cuttings: national and provincial newspapers and periodicals (part on microfilm).
Catalogues:	Card Index by programme title. Limited subject indexing (e.g. documentaries, religion, etc.).

Institutional archives and libraries: programmes

Although both types of unit in this category store programme material, either television or radio, there is otherwise a marked difference between *archives* and *libraries*. The term archive, too often used loosely for any kind of library or collection, really implies an organization with an emphasis on preservation for research purposes, and storage according to very high technical standards.

Film libraries in broadcasting organizations or commercial film libraries have as their principal function the selection and storage of programme material considered suitable for future re-use or for sale commercially as archive footage. Two types of programme material are kept by the libraries — complete programmes, suitable for repeat transmission or sale, or programme excerpts ('stock-shots' in television) suitable for re-use as establishing material, inserts, background or archive items. Television material can be stored on 35mm or 16mm film, or a variety of tape formats including broadcast-standard 1in or 2in videotape, Low band or High band U-matic 3/4in tape cassettes, or domestic-standard VHS/Betamax 1/2in tape cassettes. Radio material will be stored on vinyl discs or various audio tape formats.

ANGLIA TELEVISION
Film/Cassette Library: Anglia House, Norwich NR1 3JG; 0603 615151

Contact:	Librarian.
Access:	Anglia Television staff; no facilities for outside researchers — telephone enquiries only. Programme sales through Anglia International Sales.
Coverage:	Anglia Television programmes, 1959–, including news, magazine items, current affairs, filmed dramas, farming programmes, documentaries. Selected black and white material 1959–69; all colour material, 1969–.
Holdings:	*c.* 3,000 transmitted items per year (film/ENG). *c.* 600 various Anglia programmes (VHS/U-matic). Scripts.
Special collections:	*Bygones* feature series (on past crafts and people).
Catalogues:	Card Index: 1959–83; Computer system, 1984–.

BORDER TELEVISION
Film Library: The Television Centre, Carlisle CA1 3NT; 0228 25101

Contact: Librarian.

Access: Border Television staff; local, ITV, Channel Four and bona fide researchers, provided appointments to view are made by letter or telephone. Library can make viewing cassettes, or select and print up required footage for customers.

Coverage: Border Television programmes: black and white, 1961–74; colour, 1974–. Local news, documentaries and features (16mm film). Commercials, COI fillers, feature films and series (35mm film).

Holdings: *c.*1,200 VTR commercials, 1in tapes.
*c.*100 Betacam cassettes.
*c.*280 Low band U-matic tapes.
*c.*8,000 cans of film.
Scripts, programme notes, slides and stills held by News Department and Production Department.

Catalogues: Microfiche catalogue, 1961–74; Datex system, 1974–.

BRITISH BROADCASTING CORPORATION
BBC Film and Videotape Library
Reynard Mills Industrial Estate, Windmill Road, Brentford, Middlesex TW8 9NF; 01-567 6655

Contact: Head of Film and VT Library.

Access: BBC users only; enquiries from outside users should be made through BBC Enterprises Ltd, Woodlands, 80 Wood Lane, London W12 OTT; 01-743 5588 or 01-576 0202.

Coverage: The Library exists to store, document and make available BBC film and videotape material for re-use in programmes, as a research source and for exploitation by BBC Enterprises.

Holdings: 500,000 cans of film covering BBC film output, 1948– (limited pre-war material).
*c.*50,000 spools of videotape, mid-1960s–.
Video cassette collection, 1981–.

Catalogues: Online Title, Subject and Name catalogues for current programme output; manual catalogue covering earlier programme material gradually being incorporated.

Publication: *Guide to BBC Film and Videotape Library.*

BBC Sound Archives
Broadcasting House, London W1A 1AA; 01-927 4230

Contact: Librarian.

Access: BBC programme staff. Non-BBC users: the BBC Sound Archive also licences recordings for broadcasting and commercial purposes — 01-927 4853; listening and research facilities for non-commercial or educational purposes are available through Transcript and Tape Unit, c/o Secretariat, Broadcasting House, London W1A 1AA.

Coverage: The whole range of broadcasting — drama, music, comedy, sport and news — from all radio networks, World Service and local radio.

Holdings: *c.*250,000 recordings, mainly stored on long-playing discs and tape.

*c.*3,000 hours of new recordings are added each year, mainly BBC output, but some commissioned material.

Special collections: Sound effects recording (*c.*20,000 7in discs or tapes). News bulletins (8.00 and 18.00), 1983–.

Catalogues: Classified catalogues in card form, classified by the main programme categories: talks, drama, features, music, etc. and a section devoted to historical events in chronological order. Each card contains information on speakers, performers, cast lists, transmission and recording dates, timings and a precis of the item.

Indexes to the catalogue in book form, 1931–70; and on computer-produced microfiche, 1970–.

Publications: *Chronological list of sound recordings from the nineteeth century to December 1939* (1985).

Sound effects catalogue.

Newsletter (monthly): details of new recordings added to the archive, and anniversaries.

CENTRAL INDEPENDENT TELEVISION
Film/ENG Library: Broad Street, Birmingham B1 2JP; 021-643 9898

Contact: Librarian.

Access: Central Television users; facilities for research on a limited basis.

Coverage: ATV (1956–81) and Central Independent Television (1982–) Midland news and current affairs material on film and ENG.

Holdings: *c.*16,500 cans of film.

*c.*2,000 videotapes.

600 High band U-matic tapes.

500 Low band U-matic tapes.

Special collections: Transmission prints and tracks. ATV documentaries (copyright held by ITC Entertainment).

Catalogues: Subject/Title Card Indexes; catalogue sheets for news.

GRANADA TELEVISION
Film Library: Quay Street, Manchester M60 9EA; 061-832 7211

Contact:	Librarian.
Access:	Granada Television staff; outside researchers allowed access to the collection whenever possible.
Coverage:	Granada Television programmes, 1960–.
Holdings:	2,300 programmes on film.
	Stockshots.
	ENG — mainly North West news items and stockshots (all local news material shot since April 1986 now held in the ENG Library, Granada TV News, Albert Dock, Liverpool).
Special collections:	North West of England footage, early 1960s–.
	Disappearing World anthropological material, 1970–.
	World in Action social and political material, 1963–.
Catalogue:	Card Index.

INDEPENDENT TELEVISION ASSOCIATION
Film Library: Knighton House, 56 Mortimer Street, London W1N 8AN; 01-636 6866

Contact:	Librarian.
Access:	ITV and Channel 4 staff; bona fide film researchers and advertising agencies. Cinema available for U-matic, VHS and film viewing — advance notice required.
Coverage:	Selection of UK (and some foreign) television commercials, 1955–.
Holdings:	10,000 commercials on 35mm/16mm film.
	1,200 Low band U-matic tapes.
Special collections:	Proctor and Gamble commercials, 1957–80.
	International advertising film festival award winners.
Catalogue:	Computerized catalogue (search by product, title, date).

LONDON WEEKEND TELEVISION
Film Department: Kent House, Upper Ground, London SE1 9LT; 01-261 3690

Contact:	Extracts Liaison Officer.
Access:	Television companies and bona fide researchers.
Coverage:	LWT transmitted programmes and programme extracts (including *The South Bank Show*, etc.).
Holdings:	Videotape; 16mm film.

LONDON WEEKEND TELEVISION
Stockshot Library: Kent House, Upper Ground, London SE1 9LT; 01-261 3771

Contact:	Librarian.

Access: LWT staff; bona fide researchers and television companies, but not the general public.
Coverage: Current affairs and London material, 1980–.
                 Archive material held in Film Library and VT Library.
Holdings: 5,000 cans of film.
                 5,000 3/4in tape cassettes.
Catalogues: Microfiche catalogues: Personality/Subject (UDC), 1980–7; microcomputer, 1988–.

SCOTTISH TELEVISION
Film and Videotape Library: Cowcaddens, Glasgow G2 3PR; 041-332 9999, exts 4511/4512
Contact: Head of Library Services.
Access: Programme makers and researchers; external enquirers will be referred to the Programme Sales Department.
Coverage: Scottish Television film and videotape material, other purchased programmes for transmission on STV, and advertising commercials.
Holdings: 6,000 Betacam cassettes.
                 7,000 cans 16mm film.
                 3,500 2in videotapes.
                 7,500 1in videotapes.
Special   VHS viewing copies of selected archive programmes held in
collections: separate collection (ext. 4821).
Catalogues: Card catalogue: Title/ Subject/ Name.
                 Computer catalogue: News material.

TELEVISION SOUTH — TVS
Film-Videotape-ENG-Slides and Stills Library: Television Centre, Northam, Southampton, Hants SO9 5HZ; 0703 634211 *and* Television Centre, Vinters Park, Maidstone, Kent ME14 5NZ; 0622 691111
Contact: Librarian-in-Charge (for both addresses).
Access: TVS staff; outside users apply to Company Archivist. Programme sales through Telso, The Adelphi, John Adam Street, London WC2N 6HP.
Coverage: Southern Television news and current affairs material (*Day by Day*), 1976–81.
                 TVS news and current affairs material (*Coast to Coast* and News), 1982–.
                 All Southern Television programmes, other than the above, in vaults at Video Images (0703 422088).
Holdings: 9,000 films.
                 1,000 2in videotapes; 12,000 1in videotapes.

2,000 3/4in and 1/2in ENG, 1986–.

22,000 slides (DLS), 1988–; 7,500 stills.

Special collections:	Southern Television news and current affairs black and white negatives, early 1960s–.
Catalogue:	Computer database for VT Library and DLS Gallery 2000 slide storage and retrieval system.

TELEVISION SOUTH WEST — TSW

Film and Video Tape Library: Derry's Cross, Plymouth, Devon PL1 2SP; 0752 663322

Contact:	Supervising Librarian or Archival Librarian.
Access:	TSW staff; researchers by appointment with the Archival Librarian. Programme sales through TSW Worldwide Sales.
Coverage:	TSW (1982–) and Westward Television (1961–81) local programmes, news and documentaries, 1961–.

THAMES TELEVISION

Film and VHS Library: 306–316 Euston Road, London NW1 3BB; 01-387 9494, ext. 4464/4440

Contact:	Senior Film Librarian.
Access:	Thames Television staff only; outside enquiries through Library Sales Co-ordinator.
Coverage:	Thames Television programmes — documentaries and current affairs for re-use; commissioned programmes (Euston Films, Cosgrove Hall, etc.) as research source.
Holdings:	All Thames TV programmes (and inserts), 1968–. *c.* 5,000 VHS cassettes, 1985–.
Special collections:	Documentaries (single and series) and current affairs: *This Week, TV Eye, World at War, Hollywood,* etc.
Catalogue:	Computerized catalogue — internal use only.

TYNE TEES TELEVISION

Film/VTR/Commercial Library: City Road, Newcastle upon Tyne NE1 2AL; 091 2610181

Contact:	Supervisory Librarian.
Access:	Tyne Tees Television staff; outside enquiries will be researched by staff, but viewing facilities are limited so, where a preview is essential, only by appointment.
Coverage:	Tyne Tees Television programmes — news, current affairs, documentaries, religion, sport and farming.
Holdings:	*c.* 9,000 programme and insert VTRs. *c.* 30,000 35mm slides. 16mm news film, early 1960s–.

ENG material, local features on 16mm/35mm film.

Catalogues: Card Indexes/Kalamazoo/Files/Tape Print-outs. Quick-reference wall-mounted strip index for VTR/ENG. Indexes: Alphabetical/Numerical/Subject or Guest.

ULSTER TELEVISION

Film Library: Havelock House, Ormeau Road, Belfast BT7 1EB; 0232 228122

Contact: Archive Manager or Film Librarian.

Access: Ulster Television staff; UK and other broadcasting organizations; educational and bona fide researchers.

Coverage: Ulster Television programmes of Northern Ireland activities and interests, 1959–.

Holdings: *c.* 6,000 cans of black and white reversal and negative 16mm film stock, 1959–71.

c. 3,000 cans of colour reversal and negative 16mm film stock, 1971–83 (some to the present).

c. 8,000 EP tapes, 1983–.

c. 1,000 1in programme tapes, and 2in Archive tapes.

Special   2,500 Ulster Television black and white stills.

collections: 12,500 colour transparencies of Northern Ireland places and personalities.

Catalogue: Card Indexes: Multiple Subject Headings (Personalities/Places/Sport/Interviews/Explosions/etc.).

YORKSHIRE TELEVISION

Film Library: The Television Centre, Leeds LS3 1JS; 0532 438283, ext. 4634

Contact: Film Librarian.

Access: Yorkshire TV staff; ITV researchers by appointment. Enquiries from outside companies (other than ITV) and individuals should be made to YTV Sales (0532 438283)

Coverage: Yorkshire Television programmes and inserts, 1982–. Film and VT programmes from 1968–81 are now the copyright of AML, and are available via Chameleon Films, Leeds.

Calendar local news and current affairs, July 1968–.

Holdings: *c.* 10,000 cans of film.

c. 2,200 Betacam ENG cassettes/*c.*200 Betamax cassettes.

Catalogues: Card Catalogues: Title/Accessions; Subject/Names.

Computer Catalogue: Subject/Name/Title, 1985–.

6.2 Libraries

Specialist libraries with collections of published material on the subject of broadcasting are maintained by broadcasting authorities, trade associations and educational bodies. As in the case of the institutional archives, many of these libraries have as their principal function to provide services to their own staff or members, and only as a secondary purpose to make their collections available to outside researchers.

The book or information libraries of the ITV companies are not listed here as they are private library services providing research support for programme making and administration in their company, and are not, in any case, special libraries on the subject of broadcasting.

Public libraries with special collections on broadcasting, perhaps as a responsibility within an inter-library co-operative subject specialization scheme, are not included here; they can be traced in the directories of libraries or guides to such schemes.

The following entries for libraries on broadcasting contain the details of conditions of access for researchers, coverage, holdings, catalogues and published guides.

ADVERTISING ASSOCIATION

Information Centre: Abford House, 15 Wilton Road, London SW1V 1NJ; 01-828 2771

Contact:	Head of Information Services.
Access:	Open to the public. Appointment is advisable when in-depth research is intended.
Coverage:	Advertising, marketing, media, sales promotion and public relations mainly in the United Kingdom.
Holdings:	2,000 books.
	150 periodical titles.
	300 press cuttings files.
Special collections:	Advertising statistics.
	Advertising Association publications.
Catalogues:	Book Card Catalogue: Author/Subject.
	Periodical Articles Card Index.
Publications:	*Background Briefings*: No. 1: *Advertising and children* (2nd edn, 1983); No. 2: *How advertising is regulated* (2nd edn, 1983).
	Student Briefs: No. 1: *The advertising business*; No. 2: *The advertising media*; No. 3: *The advertising agency*; No. 4: *Advertising on television*; No. 5: *The regulation of advertising*; No. 6: *Facts and figures on advertising*.
	Reading lists for students on advertising and marketing.

BRITISH BROADCASTING CORPORATION

The BBC maintains many libraries to support administration and production within the principal output areas — Radio, Television and External Services, as well as in the Regions, the Monitoring Service and Engineering Research

Department. Most of these libraries are generalist collections servicing a wide range of information and research requirements from broadcasting administrators and production staff, and are not in themselves specialist sources on broadcasting. Only two of the units have substantial collections of research material on broadcasting — the BBC Engineering Research Department Library and the BBC Radio Reference Library Broadcasting Collection.

BBC Engineering Research Department Library
Kingswood Warren, Tadworth, Surrey KT20 6NP; 0737 832361

Contact:	Librarian.
Access:	BBC staff; external researchers by appointment.
Coverage:	Wide range of engineering topics including electronics, data communications and broadcast engineering.
Holdings:	3,000 technical books and reports. 170 current periodicals. British and international standards.
Special collections:	BBC Research Department Reports. CCIR (International Consultative Committee on Radio Communications) documents.
Catalogue:	Microfiche catalogue of the holdings of BBC Data libraries (including Research Department Library).

BBC Radio Reference Library: Broadcasting Collection
Henry Wood House, Langham Place, London W1A 1AA; 01-580 4468

Contact:	Assistant-in-Charge.
Access:	BBC staff only; enquiries from outside should be directed to the BBC Data Enquiry Service (q.v.).
Coverage:	General collection of books, pamphlets and reports on the history and development of British broadcasting.
Holdings:	5,000 books, pamphlets and reports. 30 broadcasting periodical titles.
Special collections:	*BBC annual report and accounts*, 1927–72; *BBC handbook*, 1928–87. Government publications and Parliamentary reports.
Catalogue:	Computer catalogue (BLCMP) of the holdings of BBC Data Libraries.
Publication:	*British broadcasting 1922–1982* edited by Gavin Higgens (London: BBC Data Publications, 1983).

BRITISH FILM INSTITUTE
Library Services: 21 Stephen Street, London W1P 1PL; 01-255 1444

Contact:	Head of Library Services.
Access:	Members of the BFI, ACTT, RTS, FIAF and FIAT. Daily and weekly passes available.

Coverage: The structure, personnel and programmes of UK television, covering social, economic and aesthetic aspects. World television and telecommunications are covered in more general terms.

Holdings: *c.* 3,500 books (including annual reports).
                c. 160 periodical titles.
                Press cuttings files.

Special   Press releases: BBC, Channel 4 and ITV companies.
collections: ITV Weekly Programme Schedules, 1955–.
                BBC Programmes-as-Broadcast (microfilm), *c.* 1936–.
                BBC Programme Index.

Catalogues: Card Catalogue to book stock: Authors/Titles/Subjects/ Programme Titles/Personalities.
                Index to programmes transmitted on UK television, with brief details of personnel, synopses, reviews, etc.
                Index to personalities giving references to periodical literature.
                SIFT (Summary of Information on Film and Television), an online database of information about film, television and video, compiled from the BFI data, will be available in 1988.

Publications: *British national film and video catalogue* (1963–).
                TV documentation: a guide to BFI library services and resources (1985).
                Film and television periodical holdings (1982).
                Monthly accessions list; Current awareness list (4 p.a.).

BRITISH UNIVERSITIES FILM AND VIDEO COUNCIL (BUFVC)
Information Service: 55 Greek Street, LondonW1V 5LR; 01-734 3687

Contact: Information Officer.

Access: Staff and students of BUFVC member organizations. Information Service subscribers. Other students and researchers may use the Library for reference purposes by appointment.

Coverage: Film and history; scientific film; television studies; educational technology; British newsreels.

Holdings: 1,660 books, 710 pamphlets.
                50 periodicals.
                Press cuttings.
                800 AV materials (in Audio-Visual Reference Centre).
                500 films and videos (in the Higher Education Film and Video Library).
                130 videos for sale direct from the BUFVC.

Special   Slade Film History Register.
collections: Records of the Scientific Film Association.
                British and foreign film and video distributors' catalogues.

Catalogues:	HELPIS (Higher Education Film and Video Library) online database (available through BLAISE-LINE).
	BUFVC Catalogue (annual).
	BUFVC Distributors Index (annual).
Publications:	*Researchers' guide to British film and television collections* (BUFVC, 2nd edn, 1985).
	Researchers' guide to British newsreels (BUFVC, 1983).

CENTRE FOR THE STUDY OF COMMUNICATION AND CULTURE (CSCC)
The Library: 221 Goldhurst Terrace, London NW6 3EP; 01-328 2868

Contact:	Librarian.
Access:	CSCC staff; members of the public, researchers and students may use the Library for reference purposes by appointment.
Coverage:	Communication research and media studies generally, broadcasting, advertising, film, journalism, the press, church communications and theology, international communications, media education.
Holdings:	6,000 books
	3,500 documents.
	500 periodicals (*c.* 300 newsletters, etc.).
Special collections:	Media education books and documents; theology and communications books and documents; Latin American communication studies (in Spanish and Portuguese); cultural studies.
Catalogues:	Card Catalogue, 1979–85: Author/Title/Subject.
	Computer Catalogue, 1986–.
Publications:	Library accessions list.
	Centre publications: *Communication research trends* (1980–. Quarterly); monographs; working papers; reports.

THE EUROPEAN INSTITUTE FOR THE MEDIA
Library and Documentation Centre: The University of Manchester, Manchester M13 9PL; 061-273 2754/2755/6055

Contact:	Librarian.
Access:	European Institute for the Media staff, students and researchers; members of the public. Appointment not required. Borrowing facilities.
Coverage:	Mass media and communication in the United Kingdom and other European countries, telecommunications and educational broadcasting.
Holdings:	4,500 books (with access to University Library holdings).
	80 periodicals.
	Press cuttings.

Special collections:	Press releases and annual reports from British and foreign broadcasting organizations.
	Council of Europe and Unesco publications on broadcasting.
	Media Monographs, 1984–.
Catalogues:	Card catalogue to the book stock: Author/Subject.
	Card index to periodicals.
	Card index to press cuttings (in preparation).
Publications:	*Mass communications in Western Europe: an annotated bibliography* (1985).
	Institute publications: *Media Bulletin* (quarterly newsletter) and *Media Monographs* (series of reports following research projects at the Institute).

HOME OFFICE
Information and Library Services: 50 Queen Anne's Gate, London SW1H 9AT; 01-273 3398/3043

Contact:	Information Librarian.
Access:	Home Office and Northern Ireland Office staff; genuine researchers for reference purposes by appointment.
Coverage:	Home Office interests, including broadcasting.
Holdings:	*c.*30,000 books (including *c.* 500 on broadcasting).
Special collections:	Home Office publications.
	Parliamentary debates (*Hansards*), 1743–.
Catalogue:	Microfiche catalogue to book stock: Author/Title; Subject (Library of Congress subject headings).
Publications:	Home Office List of Publications (annual).
	Information and Library Services: Publications Received.

INDEPENDENT BROADCASTING AUTHORITY
Library: 70 Brompton Road, London SW3 1EY; 01-584 7011

Contact:	Librarian.
Access:	IBA, ITV, Channel 4 and ILR staff; members of the public, students and researchers may use the Library for reference purposes by appointment.
Coverage:	British and foreign broadcasting; mass media and communications; advertising and marketing. Telecommunications and broadcast engineering covered primarily by the Technical Library, IBA Engineering Headquarters, Crawley Court, Winchester, Hants SO21 2QA; 0962 823434.
Holdings:	10,000 books, pamphlets and reports.
	300 periodicals.
	250,000 press cuttings.
	1,000 slides (IBA/ITV history and programmes).

Special collections:	IBA, Channel 4 and ITV company press releases. IBA, Channel 4, ITV and ILR company annual reports. Government and Parliamentary publications on broadcasting, 1923–. IBA Research Department audience research reports. Television audience ratings (Nielsen/Telepulse/TAM/JICTAR/BARB), 1955–. ITV Weekly Programme Schedules, 1955–. ITV/ILR/DBS/Radio Teletext franchise applications. (Associated) Rediffusion production archives and files, 1955–68.
Catalogue:	Computerized Catalogue (books, periodical articles, government reports, research reports, conference proceedings): Author/Title/Subject.
Publications:	*Broadcasting: a selected bibliography.* *IBA Library: Union list of periodical holdings.*

INDEPENDENT TELEVISION ASSOCIATION
Library: Knighton House, 56 Mortimer Street, London W1N 8AN; 01-636 6866

Contact:	Librarian.
Access:	ITV Association, ITV company and Channel 4 staff.
Coverage:	Broadcasting, advertising and marketing in the United Kingdom.
Holdings:	2,000 books. 78 periodicals. Press cuttings, 1978–.
Special collections:	ITV programme titles register (not kept in the Library). ITV franchise applications, 1980. Government publications on broadcasting. TV audience ratings (incomplete).
Catalogue:	Computerized Catalogue: Author/Title/Subject.

INTERNATIONAL INSTITUTE OF COMMUNICATIONS
Library: Tavistock House South, Tavistock Square, London WC1H 9LF; 01-388 0671

Contact:	Librarian.
Access:	IIC members; members of the public and students may use the Library for reference purposes.
Coverage:	Electronic communications, including broadcasting and telecommunications.
Holdings:	10,000 books. 200 periodicals. Press cuttings collection.

Special	Early communications satellite material.
collections:	IIC reports and publications.
Catalogues:	Card Catalogue (pre-1980 book stock).
	Card Index (periodicals and press cuttings).
	Computerized Catalogue, 1987–.
Publications:	List of periodical holdings.
	IIC Library classification scheme and subject index.

LEICESTER UNIVERSITY: CENTRE FOR MASS COMMUNICATION RESEARCH
University Library: University Road, Leicester LE1 7RH; 0533 522042

General:	The Centre does not operate a separate library, apart from a small collection of *c.*1,500 research reports and conference papers; however, the University Library has an excellent collection on mass communications.
Contact:	Reference Librarian.
Access:	Leicester University staff and student members. Non-members should apply for permission to use the Library.
Coverage:	Subjects related to the University courses from archaelogy to zoology, with large section on mass communications.
Holdings:	750,000 books and pamphlets.
	5,000 periodicals.
Catalogues:	Card Catalogue, –1983.
	Microfiche Catalogue, 1984–.

THE MEDIA PROJECT
The Library: The Volunteer Centre UK, 29 Lower King's Road, Berkhamsted, Herts. HP4 2AB; 04427 73311

Contact:	Information Assistant.
Access:	Individuals carrying out work in the field of social action broadcasting, e.g. academic researchers, broadcasters, students.
Coverage:	Written, spoken or broadcast material concerned with social action broadcasting.
Holdings:	Computerized database holding abstracts of: books; research documents; articles; and support materials to broadcast programmes on the subject of social action broadcasting.
Special	Abstracts of Media Project publications: articles; research
collections:	documents; support materials published or broadcast since 1977.
	Computerized database of radio training courses (from June 1988).
Publications:	Current awareness bulletin and selected dissemination of information service.

Media Project publications: *Action stations: the directory of social action programmes* (bi-annual); *On air/off air* (bi-monthly).

Case studies, information papers and reports.

OFFICE OF TELECOMMUNICATIONS (OFTEL)

Library: Atlantic House, Holborn Viaduct, London EC1N 2HQ; 01-822 1664

Contact:	Librarian.
Access:	OFTEL and Government department staff; members of the public for reference purposes only by appointment, unless just using the Public Registers or purchasing OFTEL publications.
Coverage:	Telecommunications; information technology; consumer affairs; privatization and competition policy.
Holdings:	Books.
	Periodicals.
	Government and Parliamentary publications.
Special collections:	Public Registers of licences made under the *Telecommunications Act 1984*: 1. Licences; 2. Contractors; 3. Apparatus.
	British and international standards on telecommunications (BSI, CCITT, ITU, CEPT, etc.).
	Annual reports of overseas posts and telecommunications organizations.
Catalogue:	Department of Trade and Industry Library Services Catalogue (BLAISE COM fiche): 1. Author/Title; 2. Subject.
Publications:	List of periodicals and newspapers.
	List of telcommunication legislation.
	Library guide.
	Reading lists and bibliographies.
	Publications List.

POLYTECHNIC OF CENTRAL LONDON: SCHOOL OF COMMUNICATIONS

Library: 37–49 Riding House Street, London W1P 7PT; 01-486 5811

Contact:	Faculty Librarian for Communication.
Access:	Polytechnic staff and student members; members of the public, students and researchers may use the Library for reference purposes.
Coverage:	Social sciences, business studies, women's studies and communication (including media, photography, film, radio, television and the press).
Holdings:	*c.*50,000 books and pamphlets.
	*c.*500 periodicals.
Special collections:	Videotapes (mainly feature films — reference only).
	Broadcasting company annual reports.

Polytechnic of Central London Archives (by appointment only).
Open University audio tapes.

Catalogues: Libertas (computerized catalogue); Okapi (computerized subject searching system); microfiche (for backup and earlier material); card catalogue for pre-1975 material.

Publications: Various guides to the Library, Libertas and other resources. Video on the Library service.

5.3 Museums

Considering Britain's pioneering role in the development of broadcasting, there have been, until recently, surprisingly few museums devoted to the subject in the United Kingdom. For some years, apart from a few temporary exhibitions to mark broadcasting anniversaries, the only major permanent exhibitions had been of the technical aspects of broadcasting in the Science Museum and the Broadcasting Gallery (1968–87) at the Independent Broadcasting Authority, which had been the first 'museum' to explain all aspects of the medium to the layman.

However, recently two national museums on broadcasting have opened: the National Museum of Photography, Film and Television in Bradford in 1986, and the Museum of the Moving Image on London's South Bank in 1988. There are also some smaller specialized museums and collections containing material of relevance to broadcasting.

The value of museums is not only in their collections of the artifacts and technical equipment of broadcasting, either originals or replicas, illustrating the techniques of radio and television engineering and production, but also in the explanation they give of the significance of the telcommunications revolution and its impact on society.

MUSEUM OF THE MOVING IMAGE (MOMI)
South Bank, London SE1 8XT; 01-928 3535

Contact: Curator.

History: MOMI, which offers a unique insight into cinema and television history, is the result of a seven-year collaboration between Leslie Hardcastle, the Controller of the National Film Theatre, and David Francis, the Curator of the National Film Archive.

Coverage: The history — technical, social and artistic — of the evolution of moving images from Chinese shadow theatre through to future film and television technologies.

Exhibits: Some forty main exhibit areas, many offering hands-on involvement, range from the earliest cinematic experiments to the coming of sound; from the first outside broadcasts to a modern TV studio. Plus changing exhibition.

Publication: *The moving image* by John Wyver (Blackwell/BFI, 1988).

NATIONAL MUSEUM OF PHOTOGRAPHY, FILM AND TELEVISION
Prince's View, Bradford, West Yorkshire BD5 OTR; 0274 727488

Contact: Keeper.

History: Opened in 1983, the Museum is an outstation of the Science Museum.

Coverage: The Museum collects, conserves and displays photography, film and television as documentary records, an expansion of human vision and as art forms.

Exhibits: Television Galleries: 1. 'Television: Behind the Screen' (how television works, and how programmes are made — a TV studio, control room, chromakey special effect, news studio and autocue, vision mixing, and a Video Box). 2. 'The Story of British Television' (history of the medium from John Logie Baird to the present, with working models, original equipment and dramatic reconstruction).
Cinema: IMAX screen (52 x 65ft), the largest in Britain.

Publication: *Television: the first fifty years* by Keith Geddes and Gordon Bussey (The Museum, 1986).

NATIONAL WIRELESS MUSEUM
Arreton Manor, Arreton, nr Newport, Isle of Wight; 0983 67665

Contact: Curator.

History: Formed by the Communications and Electronics Museum Trust.

Coverage: History of wireless from the First World War and the crystal-set era to the present day — including television from the Baird mechanical 'Televisor'.

THE ROBERT OPIE COLLECTION
Albert Warehouse, Gloucester Docks, Gloucester GL1 2EH; 0452 302309

Contact: Curator.

History: Britain's first museum of advertising and packaging is the culmination of twenty years' research and collecting by Robert Opie, and provides a unique insight into the history of the consumer society.

Coverage: Advertising and packaging material, 1850–.

Exhibits: British and American television commercials, 1955–.
Posters, display cards and printed ephemera.
Packages, bottles, tins and other consumables.
Children's toys, games, books and comics.

Publications: *The art of the label* by Robert Opie (Simon & Schuster, 1987); *Rule Britannia* by Robert Opie (Viking, 1985).

SCIENCE MUSEUM

Exhibition Road, London SW7 2DD; 01-589 3456

History: The Science Museum, more correctly the National Museum of Science and Technology, was opened in 1857. The National Railway Museum at York, and the National Museum of Photography, Film and Television at Bradford are outstations.

Coverage: The collections illustrate the development of science, medicine, engineering, transport, industries and communications.

Exhibits: 'Telecommunications: a technology for change':
                Part 1 (Gallery 25): 'The Story' (illustrating 'how telecommunications has quickened the pace of life . . .'): Telegraphy; Cables; Telephony; Wire-less Transmission and Telegraphy; Radio and Television; Teletext and Viewdata.
                Part 2 (Gallery 20): 'The Technologies': Switching; Transmission; Terminals; Radio; Overland; Submarine Cables.

Publication: *Telecommunications: a technology for change* by Eryl Davies (HMSO, 1983).

Further reading

Museum and galleries in Great Britain and Ireland. 1954–. Annual. East Grinstead, West Sussex: British Leisure Publications.
Museums yearbook. Annual. London: Museums Association.

Index